$ 75.00

INTERNATIONAL POLITICAL ECONOMY SERIES

General Editor: Timothy M. Shaw, Professor of Political Science and International Development Studies, and Director of the Centre for Foreign Policy Studies, Dalhousie University, Halifax, Nova Scotia, Canada

*Recent titles include*:

Pradeep Agrawal, Subir V. Gokarn, Veena Mishra, Kirit S. Parikh and Kunal Sen
ECONOMIC RESTRUCTURING IN EAST ASIA AND INDIA: Perspectives on Policy Reform

Gavin Cawthra
SECURING SOUTH AFRICA'S DEMOCRACY: Defence, Development and Security in Transition

Steve Chan (*editor*)
FOREIGN DIRECT INVESTMENT IN A CHANGING GLOBAL POLITICAL ECONOMY

Jennifer Clapp
ADJUSTMENT AND AGRICULTURE IN AFRICA: Farmers, the State and the World Bank in Guinea

Seamus Cleary
THE ROLE OF NGOs UNDER AUTHORITARIAN POLITICAL SYSTEMS

Robert W. Cox (*editor*)
THE NEW REALISM: Perspectives on Multilateralism and World Order

Diane Ethier
ECONOMIC ADJUSTMENT IN NEW DEMOCRACIES: Lessons from Southern Europe

Stephen Gill (*editor*)
GLOBALIZATION, DEMOCRATIZATION AND MULTILATERALISM

Jacques Hersh and Johannes Dragsbaek Schmidt (*editors*)
THE AFTERMATH OF 'REAL EXISTING SOCIALISM' IN EASTERN EUROPE, Volume 1: Between Western Europe and East Asia

David Hulme and Michael Edwards (*editors*)
NGOs, STATES AND DONORS: Too Close for Comfort?

Staffan Lindberg and Árni Sverrisson (*editors*)
SOCIAL MOVEMENTS IN DEVELOPMENT: The Challenge of Globalization and Democratization

Anne Lorentzen and Marianne Rostgaard (*editors*)
THE AFTERMATH OF 'REAL EXISTING SOCIALISM' IN EASTERN EUROPE, Volume 2: People and Technology in the Process of Transition

Laura Macdonald
SUPPORTING CIVIL SOCIETY: The Political Role of Non-Governmental
Organizations in Central America

Stephen D. McDowell
GLOBALIZATION, LIBERALIZATION AND POLICY CHANGE: A Political
Economy of India's Communications Sector

Juan Antonio Morales and Gary McMahon (*editors*)
ECONOMIC POLICY AND THE TRANSITION TO DEMOCRACY: The Latin
American Experience

Ted Schrecker (*editor*)
SURVIVING GLOBALISM: The Social and Environmental Challenges

Ann Seidman, Robert B. Seidman and Janice Payne (*editors*)
LEGISLATIVE DRAFTING FOR MARKET REFORM: Some Lessons from
China

Kenneth P. Thomas
CAPITAL BEYOND BORDERS: States and Firms in the Auto Industry,
1960–94

Caroline Thomas and Peter Wilkin (*editors*)
GLOBALIZATION AND THE SOUTH

Geoffrey R. D. Underhill (*editor*)
THE NEW WORLD ORDER IN INTERNATIONAL FINANCE

Henry Veltmeyer, James Petras and Steve Vieux
NEOLIBERALISM AND CLASS CONFLICT IN LATIN AMERICA: A
Comparative Perspective on the Political Economy of Structural Adjustment

**International Political Economy Series**
**Series Standing Order ISBN 0–333–71110–6**
(*outside North America only*)

You can receive future titles in this series as they are published by placing a standing
order. Please contact your bookseller or, in case of difficulty, write to us at the address
below with your name and address, the title of the series and the ISBN quoted above.

Customer Services Department, Macmillan Distribution Ltd
Houndmills, Basingstoke, Hampshire RG21 6XS, England

# Communication, Commerce and Power

## The Political Economy of America and the Direct Broadcast Satellite, 1960–2000

Edward A. Comor
*Assistant Professor*
*School of International Service*
*American University*
*Washington, DC*

First published in Great Britain 1998 by
**MACMILLAN PRESS LTD**
Houndmills, Basingstoke, Hampshire RG21 6XS and London
Companies and representatives throughout the world

A catalogue record for this book is available from the British Library.

ISBN 0–333–68823–6

First published in the United States of America 1998 by
**ST. MARTIN'S PRESS, INC.,**
Scholarly and Reference Division,
175 Fifth Avenue, New York, N.Y. 10010

ISBN 0–312–21071–X

Library of Congress Cataloging-in-Publication Data
Comor, Edward A., 1962–
Communication, commerce, and power : the political economy of
America and the direct broadcast satellite, 1960–2000 / Edward A.
Comor.
p.   cm. — (International political economy series)
Includes bibliographical references and index.
ISBN 0–312–21071–X
1. Direct broadcast satellite television—United States—History.
2. Television broadcasting—Government policy—United States-
-History.   3. Direct broadcast satellite television—History.
4. Television broadcasting—Government policy—History.   I. Title.
II. Series.
HE9721.U5C646  1998
384.55'45'0973—dc21                                        97–18332
                                                                CIP

This book is printed on paper suitable for recycling and made from fully managed and
sustained forest sources.

10   9   8   7   6   5   4   3   2   1
07   06   05   04   03   02   01   00   99   98

Printed and bound in Great Britain by
Antony Rowe Ltd, Chippenham, Wiltshire

# Contents

Preface                                                              vii

List of Acronyms                                                       x

1  INTRODUCTION                                                        1

   1.1  DBS, the United States, and the Information
      Economy                                                      3
   1.2  Chapter Previews                                             9
      Notes                                                       13

2  CRITICAL PERSPECTIVES ON US FOREIGN
   COMMUNICATION POLICY                                            17

   2.1  The Cultural Imperialism Paradigm                          17
   2.2  Culture as the Object of Inquiry                           21
   2.3  Culture and Critical International Political
      Economy                                                     23
   2.4  Mediators of the International Political Economy           29
   2.5  Conclusions                                                37
      Notes                                                       38

3  TELESATELLITE POLICY AND DBS, 1962–1984                            41

   3.1  Formative Telesatellite Developments                       42
   3.2  The Opportunity and Threat of Telesatellite
      Technology                                                  52
   3.3  Toward 'Open Skies' and the Political
      Feasibility of DBS                                          55
   3.4  The Rise and Fall of Domestic DBS: 1980–1984              60
   3.5  Conclusions                                                63
      Notes                                                       66

4  FOREIGN COMMUNICATION POLICY AND
   DBS: 1962–1984                                                  75

   4.1  US Propaganda Broadcasting                                 76
   4.2  The Free Flow of Information and
      International Law                                            79
   4.3  US Responses to the Free Flow Imbroglio                    87

4.4   DBS, UNESCO and the NWICO                        91
4.5   Conclusions                                      96
      Notes                                            99

5  DBS AND THE STRUCTURE OF US POLICY
   MAKING                                              107

5.1   Policy Agents and the Fragmented Character
      of US Policy                                     108
5.2   The US Policy Process and WARC-79                113
5.3   Shifting Demands and Structural Reforms          117
5.4   Conclusions                                      123
      Notes                                            124

6  EXPORTING LIBERALIZATION AND THE
   ASCENDANCY OF TRADE                                 131

6.1   The Failure of Free Flow                         133
6.2   The Emergence of Free Trade                      137
6.3   Free Trade and International Institutions         144
6.4   Conclusions                                      149
      Notes                                            152

7  CAPITAL, TECHNOLOGY AND THE UNITED
   STATES IN AN 'OPEN MARKET' REGIME                   161

7.1   DBS in an 'Open Market'                          164
7.2   DBS, Digitalization and HDTV                     170
7.3   DBS and Global Markets                           178
7.4   Conclusions                                      185
      Notes                                            187

8  CONCLUSION: COMMUNICATION, CULTURE AND
   AMERICAN HEGEMONY                                   193

8.1   Assessing Cultural Imperialism                   196
8.2   The Internationalizing State and US Hegemony     199
8.3   Hegemony, Culture and Mediators of the
      International Political Economy                   204
8.4   DBS and the Twenty-first Century                 207
      Notes                                            211

*Bibliography*                                         213
*Index*                                                245

# Preface

Talk about globalization in the international political economy – particularly discussions focusing on communication technology developments – all too often convey the dawning of seamless human interactions linked in a complex web of commercial relations. This certainly is the view held by most American state officials at the end of the twentieth century. From the official Cold War policy of 'containment', the United States has turned to the awkward unofficial term 'enlargement' – enlargement of institutions friendly to open markets, liberal democracy and corporate-friendly transnational technologies. In the updated version of the old General Motors claim that 'what's good for GM is good for America', today 'what is good for America is deemed to be what is good for Boeing's exports, for Microsoft's penetration of the world's computer operating systems and for Hollywood's screenings in cinemas across the globe'.[1] Indeed, communications and information commodity activities together constitute the largest and fastest-growing sector of the world economy.[2]

What all this really means and precisely how 'enlargement' is taking place remain remarkably under-assessed. This book is a contribution to understanding this. In the following pages I argue that people make history, and technologies, organizations, institutions and international regimes are the vehicles and mediators of its construction. I also argue that in the next century, the position of the United States in the international political economy in large part will be determined by human agents whose interests are directly shaped by past ways of organizing and thinking. Nevertheless, because people are capable of changing these ways of organizing and thinking – capable of changing the structures of everyday life – the world of tomorrow is far from being altogether mapped out. The fact that technologies, organizations, institutions and regimes require human intervention, both at the time of their creation and as a condition of their perpetuation, gives cause, I believe, for guarded optimism.

Perhaps the most important and recently most neglected institution shaping this future is the nation state. As Leo Panitch writes, 'states have become the authors of a regime that defines and guarantees, through treaties with constitutional effect, the global and domestic rights of capital'.[3] In this book, the history of US policy in relation to one of the most significant technologies of the so-called information economy – the Direct Broadcast Satellite (DBS) – is assessed and contextualized. Originally, the decision to focus on DBS and its relationship to the American state was based on my interest in exploring cultural imperialism and the role it plays in more general political-economic processes. But over time, primary sources – mostly US government documents and interviews with American state personnel–compelled me to pursue a somewhat more concentrated analysis. These also led me to consider some more complex theoretical issues, particularly those of concern to 'critical' or Gramscian students of international political economy. Rather than finding an American state working in imperialistic harmony with private sector mass media, telecommunications and more general information economy interests (all perpetuating a US-centered world order based on consent rather than coercion), innumerable inter-corporate and intra-state tensions and conflicts generated a still more pressing question: *What is the precise role of the American state in the process of cultural imperialism?* Predictably, this opened the door to other questions involving American hegemonic capacities in relation to the ascendancy of communication and information activities in the international political economy.

The direct broadcast satellite, as arguably the most powerful, far-reaching and culturally intrusive of all new communication technologies, remained the logical analytical staging post from which to explore such issues. At this juncture in history – one in which the vagaries of capitalism have become almost universally accepted – a concerted effort to understand how the 'common sense' of open markets, free trade and neo-liberal development policies have been constructed and are being maintained constitutes, I believe, an essential step in efforts to redress the potential narrowing of the human imagination. This book aims to inspire more work of this type – work that recognizes the importance of understanding the complex dynamics underlying 'what we know' to be a fundamental concern of the critical social scientist.

What follows is a revised version of my doctoral dissertation completed for the Department of Political Science at York University in Toronto. During these years, Martin Hewson, David Leyton-Brown, Steve Patten, J. Magnus Ryner, Timothy J. Sinclair, Anne Stretch, Graham Todd and Reg Whitaker all made significant personal and professional contributions. Financial support from Canada's Social Science and Humanities Research Council and the Ontario Graduate Scholarship Programme were essential to its completion. While at

York, and during my subsequent tenure at the School of International Service, American University, many others have provided ideas and encouragement. Among these are Henry Comor, Robert W. Cox, Ken Donow, Elizabeth Hagg, Beth Haverkamp-Powers, Sara Fletcher Luther, Ted Magder, James Mittelman, Vincent Mosco, Hamid Mowlana, Mustapha Pasha, Dino Rosati, James N. Rosenau, Christopher Rossi, Rohan Samarajiva, Harry Trebing, Paul Wapner, and Macmillan IPE series editor Timothy M. Shaw. Thank you one and all.

Thanks also to research assistants Kristen Comeaux, Cynthia Dowdell, Peter Haney, Alan Kronstadt, Rachel Kuennen, Allison Levine and Kathleen Lewis-Workman.

I am compelled to convey heartfelt thanks to Leo Panitch for his drive, critical contributions, and the tremendous faith he had in his student. I also must thank Ian Parker for his years of friendship, support, and willingness to introduce me to the pleasure and pain of critical thinking. Their scholarly work and political principles are sources of continuing inspiration.

Finally, I would like to acknowledge the role played by friends, old and new. Against the constraints of common sense, I have little doubt that my guarded optimism has something to do with their passion, understanding and unflagging generosity.

Edward Comor
Washington, DC
June 1997


**NOTES**

1   Martin Walker, 'Foreign Policy Goes to Market', *Manchester Guardian Weekly* (12 January 1997) p. 6.
2   Robert W. McChesney, 'The Global Struggle for Democratic Communication', in *Monthly Review*, 48(3) (July–August 1996) 5.
3   Leo Panitch, 'Globalization, States, and Left Strategies', in *Social Justice*, 23(1–2) (1996) 80.

# List of Acronyms

| | |
|---|---|
| ABC | American Broadcasting Company |
| ATS | Applications Technology Satellite |
| AT&T | American Telephone and Telegraph Company |
| BBC | British Broadcasting Corporation |
| BSS | Broadcasting Satellite Services |
| CBS | Columbia Broadcasting System |
| CIA | Central Intelligence Agency |
| CNN | Cable Network News |
| Comsat/COMSAT | Communications Satellite Corporation |
| COPUOS | Conference on the Peaceful Uses of Outer Space |
| DBS | Direct Broadcast Satellite |
| DoD | Department of Defense |
| DoJ | Department of Justice |
| DTH | Direct-to-Home |
| EC | European Community |
| EU | European Union |
| FCC | Federal Communications Commission |
| FSS | Fixed Satellite Services |
| FTA | Free Trade Agreement |
| GAO | General Accounting Office |
| GATS | General Agreement on Trade in Services |
| GATT | General Agreement on Tariffs and Trade |
| GDP | Gross Domestic Product |
| GE | General Electric |
| GII | Global Information Infrastructure |
| GM | General Motors |
| GSO | Geostationary Orbit |
| HBO | Home Box Office |
| HDTV | High Definition Television |
| IBM | International Business Machines |
| ICIP | International Communications and Information Policy |
| IIPA | International Intellectual Property Alliance |
| IMF | International Monetary Fund |
| Intelsat | International Telecommunication Satellite Organization |

| | |
|---|---|
| IPDC | International Program for the Development of Communication |
| IPE | International Political Economy |
| ITU | International Telecommunications Union |
| ITV | International Television Service |
| LDC | Less Developed Country |
| MAC | Multiplexed Analogue Component |
| MFN | Most Favored Nation |
| MPAA | Motion Picture Association of America |
| MTV | Music Television |
| NAB | National Association of Broadcasters |
| NAFTA | North American Free Trade Agreement |
| NAS | National Academy of Sciences |
| NASA | National Aeronautics and Space Administration |
| NCTA | National Cable Television Association |
| NFTC | National Foreign Trade Council |
| NHK | Japanese Broadcasting Corporation |
| NIEO | New International Economic Order |
| NSA | National Security Administration |
| NSC | National Security Council |
| NSCDD | National Security Council Decision Directive |
| NTIA | National Telecommunications and Information Administration |
| NTSC | National Television Systems Committee |
| NWICO | New World International Communications Order |
| OECD | Organization for Economic Cooperation and Development |
| OIA | Office of International Affairs |
| OICP | Office of International Communication Policy |
| OPEC | Organization of Petroleum Exporting Countries |
| OST | Outer Space Treaty |
| OTP | Office of Telecommunications Policy |
| PAL | Phase Alternation Line |
| PRC | People's Republic of China |
| PTT | Post Telephone and Telegraph |
| RBOC | Regional Bell Operating Company |
| RCA | Radio Corporation of America |
| RFE | Radio Free Europe |
| RL | Radio Liberty |

| | |
|---|---|
| SBCA | Satellite Broadcasting and Communication Association |
| SBS | Satellite Business Systems |
| SECAM | Sequential Couleur à Memoire |
| SIG | Senior Interagency Group |
| STC | Satellite Television Corporation |
| TCI | Tele-Communication Incorporated |
| TNC | Transnational Corporation |
| TRIPS | Trade-related Intellectual Property Rights |
| UAR | United Arab Republic |
| UN | United Nations |
| UNCTAD | United Nations Conference on Trade and Development |
| UNESCO | United Nations Educational, Scientific and Cultural Organization |
| US | United States |
| USCI | United States Communications Incorporated |
| USIA | United States Information Administration |
| USSB | United States Satellite Broadcasting |
| USSR | Union of Soviet Socialist Republics |
| USTR | United States Trade Representative |
| VCR | Video Cassette Recorder |
| VoA | Voice of America |
| WARC | World Administrative Radio Conference |
| WARC-ST | World Administrative Radio Conference on Space Telecommunications |
| WATTC | World Administration Telegraph and Telephone Conference |
| WTO | World Trade Organization |

# 1 Introduction

In the first term of the Presidency of Ronald Reagan, Dennis LeBlanc – formerly a California state trooper, a chauffeur for Governor Reagan, and a boyfriend to one of the President's daughters – was made Associate Administrator of Telecommunications Policy in the US Department of Commerce. On two occasions in the summer of 1982, a US military aircraft flew LeBlanc to California from Washington, DC. The special assignment that LeBlanc was selected to perform involved work at the President's holiday home, Rancho del Cielo, cutting wood and clearing underbrush.

The official auditor for Congress, the General Accounting Office (GAO), took issue with LeBlanc's summer activities. When appointed to work in the Commerce Department, LeBlanc acknowledged, 'I have no communications background.' Nevertheless, LeBlanc accepted the job of supervising twelve federal employees in the task of developing vaguely defined aspects of US telecommunications policy. In response to the GAO disclosure of his Rancho del Cielo responsibilities, LeBlanc told a reporter, 'I think it's nitpicking.' A Commerce Department spokesperson was more defiant. LeBlanc, she said, will 'continue to make trips when the President requests it. The President is the Commander in Chief.' Dennis LeBlanc resigned ten months later.[1]

Although the LeBlanc incident was extraordinary, it was not exceptional. According to an unnamed state official quoted in a 1982 news report on Commerce Department telecommunications activities, 'There is no expertise and virtually all of the appointees in top and second level positions of authority are unqualified and unknowledgeable.' In 1983, a well-known Washington telecommunications consultant, Roland S. Homet, Jr, warned Congress that 'A field that is treated like a dumping ground begins to look like one.'[2]

Despite the concerns of private sector spokespersons and the inaccurate perceptions of innumerable academic policy analysts, the neglect of US foreign communication policy and the dumping-ground mentality related to it persisted for many years. Indeed, the importance, if not centrality, of the information and communication commodity sector for the late-twentieth-century economic development of the United States only became widely recognized in the 1980s. This

1

consciousness first emerged about a decade earlier – a period marking America's relative political-economic decline. Of course a more direct factor fueling this awareness was mounting empirical evidence of the strength and growth opportunities afforded by information and communication activities.

In 1986, American companies were responsible for over 43 per cent of world revenues in this rapidly growing sector and this dominance was particularly strong in information-based services, where US corporations generated 47 per cent of international revenues.[3] Not only was the United States the world's largest services exporter *prior to* the opening up of world markets through the Uruguay Round General Agreement on Tariffs and Trade (GATT), it also held the largest services trade surplus. While from 1987 to 1992 the US trade surplus in services increased almost four-fold, reaching US$60.6 billion[4] in 1992, the US trade deficit in goods was reduced from –$159.5 billion in 1987 to –$96.2 billion in 1992. As a result of the services surplus, in 1987 the US trade deficit was lowered by 8 per cent, and in 1990 services exports reduced this by 36 per cent. In 1992, the US trade deficit was reduced by 63 per cent as a result of America's relative strength in services.[5]

Taken together, what can be classified as core US information-based industries (defined here as those industries primarily engaged in the production and dissemination of copyrighted materials) – including newspapers and periodicals, book publishing, radio and television broadcasting, cable television, records and tapes, motion pictures, advertising, computer software, and data processing – in real value-added terms, grew from $96.4 billion in 1977 to $238.6 billion in 1993. As measured in relation to national Gross Domestic Product (GDP), these industries constituted 2.2 per cent of US GDP in 1977 and 3.74 per cent in 1993.[6] Applying a broader definition of information-based industries,[7] their total value rose from $163.5 billion in 1977 to $362.5 billion in 1993. In relation to the rest of the US economy, these industries constituted 3.73 per cent of GDP in 1977 and 5.69 per cent in 1993. Employment in core information-based industries rose from 1.5 million jobs in 1977 to almost 3.0 million in 1993. Again, applying a broader definition of information-based industries, employment increased from 3.0 million to 5.7 million. Also from 1977 to 1993, employment in information-based industries, measured either narrowly or broadly, grew by an average of 4.5 per cent each year while employment in the US economy as a whole grew at an average rate of 1.7 per cent.[8]

The disjuncture between the rising importance of information and communication activities for the United States in the international political economy and its apparent neglect within the American state – as illustrated by the case of Dennis LeBlanc – also underlines a general absence of a comprehensive understanding of how the American state operates in relation to the ever-changing political, economic, technological and cultural circumstances related to this increasingly important policy area. In the early 1980s, the urgent need to forge a global free flow of information – America's long-established quest for an international regime in which the right to move information into and out of nation states would, under most circumstances, trump the right of governments to exercise national sovereignty – was becoming a core issue for more and more US and foreign-based corporations. They sought the reform of national and international institutions and regulatory regimes in ways that would facilitate their use of transnational services through applications of information and communication technology. The development and implementation of the direct broadcast satellite (DBS),[9] while one of several significant technologies to have emerged in the 1980s, reveals a number of crucial insights into this more general history.

## 1.1. DBS, THE UNITED STATES, AND THE INFORMATION ECONOMY

Particularly since 1945, American public and private sector officials have acted as the *provocateurs par excellence* of international communications. The telecommunication satellite (telesatellite) constitutes the most powerful of US-led communication developments, and DBS has emerged to be perhaps the most significant of these. Because of its unprecedented capacity to penetrate sovereign borders with electronic signals, in the 1970s DBS became a front-line issue in an almost universal resistance to US communication policy initiatives. By the mid-1980s, the DBS issue was somewhat marginalized. Telesatellites generally were treated as components of more comprehensive developments involving the reform of international institutions and regimes. These reforms were seen to be the essential prerequisites for the development of a global information economy. Again, at the end of the twentieth century, DBS has become a technology of extraordinary political, economic and social importance. DBS applications have expanded the opportunities and stakes involved in contemporary political-economic developments. DBS is an ideal medium through which information-based commodities can enter transnational markets, and its history and the context of its development provide insights into, among other things, world order possibilities and the hegemonic capabilities of the United States.

A DBS system is made up of a ground station that processes and radiates a signal to a satellite in geostationary orbit 36,000 km above the earth's surface.[10] In the satellite, the signal is reprocessed and amplified for its transmission back to earth. Finally, the system involves a ground receiver that includes a 'dish' or 'squarial' which collects the signal and processes it for viewing on a television screen or for use on a computer terminal. DBS systems are unique because of the tremendous power used to amplify signals for the downlink. In their most powerful, sophisticated and expensive form, DBS transmissions can be received directly from space by a dish measuring as little as 18 cm in diameter. One DBS system has the capacity to service simultaneously households and businesses located over one-third of the earth's surface, and its transmissions can consist of a combination of anything from compact disc-quality audio to computer software, from database information to video signals accompanied by multiple language tracks.

Beyond these stand-alone capabilities, recent developments in digital technology have provided DBS distributors with unprecedented signal integration and compression capacities, and corporations now are beginning to make use of a range of information and communication technologies in order to take advantage of these. Through the launch of Hughes Communications' DirecTV in 1994, DBS has become a core technology in the development of what the Clinton administration has called the Global Information Infrastructure (GII) – a mass market, inter-active transnational communications system involving the virtually seamless integration of different telecommunication and information services. The very presence of direct broadcasting and its utility in creating transnational non-wired communication opportunities itself has stimulated GII-related developments. Rupert Murdoch's News Corporation International (News Corp), for example, the controlling interest of the most successful DBS service in Europe, BSkyB, and the dominant DBS service in Asia, StarTV, is planning to provide North and South America with a full menu of digitalized direct broadcast services. This involves News Corp in a partnership with US-based telecomunications company MCI (itself purchased in 1996 by British Telecom). In Europe, News Corp and British Telecom are working with Canal Plus and Bertelsmann – the largest mass-media corporations in France and Germany – to standardize and subsequently control the digital broadcasting standard for Europe. By design, News Corp subsidiary News Datacom stands ready to manufacture the digital conversion equipment that all households will require to receive this new standard for digitalized signals.[11]

Through its dominant position in European and Asian DBS, and its plans to launch a 200-channel digital direct broadcast system with MCI/British Telecom in the United States, News Corp is striving to become *the* gatekeeper of the global information infrastructure. Of course other transnational corporations hold these aspirations also. Not coincidentally, the world's other leading digital DBS system is making similar plans. DirecTV, owned by Hughes Communications (a subsidiary of General Motors), has forged a partnership with the largest telecommunications company in the world, AT&T, to develop transnational DBS services capable of rivaling News Corp and its partners. Another subsidiary of Hughes has merged with one of the world's largest telesatellite service providers, PanAmSat, to provide North, Central and South America with an integrated range of tele-communications services, including DBS.

At this stage in the history of technological development, British Telecom, MCI and AT&T all recognize DBS to constitute the best vehicle through which household and business customers can be provided with a range of integrated information services well before their own terrestrial cable infrastructures are completed. DBS provides these companies with an instantaneous global reach. More-over, most still require several years of work and investment before their domestic infrastructures, through fiber-optic cabling and other modifications, are ready to handle large-scale digital transmission activities. As such, by establishing a full-service digital network with DBS, the potential for other telecommunications corporations or established cable television companies (already possessing relatively superior cable infrastructures) to control the future GII marketplace can be significantly reduced. For News Corp and Hughes, because the owner of a DBS reception unit can only communicate to the direct broadcaster through some form of cable or telephone connection, British Telecom, MCI and AT&T provide the interactive capabilities and marketing reach needed to compete against prospective cable-based services.

At the end of the twentieth century, DBS has become *the* technology through which digitalized services can be introduced to transnational consumers – from mass and niche market television entertainment to database information and software services tailored for specialized needs. The importance of its digital signal capabilities and enormous geographic reach cannot be understated. Digital broadcasting probably constitutes the qualitative and quantitative technical improvement required to attract consumers to become participants in a prospective GII. Most importantly, digital signals provide corporate interests with the capacity to merge all forms of electronic communications into a single, inter-active and virtually seamless system. Moreover, because the costs of this potential mega-network are enormous (the least expensive component being a $1 billion DBS system), it is doubtful that once a corporation or conglomerate of interests establish such a mega-network in one region of the world, little if any direct competition is likely to emerge.[12]

Of course DBS systems are more than just unprecedented vehicles through which world information markets can be penetrated and subsequently controlled. Direct broadcast satellites also are media through which corporate 'free speech' and the ideal of individual 'choice' can be promulgated. The latter can take place most directly through the individual's day-to-day *use* of his or her 'own' DBS receiver, which provides that person with seemingly uncensored access to mostly commercial information and entertainment service providers from the outside world. In relation to more general international infrastructural developments, DBS operators have become, to some extent, the first comprehensive transnational multiple service corporations, providing digitalized products to specialized and mass audiences. Digital DBS constitutes not only the vehicle through which complementary *transnational* information-based services can be offered, it also constitutes a medium through which particular lifestyles and political-economic perspectives can be propagated. With DBS, both the medium and the message may be used to promote the interests of the very companies that may become the gatekeepers of the information economy.[13]

Despite or perhaps because of these prescient capabilities, DBS developments have followed a rather bumpy and problematic path. The theoretical feasibility of direct broadcasting was established as early as the mid-1960s. Subsequently, DBS only became a widely debated political issue in 1972 when the United Nations General Assembly approved a Soviet Union proposal that the UN develop guidelines to govern transnational broadcasting. This proposal won the consent of every country except the United States. For many European and Canadian interests, DBS represented the threat of further penetration by US mass media into international markets. For many less developed countries (LDCs) – responding to the ongoing concentration of telecommunication capabilities in relatively advanced nation states – a collective resistance to American dominance was formalized in a 1973 declaration drafted at the first Conference of Ministers of Information of Non-Aligned Countries. It stated that a 'new world communication order' should be organized. Recognizing that DBS systems could service LDC needs in mass education, health care and agricultural development, most of these countries feared that commercial priorities instead would lead to its use in extending North–South dependency relations.

Given the public nature of this conflict, perhaps it is not surprising that existing studies of the political-economic history of direct broadcast technologies tend to focus on America against 'the world,' or US interests versus LDC development aspirations. These works are largely descriptive analyses of the international debates that emerged through the DBS issue, mainly focusing on the legality and assumed implications of a successfully applied US free flow of information policy. More critical scholarly work explicitly or implicitly makes use of the cultural imperialism paradigm introduced to many by Herbert I. Schiller in 1969.[14] With few exceptions, however, these critical efforts, despite the provocative and important issues raised, suffer from the tendency to make theoretical generalizations based on political assumptions or inadequate empirical research.

This book is different. It reviews the history of US foreign communication policy from the early 1960s to the end of the 1990s and focuses on the relationship of the American state to DBS in the context of the hegemonic crisis facing the US since the early 1970s. Its approach involves a critical reassessment of the cultural imperialism paradigm and aspects of work by 'critical' and Gramscian international political economists. It shows that in the United States the corporate proponents of DBS, until recently, have been marginally situated in terms of their influence on foreign communication policy. In fact, the media conglomerates that most proponents of the cultural imperialism paradigm believe were the champions of DBS were, at various times, altogether opposed to its domestic application, indifferent to its international implementation and intimidated by other corporate interests to such an extent that some even conspired against its introduction. Despite the fact that direct broadcast technologies initially were developed by the cooperative efforts of American state agencies and some domestic satellite manufacturers, the first transnational DBS applications took place in Europe and Asia and were by no means dominated by US corporate investments. As such, the underlying empirical question pursued over the course of the following pages is this: what have been the historical forces shaping the retardation of US-based DBS developments during a period in which the American state sought the entrenchment of free flow of information principles?

Perhaps more importantly, the following chapters examine this history in order to assess three issues of contemporary empirical *and* theoretical importance. One of these is the role of the American state in contemporary globalization developments. Through this analysis of DBS and US foreign policy, the nature of relationships involving American state agents, private sector interests and international institutions are elaborated. *Specifically, this history compels us to ask what has been role of the American state and other state structures in globalization processes? How have nation state structures been modified through these developments? And what strategic lessons can be garnered from a historical analysis of a cutting-edge transnational communication technology – DBS – in the context of the assumed hegemonic decline of the United States and related shifts in the international political economy?*

A second and related issue to be addressed involves the capacity of the United States to reassert or reform its hegemonic position. If hegemony is a process involving economic dominance, military superiority *and* the maintenance of international *consent*, the subject of the present study appears most relevant. Critical students of international political economy, for example, have long recognized the existence of a dialectical relationship between the changing material conditions of life and the presence and perhaps predominance of certain ideas or ways of thinking. However, little work has been done specifying how this knowledge maintenance or creation process takes place. *Through the present analysis of what can be viewed as one of the most significant transnational communication technologies in history, this book directs us toward some important theoretical correctives. Both the cultural imperialism paradigm and the Gramscian concept of hegemony will be used, tested and constructively critiqued.*

A final issue pursued in the following pages concerns the need to specify better the complex role being played by key institutional, organizational and technological media in the international political economy. In recognizing that regimes, institutions, organizations and technologies mediate and hence modify individual, group, corporate and nation-state relationships and perspectives, this history serves as a vehicle by which to pursue more general theoretical concerns. DBS, of course, constitutes a core transnational medium by itself. However, its development and application also have affected and have been affected by other mediators, broadly defined. *A more general goal of this book involves an articulation of this complex process and the nature and effects of such mediations in contemporary history.*

## 1.2 CHAPTER PREVIEWS

These issues – the role of the American state in globalization processes; the hegemonic capacity of the United States in the emerging international political economy; and the role of international regimes, institutions, organizations and technologies as mediators of contemporary history – are pursued in the following chapters. Chapter 2, 'Critical Perspectives on US Foreign Communication Policy,' presents an introduction to some of the theoretical perspectives that will be applied in assessing the history at hand. It includes a critique of the cultural imperialism paradigm, a theorization of what is called 'cultural power,' and an introduction to how we may best conceptualize the state (as an institution) and other core media in the context of contemporary globalization developments.

Chapter 3, 'Telesatellite Policy and DBS, 1962–1984,' focuses on a US policy paradox. While preliminary DBS developments were funded largely through American state agencies, and although US officials responsible for overseas propaganda activities recognized the advantages of its implementation, private sector efforts to develop DBS services were repeatedly suffocated. The obstructionist activities of AT&T and other interests against the ambitions of Hughes Aircraft and other prospective DBS manufacturers are discussed in the context of more general American state interests and the formative Communications Satellite Act of 1962. In contrast to the cultural imperialism paradigm, this chapter underlines the presence (at least in the 1960s) of some degree of American public sector disdain for private sector mass-media exports, referred to by some government officials as 'second rate' and even 'irrelevant.' However, in the 1970s, with an expanding number and range of corporate interests involved in the application of new communication technologies, this perspective faded (at least in public) and AT&T and other monopolies were subjected to widespread attack.

The paradox discussed in Chapter 3 and its implications are addressed in a foreign policy context in Chapter 4, 'Foreign Communication Policy and DBS, 1962–1984.' Despite hostile domestic interests, and the repeated assurances of American state officials, this period was characterized by the use of DBS by mostly less developed countries *as an issue* to facilitate political mobilization against US power and in efforts to construct a so-called New World Information and Communication Order (NWICO).

This chapter examines the role that both DBS as an issue and DBS as a technology played in US foreign communication policy. It argues that the DBS issue not only played a significant role in mobilizing the NWICO movement, but this mobilization, in turn, was used by the Reagan administration as a propaganda vehicle facilitating an assault on foreign opposition to American and 'free market' capitalist interests in less developed regions of the world. In the 1980s, the mounting economic urgency to advance the international free flow of information impelled the Reagan White House to entrench the United States in a 'no-compromise/take-no-prisoners' response to LDC demands. More importantly, Chapter 4 contextualizes this conflict. It argues that the early 1980s was a crisis period in US foreign communication policy. The America-versus-NWICO conflict more fundamentally reflected efforts to redress the hegemonic crisis involving the radical restructuring of the domestic and international political economy and, of necessity, a restructuring of the American state itself. The emerging importance, at the dawn of a 'post-Fordist' regime of accumulation, of communication and information activities involved an urgent push for new and reformed state capabilities and new and reformed international institutions.

Chapter 5, 'DBS and the Structure of US Policy Making,' pursues this crisis and transition period in more detail. Through an examination of the fragmented and largely *ad hoc* character of American foreign communication policy, particularly in the 1980s, it argues that the long-standing influence of predominant private and public sector vested interests, the divisive and conflictual nature of American political structures, and the relatively entrenched market positions of direct broadcasting's prospective competitors, all produced a decidedly unpromising environment for the domestic application of DBS technologies. Predictably, every one of the Federal Communications

Commission's (FCC's) initial DBS licensees, granted in the early 1980s, failed to establish viable services. More generally, the historical and structural conditions that had produced an ensemble of federal agencies incapable of making and implementing cohesive and long-term foreign communication policies were unintentionally made even less effective through reform efforts involving neo-liberal re-regulatory developments during this period. While the Reagan administration attacked established international institutions, intra-state efforts to coordinate US foreign communication policy better remained lacking primarily due to the absence of an undisputed leader among state agencies. The Office of the United States Trade Representative (USTR) and its expanding mandate to reform international trade institutions emerged to fill this vacuum. By the mid-1980s, a complex overlapping of communications with trade policy had taken root. Free-flow policy aspirations now were to be achieved through free trade. US corporations directly concerned with free flow developments considered this trade approach to be a viable means of overcoming foreign resistance, while other American companies came to recognize themselves to be increasingly dependent on transnational communication capabilities.

Inadequate US policy-making structures led to a foreign communication policy crisis and the compulsion to restructure the American state. In Chapter 6, 'Exporting Liberalization and the Ascendancy of Trade,' this complex and often problematic process is related both to agency and structure involving a growing demand, initiated by mostly US-based financial services, computer services and telecommunication equipment companies, for the neo-liberal re-regulation of domestic and international activities. A remarkable effort driven by the private sector to promote the ideals of competition and trade reciprocity for information-based products and services emerged from this. These forces and this crisis also involved the ascent of the USTR as America's front-line state agent, both promoting free trade and resisting foreign and international legal precedents that could be used to retard future communication policy aspirations.

A push to include service sector activities and intellectual property rights in the Uruguay Round GATT negotiations subsequently constituted the core international institutional reform pursued in efforts to redress the American foreign communication policy crisis. And while DBS plans and applications played a marginal role in what turned out to be a generally successful strategy, the emergence of a *de facto* international free flow regime through trade-based agreements, the collapse of Soviet and East European communism, and the development of significant advancements in digital and other technologies, all facilitated a growing appreciation that information-based products and services *themselves* constitute a significant cultural-power tool in America's foreign policy ensemble.

In Chapter 7, 'Capital, Technology, and the United States in an "Open Market" Regime,' examples of late-twentieth-century US public and private sector information and communication activities are presented to illustrate empirical and theoretical points raised in Chater 6. The US Telecommunications Act of 1996, for example, is treated as one of the most significant steps yet taken by the American state in its role as a core mediator of corporate interests in international markets. Beyond the further 'freeing up' of private sector interests in efforts to construct some form of domestic and international information highway, the Act fuels its development not despite but precisely because of the oligopolistic tendencies it releases. Related to this development are digital technology applications involving DBS and the introduction of high definition television. From this discussion, I argue that the disparate character of the American state ironically has provided US-based capital with unanticipated competitive advantages in most information economy developments. European and Japanese efforts to challenge American-based interests, for instance, have been handicapped both as a result of the wealth and resiliency of the American market and (ironically) due to the structural *inability* of the American state explicitly to organize private sector interests in communication and information activities – activities now predominantly characterized by technological dynamism.

In response to the history presented in the previous chapters and the issues raised and elaborated in them, Chapter 8, the book's 'Conclusion,' suggests general theoretical revisions to the cultural imperialism paradigm that may facilitate a more precise assessment of foreign communication policy and more general developments in world order. Aspects of the conceptualization of hegemony formulated by Robert W. Cox are emphasized as developmental supplements to this paradigm. However, as a result of the role played by the American state as the core but complex mediator of what will be described as an emerging hegemonic bloc of interests, this final chapter emphasizes the role of the nation state in contemporary globalization processes. An aggressive US-mediated process is portrayed in which the American state has acted to reform the conditions in which a prospective US-based and corporate-led global information infrastructure can be developed. Finally, the Conclusion points to implications and potential contradictions stemming from contemporary strategies involving international communications. In light of the book's findings, general suggestions are made as to the role of communication in ongoing efforts by US interests to resist political-economic decline and construct a twenty-first-century *Pax Americana*.

Out of hegemonic crisis, new economic interests have emerged and have ignited a range of domestic and international reforms. The case of Reagan appointee Dennis LeBlanc was a comedic reflection of the structural conditions that handcuffed American state officials in their work to service the emerging demands of diverse information economy interests. The American state subsequently became the target of a remarkable effort toward domestic reform. Only then was the United States able to reform core institutions in the international political economy. But before this history is elaborated using DBS as a narrative guide, I present the theoretical issues and conceptual tools explicitly and implicitly used in subsequent chapters.

## NOTES

1    Dennis LeBlanc quoted in Helen Thomas, 'Federal Exec Doubles as Ranch Hand,' UPI Release (19 December 1982) n.p. Also see Thomas, 'Commerce Administrator-Ranch Hand Resigns,' UPI Release (7 November 1983) n.p.

2    Homet quoted in US Congress, Senate, Committee on Foreign Relations. Subcommittee on Arms Control, Oceans, International Operations and Environment. Hearings on 'International Communication and Information Policy.' 98th Congr., 1st sess. (19 and 31 October 1983) p. 173.

3    These figures are from a 1986 UNESCO study that subdivided information economy activities into four sub-sectors: 'media' (including the producers of information content, such as film, video, music, radio, the press and television); 'services' (constituting those industries that process and disseminate information, including data processing, software, on-line data bases, computer services, telecommunication carriers and postal services); 'equipment' (referring to manufacturers of capital goods needed for both 'media' and 'services'); and the 'components' sub-sector (referring to other products and services that are direct inputs for 'media,' 'services' and 'equipment'). UNESCO, *World Communication Report* (Paris: UNESCO, 1989) p. 83.

4    Hereafter, all references to dollars will refer to US currency unless otherwise indicated.

5    Coalition of Service Industries, *The Service Economy*, 7(3) (July 1993) p. 13.

6    Stephen E. Siwek and Harold Furchtgott-Roth, *Copyright Industries in the US Economy, 1977–1993* (Washington, DC: International Intellectual Property Alliance, January 1995) Tables 2 and 3.

7    If industries producing and disseminating a product that is only partially copyrighted are included, such as architectural services; industries that distribute copyrighted materials only, such as libraries and transportation services; and related industries that produce and maintain equipment used exclusively for copyrighted materials, such as computer and television manufacturers, the scale and relative importance of these activities increase substantially.

8    Siwek and Furchtgott-Roth, *Copyright Industries in the US Economy, 1977–1993*, Tables 2, 3 and 6. General comparisons with the US automobile sector illustrate the significance of this economic strength in information and communication activities. In 1977, the motor vehicle industry constituted 4.8% of US GDP. By 1993, it had declined to 3.5%. In 1977, 947,000 workers were employed in motor vehicle manufacturing. In 1993, only 833,000 worked in this industry. Despite the 'recovery' of the American automobile sector since the early 1980s, the US trade deficit in manufactured motor vehicle products, from 1987 to 1992, fell by just $12.9 billion (from −$57.6 billion to −$44.7 billion). Statistics provided by American Automobile Manufacturing Association in private correspondence, 1 July 1996, from data generated by the US Department of Commerce, Bureau of Economic Analysis.

9    DBS alternatively is referred to as direct-to-home (DTH).

10   Satellites in geostationary orbit are stationary in relation to a location on earth. This orbit must take place over the equator to ensure that the satellite's speed equals that of the earth's rotation. To maintain this orbit, the centrifugal force generated by the satellite pulling it away from earth is counter-balanced by the earth's gravitational pull. Therefore, as the satellite's altitude increases, the slower its orbital speed must be. Because of the necessity of a 24–hour orbit, geostationary locations are limited to the altitude of 35,786 km. Only some locations at this altitude are suitable for DBS. To prevent interference, direct broadcast satellites require predefined radio frequencies and the satellites ideally are spaced at least 9 degrees (or over 3,600 km) apart. And while the circumference of the geostationary orbit is 265,000 km – a distance that certainly helps prevent overcrowding – some locations are far more preferable than others since location will largely determine the potential coverage area on earth. These conditions have made DBS orbital positions and frequency assignments limited resources. See F.A. Wilson, *An Introduction to Satellite Television*, rev. ed. (London: Bernard Babani, 1989) pp. 1 and 23.

11   The most probable household technology through which digital broadcasts and other such communications will be delivered to mass market consumers are high definition television (HDTV) sets. HDTV utilizes digital technology to produce a picture quality approximating cinema film and the sound of a compact disc player.

12   The advantages of telesatellites in efforts to establish a virtually seamless global electronic communication system in relation to terrestrial systems

include the minimal ground-based infrastructure needed to receive and send transmissions; the virtually unrestricted geographic mobility of signal receivers and transmitters; and the economic efficiencies of tele-satellites in relation to terrestrial systems (i.e., cable lines) as calculated on a cost-per-user versus overhead and maintenance costs basis. See William B. Scott, 'Satellites Key to "Infostructure",' *Aviation Week & Space Technology* (14 March 1994) 57–8.

13    On this potential, see Henry Porter, 'Keeper of the Global Gate,' *Manchester Guardian Weekly*, 155(26) (29 December 1996) 16–17.

14    Herbert I. Schiller, *Mass Communications and American Empire* (Boulder, Col.: Westview Press, 1969).

# 2 Critical Perspectives on US Foreign Communication Policy

The underdevelopment of a theory of culture among both critical international political economists and agents of US foreign policy is remarkable. In these pages I begin to redress this gap by focusing on the role of the American state in shaping cultural capacities as a method of constructing and maintaining international consent. This effort is pursued through a critique of aspects of the cultural imperialism paradigm – something of a staple among students of international communications since the late 1960s – and some discussion of 'knowledge' as a neglected concept among students of political economy. In what follows, the practical nature of culture in the dialectical construction, maintenance or annihilation of a hegemonic order is pursued. More than a critique, this chapter also presents theoretical tools of use both in this book's analysis of DBS and US foreign communication policy and, it is hoped, in the more general theoretical and strategic efforts of critical social scientists.

## 2.1 THE CULTURAL IMPERIALISM PARADIGM

In 1979, the United Nations Educational, Scientific and Cultural Organization (UNESCO) released the report of its International Commission for the Study of Communication Problems – more commonly called the MacBride Report. Its conclusion that the '[i]mbalances in national information and communication systems are as disturbing and unacceptable as social, economic, cultural and technological disparities', and that the 'rectification of the latter is inconceivable...without elimination of the former,'[1] was to some degree the product of concern about the early unilateral development of DBS systems by American-based interests. Luiz Felipe de Seixas Correa, a Brazilian representative to the UN, expressed this in 1974: 'it is inconceivable that a field so pregnant with far-reaching implications [international communication] should be allowed to evolve

17

without the benefit of rules and norms incorporating the views, interests, concerns, and aspirations of all States.'[2]

Analyses of DBS developments and more general research on US foreign communication policy have been directly influenced by this kind of perspective. In turn, these views have influenced and perhaps have even limited attempts to specify the role and precise nature the American state in late-twentieth-century international information and communication developments. Herbert Schiller, for example, has portrayed American state policy agents as the instrumental functionaries of both the US military and US-based transnational corporations (TNCs). He argues that new communication technologies, including DBS, not only were developed and applied to further US military and commercial influence over other countries, but also that American public and private sector officials were engaged in a sometimes conscious effort to dominate the world through the exercise of ·some form of cultural power. Schiller assumed, for instance, that America's resistance to restrictions on transnational broadcasting (namely, its promotion of free flow of information principles) constituted a prime expression of a cultural imperialism strategy. According to Schiller, cultural imperialism is 'the sum of the processes by which a society is brought into the modern world system and how its dominating stratum is attracted, pressured, forced, and sometimes bribed into shaping social institutions to correspond to, or even promote, the values and structures of the dominating center of the system.'[3] In this effort, the United States is assumed to represent most directly the interests of 'a handful of media conglomerates...[who] already dominate the international flow of news, films, magazines, TV programs, and other items.'[4]

Cultural imperialism, according to Schiller, thus has been a significant component of both America's domestic military-industrial complex and US imperialism writ large. Primarily through complex networks of elite relations, Schiller believes that US mass media export efforts have been part of larger attempts to mute foreign opposition to American policies and corporate activities. Mostly military-based research and development funds have subsidized and continue to subsidize private sector manufacturers. To varying degrees, public and private sector participants in this relationship have used television and other mass media both to secure foreign markets and to enhance political-military security by transforming 'publics' into 'consumers.' Advertisers, producers and other mass-media interests are assumed to have been aware of these American 'needs' and to have been naturally interested in expanding their markets overseas.

As Schiller explained in 1991, there were three 'essential assumptions undergirding' his thesis. First, he assumed that cultural imperialism was a significant sub-set of a more comprehensive American imperialism. His second assumption was that because corporate security or expansion efforts require the presence of at least some consumerist values, 'the cultural and economic spheres are indivisible.' And third, Schiller cited empirical evidence indicating that the historical growth of the mass-media sector had accompanied the growth of other US exports. This, he believed, indicated that 'the corporate economy is increasingly dependent on the media-cultural sector.'[5]

While elite theory informs much of his work,[6] Schiller suggests that the structural dynamics of the US political economy constitutes the primary force underlying the perpetuation of cultural imperialism. In essence, this theorization is an elaboration of the warnings made by President Eisenhower regarding America's military-industrial complex. Schiller makes the point that the 'fixed costs' mobilized in this complex, involving communication corporations that both receive substantial military research and development funds and hold significant mass media interests (such as the RCA Corporation), constitute an 'inertial force, repulsing ... efforts at change.'[7] Schiller adds that

the mechanics are simple and automatic. Control of [military-related] research enjoys an already-privileged position that is powerful enough to secure the research appropriations in the first place. The fruits of discovery further strengthen the existing power structure and, when applied practically, the material investment becomes a new obstacle to further change and flexibility.... The mutual reinforcement that the military and the communications industry power concentrates offer each other is strengthened additionally by their deep penetration into the highest levels of governmental bureaucracy.[8]

While this elite theory-structural perspective impels him to address important issues, Schiller and others interested in constructing a critical approach to US foreign communication policy have failed to develop this paradigm in an appropriately nuanced way. While in *Mass Communications and American Empire* Schiller provides an intriguing survey of interlocking public and private sector agents, for the most part he assumes these relationships to be largely unproblematic.

Because RCA owns NBC, and because RCA owns shares in the state-established Communications Satellite Corporation (Comsat), and so forth, a self-perpetuating systemic monolith of public and private sector interests are assumed to be working in imperialistic harmony.[9]

The history of DBS and related developments, however, reveals not just a more complex relationship among these interests, it also suggests that different policy outcomes should sometimes be anticipated. While, in the 1960s, RCA (which held significant satellite manufacturing interests) had received some money from the Department of Defense to perform preliminary DBS research, NBC, as its terrestrial broadcaster, had no interest in the domestic competition represented by direct broadcast applications. And while Comsat officials were similarly uninterested in DBS-type advancements – largely due to the potential of direct broadcasting to harm aspects of AT&T's (Comsat's major shareholder) established telecommunication infrastructure – American military officials indeed were interested in the development of *any* far-reaching and relatively cost-effective communications technology. With few exceptions, critical analysts of US foreign communication policy have glossed over such schisms and their complex implications, and instead have tended to assume that, because new space satellite technologies will improve the general international power capacities of the US government and US-based corporations, they will be developed and implemented.[10]

The main point to be made from this trivialization of conflict is that the cultural imperialism paradigm, if it is to be developed into a means of accurately assessing US policies and capacities, requires the analyst to recognize the usually problematic nature of the intra-state, inter- and intra-corporate, and intra-structural relationships that directly influence nation-state activities and international developments. The history of DBS and more general US foreign communication policy developments reveal cultural imperialism to be an essentially reductionist, non-dialectical approach to a complex and extraordinarily important scholarly project.

Complex systemic and incidental factors have directly shaped the history of US foreign communication policy and DBS – systemic and incidental factors that serve to clarify and correct these generalizations. US foreign communication policy has been remarkably un-coordinated and at times riddled with paradoxes and contradictions. Rather than a policy field characterized by an ongoing drive to build overseas markets, US telesatellite policy has been dominated (until recently) by vested interests associated with AT&T's domestic monopoly and the presumed security needs of the West as expressed through the Department of Defense (DoD). In fact, the potential economic and cultural-power benefits of developing and implementing DBS technologies, although occasionally recognized, were more usually suppressed or diverted to protect these and other interests.

## 2.2  CULTURE AS THE OBJECT OF INQUIRY

US foreign communication policy, as characterized through the lens of the cultural imperialism paradigm, is the expression of a complex and systemic collaboration among media-based conglomerates and other corporations, the US military establishment and other state agents. Despite the presence of structural incoherence in this policy field, proponents of the cultural imperialism paradigm continue to argue that a conscious and/or systemic strategy has promoted and continues to promote mass public compliance with the assumed interests of US-based capitalists.[11] Beyond the vagueness of such positions, theorizations of how the American state does this and how technologies, organizations and institutions facilitate compliance and/or resistance to US interests remain underdeveloped. Moreover, proponents of the cultural imperialism paradigm have provided little or no precise explanation of how international consent is maintained or, directly related to this, how a counter-hegemonic consciousness can be generated.[12]

What generates these and related problems in applying the cultural imperialism paradigm is its remarkably underdeveloped understanding of the nature of culture itself. For Schiller and other cultural imperialist theorists, control over the political and economic lives of others is complemented by control 'over those practices by which collectivities make sense of their lives.'[13] But beyond this generalization, this cultural control apparently has involved specific messages carried over the mass media,[14] to a more complex promotion of world-wide consumerism,[15] to the all-encompassing invasion of capitalism writ large as itself a kind of cultural formation. This latter position understands capitalism to be an imperialist system and contemporary globalization developments as the most recent formulation of this systemic drive. As mentioned above, this occlusion of agency in cultural imperialism recently has been embraced by Schiller. Transnational corporations or capital writ large, rather than the United States, is now the imperialist. Again, a precise explanation of who these imperialists are, their motivations, and the complexities of their efforts to dominate others is missing.

Because culture, as the object of inquiry, is itself under-theorized, efforts to specify how cultural imperialism works (or does not work) remain largely unrealized. As long as culture is conceptualized as little more than something that can be readily manipulated by controlling information flows or, more generally, as a functional derivative of the systemic needs of capital, little progress will be made following the prescient work of Schiller and others. Assuming that human beings are not intellectual sponges – soaking up, for instance, consumerist messages sent by corporations and 'the West' – and assuming that more general capitalist and imperialist processes are complex and problematic, involving both systemic forces and human agency, our goal must be the specification of cultural imperialism rather its dismissal.

Specificity is essential both to understand the role of culture in American foreign communication policy and hegemony *and* for the political task of locating where and how consent is constructed or deconstructed. Existing theories of cultural imperialism afford remarkably little opportunity for such strategic concerns. Given the monolithic nature of the American state and capital writ large, significant opportunities for resistance are present only at the peripheries of capitalism. A united front of Third World countries or a mass movement of a disillusioned First World underclass appear to be the only opponents to the imperialist tidal wave. Schiller and others are correct in understanding capitalism to be dynamic and ever-expanding, systemically orientated toward cultural penetration and possibly cultural domination. They also are correct in recognizing the American state to have been its core agent forging the conditions necessary for its development. This view of cultural imperialism fails, however, in its comprehension of the problematic nature of 'the system.' It lacks a theorization of the internal contradictions characterizing capitalism itself. Perhaps most remarkably, it contains little or no recognition that the American state itself is not, and indeed *cannot be*, the monolithic servant of capitalism – even if the complex that is capitalism could ever be unproblematically represented as *an* interest.

Specification of the complex nature of capitalism, cultural imperialism and the workings of the American state constitute primary concerns in this study on DBS. This empirical *and* theoretical investigation is concerned with both analytical accuracy and strategic opportunity. As I have suggested elsewhere,[16] the work of Gramscian or critical international political economists remains underdeveloped on the subject of culture despite its central position in relation to the question of consent in world order. Nevertheless, the work of Robert Cox and others constitutes a rich point of departure for the study at hand.

## 2.3  CULTURE AND CRITICAL INTERNATIONAL POLITICAL ECONOMY

Robert Cox, like Schiller, understands that a broad range of capitalist globalization activities are contributing to cultural tendencies toward homogenization in world order. But unlike Schiller, Cox conceptualizes this core-to-periphery movement to be 'countered by the affirmation of distinct identities and distinct cultural traditions.'[17] Cox also considers states to be core structural mediators of these cultural meetings. For Cox, states may facilitate or impede cultural homogenization. The latter response may take place through the protection of strategic home industries through state-based mechanisms, such as legal protections or economic subsidies for domestic mass media, nationalist educational policies, support for a range of domestic institutions and infrastructures, and so forth.

For Cox and many other critical students of international political economy (IPE), the role of culture in world order is conceptually part of a more general Gramscian approach. The concept of hegemony is central to this. It refers to a process of political, economic, military *and* cultural predominance involving relations among classes, states and international institutions. As Stephen Gill writes, 'hegemony is not simply a form of direct ideological domination. Hegemony is won in the context of a political struggle and its central goal is to obtain political legitimacy for the arrangements preferred by the dominant class.'[18] In effect, hegemony, as I understand it, represents a *process involving the capacity to engage in and dominate institutional developments and, when necessary, control the form of mediated compromises.* On the role of culture in relation to this more elaborate process of hegemony, it is worth quoting Cox at length:

> The cultural challenge goes to the heart of the question of hegemony. 'Hegemony' is...a structure of values and understandings about the nature of order that permeates a whole

society,... a world society composed of states and non-state corporate entities. In a hegemonic order these values and understandings are relatively stable and unquestioned. They appear to most actors as the natural order of things. They are the intersubjective meanings that constitute the order itself. Such a structure of meanings is underpinned by a structure of power, in which most probably one state is dominant but that state's dominance is not sufficient by itself to create hegemony. Hegemony derives from the ways of doing and thinking of the dominant social strata of the dominant state or states insofar as these ways of doing and thinking have inspired emulation or acquired the acquiescence of the dominant social strata of other states. These social strategies and ideologies that explain and legitimize them constitute the foundation of the hegemonic order. Hegemony frames thought and thereby circumscribes action.[19]

Unlike non-Gramscian international political economists – who either focus on conflictive and essentially Hobbesian inter-state relations as the essence of international relations or the role of complex institutions and regimes of inter-state interdependence – Cox, Gill and others also consider international and domestic consent to be both extraordinarily difficult to explain and, in particular locations at certain historical junctures, the most important component of world order. As indicated by Cox, cultural conflicts constitute the loci of essential power struggles precisely because their outcome will define the parameters of individual and collective values and understandings that, in turn, shape the very parameters in which policy options are imaginable or unimaginable, feasible or not feasible.

In both the quotation above and elsewhere, Cox associates the capacity to naturalize 'the way things are' with hegemonic struggle generally and cultural development more particularly. Periods of relative cultural stability – a shared 'structure of meanings' – are directly but *problematically* associated with 'a structure of power.' States here are the necessary mediators of such structures both domestically and internationally. For Cox, culture is a central concept in the process of hegemony and in world order writ large and it is through the state – perhaps the core arbiter of setting or unraveling the political, economic and legal structures shaping cultural conditions – that its ongoing development is directly shaped rather than determined.

When compared to Schiller, this approach directs us toward a more accurate conceptualization of the role of culture in the global political economy. However, a precise elaboration of culture, as an essential subject of inquiry, remains underdeveloped. To explain this, it is helpful to introduce the term 'cultural power' as an organizational concept. I will use this term in order to pull together the complexities involved in examining both culture and hegemony. Specifically, cultural power refers to the capacity to shape the intellectual tools that all human beings use in constructing realities – what will be referred to as 'conceptual systems.' The rapid growth of information as commoditized products and services (facilitated by new communication technologies) suggests that this concern with the cultural-power implications of DBS, for example, must go well beyond an analysis of where information is produced and where it flows. Because the production and distribution of information-based commodities implies the capacity to modify human perceptions and habits (as multi-billion-dollar international marketing and advertising activities, for example, indicate), their social penetration and consumption by individuals tend to modify cultural environments most cogently through their impacts on conceptual systems.

References to culture in this book reflect the recognition that human beings are neither the passive recipients of information nor innately capable of processing information in necessarily rational, critical or creative ways.[20] One's culture directly influences the capacity of the individual and the collectivity to process and make use of information.[21] Information, by itself, is largely meaningless without the presence of conceptual systems that facilitate particular understandings and applications. As such, the capacity of some individuals or groups to shape directly how such conceptual systems are formed and used by others is an issue of fundamental importance. As Ian Parker puts it,

> changing social-economic conditions and the changes in structures of power that accompany them alter social definitions of reality and unreality.... The boundaries of reality are inextricably linked to the capacity to exclude the irrational, as defined principally by those with the power to enforce their definition.[22]

Fundamental in the construction of such realities is the capacity to manipulate conceptual systems and hence knowledge through communication media. Beyond the growing importance of international trade reforms establishing a 'free' trade in services and an enforceable intellectual property rights regime, for instance, the reorganization of US power capacities has increasingly become dependent on the complementary internationalization of liberal and consumerist ideals.

Among critical students of IPE, questions concerning cultural power have been addressed through notions of knowledge structures and the Gramscian concept of consent. The former remains underdeveloped due to its lack of theoretical precision and the latter largely as a result of the need for more sociological rigor.

According to Susan Strange, 'Structural power... confers the power to decide how things shall be done, the power to shape frameworks within which states relate to each other, relate to people, or relate to corporate enterprises.'[23] For Strange, 'the knowledge structure often lies as much in the negative capacity to deny knowledge, to exclude others, rather than in the power to convey knowledge.'[24] But in explaining this, Strange lacks a full appreciation of knowledge as a process. Technology and scientific knowledge are highlighted by Strange as the most valuable knowledge resources sought by contemporary corporations and nation states.[25] At one level this is correct. But in the context of her own definition of the importance of the knowledge structure – the power to 'deny' and/or 'convey' knowledge – this conceptualization is underdeveloped. While recognizing that 'belief systems... underpin or support the political and economic arrangements acceptable to society' – including those that support the investments and property rights associated with science and technology – Strange lacks a sophisticated theory of the relationship between information and knowledge. This, writes Strange, 'is a semantic question... which is puzzling but not very important. Is there a difference between knowledge and information? For many purposes, the two terms are interchangeable.'[26]

A less apparent shortfall is found in the work of Robert Cox. Through his explicitly dialectical approach and his interest in the complexities of national and international civil society, Cox makes effective use of an analytical category he calls 'ideas' in the international political economy. Ideas entail shared practices and meanings as well as differing perspectives. Under this category, diplomatic conduct, economic theory and even gender roles are included in his analysis and are directly related to the material capabilities (that is, the natural, technological and organizational resources available) and the institutions (namely, organized expressions of particular orders and power relations) that he believes reflect and shape world order.

Far from being unimportant, the information–knowledge distinction, its theorization and subsequent application to critical analyses are crucial. Aspects of Cox's work complement this perspective. Since the 1980s, the American state has been restructured in ways that have prioritized international developments in the free flow of information mostly through trade-related institutions. In keeping with Cox's critical approach, the complex forces at work have involved and reflected a realignment of dominant class relationships. While production and class relations are central, 'other factors enter into the formation or nonformation of real historical classes.' These, Cox explains, include 'agencies of collective action that can evoke and channel class consciousness.'[27] Capital–labour relations are understood by Cox to be dynamic and directly conditioned by the organizations and institutions that mediate them. These mediations directly influence the intellectual capacities of human agents. To some extent, the widespread establishment of such relations over time constitute historical structures, consecrating dominant structural forms both institutionally and ideologically. It is through the success of America's free-trade victory in the Uruguay Round of GATT and the subsequent growth and intensification of information and communication commodity activities that the media of hegemonic power – from private sector service corporations to international organizations and institutions – are now implicitly and explicitly reshaping (but *not* determining) the ways in which much of the world thinks about capitalism and the role of transnational communication and information developments.

It is on this point that Strange's dismissal of the importance of the information–knowledge relationship and Cox's under-theorisation of his category of ideas must be redressed.

An individual's knowledge of his or her life and world can be represented as a complex set of conceptual systems constantly applied to the ongoing tasks of perceiving and interpreting. These conceptual systems are not only used to mediate reality, they are also subjected to continual reaffirmations or modifications in accordance with individual experiences. Information flows, in whatever form, thus are continually subjected to interpretation. Simply put, culture provides the individual and the collectivity with a social-environmental reference point or social compass on which conceptual systems can be used or modified to interpret information.[28]

To some degree, technologies, organizations and institutions represent reifications of complex social constructions. They play a mediating role in the ongoing interaction and modification of conceptual systems and cultures. This way of conceptualizing information directs the analyst beyond assumptions that a predominantly one-way flow of information from a capitalist metropole inevitably will subject a receiving population to consumerist desires and liberal ideals. Instead, what this alternative suggests is that a concern with the *capacity* of receiving individuals and collectivities to interpret and make use of information constitutes a more significant analytical task. This is not to say that such flows are unimportant, only that, as the subject of study, culture must be understood as a problematic process rather than a relatively straightforward power resource akin to economic wealth or military might.

The importance of developing a precise and relatively sophisticated understanding of culture can be illustrated by contemporary problems involving capital flexibility and mobility developments involving new communication and information technologies and reformed international legal and economic regimes (that is, the formation of the World Trade Organization). For the most part, analyses of this development lack precise theorizations of the state and its necessary role as a core structural *and conceptual* mediator of such historic developments. While mostly commercial forces are making significant strides in the quest to globalize capitalism and the logic of 'the free market' and other such cultural efforts, an essential contradiction has emerged. While capital systemically tends to universalize itself, the territorially and historically bound nation state remains the core arbiter of this process. As Stephen Gill observes,

> Whereas capital tends towards universality, it cannot operate outside of or beyond the political context, and involves planning, legitimation, and the use of coercive capacities by the state. This forms the key substantive problem for a theory of international relations, at least as seen from an historical materialist perspective. In this context, one of the main tasks of political economy today is to understand and theorise the possibilities for the transformation of these dimensions of world order, in the context of consciousness, culture, and material life.[29]

Capitalism and capitalist social relations, over time, must expand and evolve. However, because this does not take place in a historical vacuum, contradiction is an inherent condition of the process. This involves the barriers that capital must overcome in the form of pre-existing political, economic and cultural structures. The state remains a core institution in international relations. While the state itself necessarily is utilized to support this systemic growth, competing capitalist interests use states as vehicles through which domestic and international structures are reformed to accommodate their particular needs. Moreover, states, as institutional structures, themselves are usually reformed in order to take on such tasks on behalf of dominant private sector interests. Deepening the complexity of this process are the more general dimensions of consciousness, culture and the conditions of day-to-day life. If the globalization of capitalist production activities and social relations is being facilitated by DBS and related transnational technologies, the task of specifying the complex and contradictory processes at work – substantively beyond the generalizations provided by the cultural imperialism paradigm – now constitutes a rather urgent undertaking.

## 2.4 MEDIATORS OF THE INTERNATIONAL POLITICAL ECONOMY

The American state stands as a core institution and DBS an extraordinary transnational technology in the contemporary international political economy. The recent history of DBS and related developments reveal the United States and other states to be complex structures, institutionally entrenched but nevertheless dialectically responsive to internal and external forces in ways that are directly biased by pre-existing structures. Changes in intra-state structures, for instance, that affected US foreign communication policy in the 1980s were directly influenced by corporate forces seeking a stable international free flow-cum-free trade regime. However, the capacity of the American state to modify *itself* in order *then* to reform international institutions was limited and the particulars of this history were directly influenced by the characteristics of existing state structures. It is in this sense that an elaboration of American state capacities can be pursued by explicitly conceptualizing the state as a complex mediator of private and public sector agents. To repeat, the structural and historical conditions in which the state performs these mediations are biased in ways that, at any particular time, are largely out of the *direct* control of any particular agent or bloc of interests.

An analysis of the American state as a complex medium of organization and conflict, and on the efforts of mostly private sector agents to forge new intra-state structures as an essential step in reforming inter-state relations, compels a reassessment and elaboration of the forces and processes shaping state structural capacities. Relatively sophisticated models of state policy exist, of course, and several of these have emphasized how the institutional and organizational capacities of a particular policy environment are related to perspectives, decisions and their implementation. Theda Skocpol, for example, has listed a number of significant variables that can be applied when examining the capabilities of particular state agents to formulate and implement relatively autonomous policies. Particularly in periods of social-economic crisis, 'distinctive state strategies', according to Skocpol, may be developed most readily by 'organizationally coherent collectivities of state officials, especially collectivities of career officials relatively insulated from ties to currently dominant socioeconomic interests.'[30] Generally, these conditions most often are held by officials in charge of 'domestic order-keeping functions' and those involved in 'the international orientations of states.'[31] In the United States, however, even among agents responsible for these functions, instances of apparent policy-making autonomy essentially do not exist.

Material and historical conditions, such as the limited availability of frequencies in the radio spectrum and the competing demands of US private sector and defense-based agents; the export and overseas aspirations of domestic corporations involved in the production and distribution of information-based commodities; and the relationship between military and intelligence-related research money and the export interests of domestic companies have led to American state officials typically being located in a broad range of government agencies with overlapping foreign and domestic policy responsibilities. Since the 1980s, the complexity of this domestic policy–foreign policy relationship has deepened as a result of the emerging significance of US-based corporations directly involved in international information and communication activities, rather than simply exporting hardware and software to foreign markets. At various times, amidst changing historical circumstances, DBS policy developments have been the expression of these structural conditions and, as such, this study of DBS developments serves to elaborate these in relation to this book's broader concern with both hegemony and cultural imperialism. Again, the focus of this inquiry must be on the role of the state in mediating not only the various agents of history but also its direct and indirect role in shaping cultural environments.

According to Robert Cox, 'The nature of the state is... [in part] defined by the class structure on which the state rests.'[32] Rather than portraying a crude dominance of a ruling class, in which dominant agents use the state instrumentally, Cox agrees with Skocpol in understanding that the actions of state actors are directly influenced by historically based structural capacities. According to Cox,

state actions are constrained by knowledge on the part of the state's agents of what the class structure makes possible and what it precludes.... The structure defining these tasks and limits, which becomes part and parcel of the state itself, is ... called the historic bloc.[33]

Cox explains a historic bloc to be a 'complex of social class relations... [which] sets the practical limits for feasible goals and methods of exercising power.' Significant social-economic movements and related power shifts will generate disruptions within a bloc. In such disruptive periods, 'classes and ideologies and the political parties that shape and guide them form rival historic blocs contending over the very nature of the state. If one bloc,' says Cox, 'displaces another, a new state is born and with a new *raison d'état.*'

In sum, a historic bloc is a complex alliance of interests which both reflect and direct the character of dominant political-economic activities at a given period of capitalist history.[34] Directly linked to such historic blocs and their capacities are more general complexes of national and international production relations and classes, and these both influence and are influenced by a particular world order. Cox and other Gramscian international political economists (such as Stephen Gill) deem such a world order to be hegemonic if 'the dominant state creates an order based ideologically on a broad measure of consent.' Cox continues that in such an order,

production in particular countries becomes connected through the mechanisms of a world economy and linked into world systems of production. The social classes of the dominant country find allies in classes within other countries. The historic blocs underpinning particular states become connected through the mutual interests and ideological perspectives of social classes in different countries, and global classes begin to form. An incipient world society grows up around the interstate system, and states themselves become internationalized in that their mechanisms and policies become adjusted to the rhythms of the world order.[35]

Cox identifies a process he calls the 'internationalizing of the state' in which the tension between national and global influences shaping state structures, in the late twentieth century, is being weighted toward the latter. This involves states being reshaped in response to changes and pressures from external agents and forces and related realignments of domestic groups and forces. Specifically, Cox argues that the internationalizing of the state involves adjustments to 'the internal structures of states'. . . so that each can best transform the global consensus into national policy and practice.'[36] In other words, the internationalizing state entails not only an adjustment of what intra-state agencies do and their relative power capacities, it also involves a realignment of the historic bloc – the complex relationship among dominant social and economic groups.

Rather than simply characterizing the American state as a dominant agent modifying the global political economy – a position generally endorsed by critical scholars of US foreign communication policy – or as itself a direct respondent to changing international conditions, Cox instead recognizes the state to be a complex mediator. The state has both been a facilitator and (in some instances) a barrier to the growth and evolution of late-twentieth-century capitalism. While the US public sector very much reflects the needs and conflicts of private sector interests, the American state also is a complex institution by itself.

Reforms to the intra-state structures of direct concern to DBS developments and foreign communication policy themselves have been shaped by the ability of the American state to change. Indeed, the particulars of the history presented in this book cannot be explained without an understanding of intra-state structures, and this requires an explicit recognition that the state is a complex mediator of often conflicting vested interests. The structural and historical conditions in which the state performs these mediations are shaped in ways that are most often out of the *direct* control of any particular agent or bloc of interests.

Conceptualizing the American state, or any state, to be influential in this way requires an understanding of the historical underpinnings of its structural biases. Because they are ongoing institutional constructions, necessarily incorporating past ways of organizing, understanding and doing, elements of state practices are, to some degree, 'fixed.' In other words, the complex ways of doing state business, although historically determined, are shaped by structural rigidities. These established ways of doing directly influence the intellectual capacities of state agents, while their ways of seeing and doing, in turn, may be used to reinforce or revise state structures. The biases of US foreign communication policy officials, at any particular time, thus are directly shaped by the peculiarities of existing state structures – structures that are shaped by the material and intellectual capacities and interests of a usually complex array of private and public sector agents.

Through empirical evidence and the application of critical political-economic theory, this book shows that the systemic and structural relationship of the American state with US-based capital in foreign communication policy has involved far more complex processes than the cultural imperialism paradigm can reveal – at least as it now stands. Rather than a structurally entrenched American imperialism defining the course of US policy, historical shifts in policy-making priorities, capacities and outcomes instead have generated multiple and even disparate centers of policy leadership. In specifying these, their contexts and the forces underlying them, a relatively sophistic-ated representation of cultural imperialism can be developed.

As shown in Chapter 6, the mediating role of the American state was crucial in the success of a trade-based foreign communication policy strategy as represented by the Uruguay Round of GATT. Both it and the American state now can be viewed as essential components of late-twentieth-century international information and communica-tion developments. In this contemporary history, different states and different officials within each state act in response to domestic and international as well as intra-state forces. Cox elaborates on this:

> Each state has evolved, through its own institutions and practices, certain consistent notions of interest and modes of conduct that can be termed its particular *raison d'état*. This autonomy is, however, conditioned by both internal and external constraints. State autonomy, in other words, is exercised within a structure created by the state's own history.[37]

What remains to be elaborated is the nature of these constraints at any particular time, in any particular nation state, and on any par-ticular issue or policy question. Of course these internal and external constraints are dialectically influential. For example, the hegemonic crisis facing the United States from the 1970s and the subsequent response of the American public and private sectors to it involved the disassembling of Fordist and Keynesian accumulation models. But rather than portraying this crisis and its response as the manipulation of states on behalf of a national or international ruling class (somehow forging and then imposing a coherent master-plan on state officials to reform domestic and global institutions), the actions of both dominant private sector interests and state actors have been directly influenced by the historically constructed structural conditions in which they think and work.

The American state, since the mid-1980s, itself has been restructured in ways that have prioritized the neo-liberal reordering of domestic and international relations. State officials have come to champion TNC interests seeking a stable international regime in which to exploit communication and information technologies and/ or expand market opportunities. In response to a foreign communication policy crisis in the 1980s, components of the American state were reformed in order to facilitate its mediation of comprehensive global restructuring activities. The American state – through the ascendancy of trade – underwent reforms enabling it to service the political and legal needs of mostly TNCs and international business consumers directly involved in information economy developments. These modifications, in turn, altered aspects of American state relations with domestic and transnational capital.

The historical context in which these intra-state reforms unfolded involved what has been called the crisis of the Fordist regime of accumulation, the pursuit of a more flexible regime of accumulation and the related crisis of US hegemony. The OPEC cartel, the Vietnam War, the relative strength and subsequent wage demands of unionized workers, and the emergence of mostly Asian-based economic competitors, all contributed to a burgeoning demand for technological innovation and lower production costs among Western corporations beginning in the 1970s. Organizational and production-based innovations involving lower costs in communication and information-related activities were achieved through ongoing research and development investments (particularly those provided by the American state), the disciplining of labor (zealously pursued through 'Thatcherism' and 'Reaganomics'), and the promotion of competition in the telecommunications and computer industries.[38]

Beyond lowering production costs and the provision of new services useful in the promotion of production process innovation, flexibility and efficiency, new communication and information technologies modified distribution and consumption capacities: information-based services facilitated the rapid turnover of capital investments; corporate abilities to respond to consumer and market demands were enhanced; globalized and instantaneous personal credit facilitated market expansion efforts; and through the more comprehensive and accurate monitoring of lifestyles and price system activities, potential consumers were approached in ever more enticing ways.

The opportunities provided to service sector-based corporations as a result of these complex developments, coupled with the ongoing crisis in the US economy (particularly in relation to the decline or stagnation in real incomes and the disintegration of secure middle-class employment opportunities) – and the collapse of the Soviet Union as a counter-weight to capitalist models – facilitated the radical reform of international communication and information regimes dating from the late 1980s. This has involved the American state as the complex mediator of mostly neo-liberal reforms in a range of international organizations, including the ITU and, most importantly, the GATT. In its institutionalization of a free trade in services and requisite intellectual property rights (when viewed in conjunction with ongoing technological innovations and applications), the recently institutionalized World Trade Organization (WTO) now constitutes a dramatic step forward in efforts to open world markets to producers and distributors of information-based commodities.

The American state has been affected by and has affected these changes. As Cox has generalized, the role of states has been transformed during this period. Rather than an institutional buffer, mandated to protect and develop domestic interests, state priorities have shifted toward 'adapting domestic economies to the perceived exigencies of the world economy.'[39] This internationalizing of the state has involved the ascendancy of state departments and personnel directly involved in foreign relations and international economic affairs and the relative subordination of domestic-orientated intra-state agencies. As a result, says Cox, state structures have been recast to facilitate the incorporation of world-economy developments into the decision-making processes of domestic policy makers.[40]

States, of course, were not and are not the only institutions mediating the international political economy. International institutions, such as the WTO and the ITU, play decisive roles in contemporary information and communication developments. As with states, the ways in which these institutions are structured will facilitate and/or inhibit the development of capitalism in general and the interests of particular dominant class fractions in particular. The history presented in this book reveals various domestic and transnational political-economic agents to have sought the mobilization and/or reformulation of state structures as their primary means of reforming the international institutions through which their aspirations could be pursued.

The historical development, implementation and implications of communication technologies – such as DBS – has not only involved struggles that are contextualized and mediated by established structural conditions; once established and part of daily life, such technologies constitute new mediators in the historical process. But beyond the capacities afforded by historically constructed ways of doing and thinking, the capacity of a technology like DBS – and thus its role as a mediator in the international political economy – also is directly shaped by its material capabilities. While the economic, political and military interests of US-based agents constitute essential dynamics underlying how DBS has been perceived and used, such dynamics have affected and have been affected by the very specific limits and opportunities prescribed by the laws of physics and more general levels of scientific, entrepreneurial and strategic knowledge present at a given place and time.

The advantages of this dialectical understanding of the role of institutional, organizational and technological media for the cultural imperialism paradigm and Gramscian conceptions of hegemony and consent are elaborated in the following chapters. At this stage, however, a number of preliminary points should be underlined. For cultural imperialist theorists, the perspective presented in these pages suggests that multiple levels of analysis are required in order to explain, for instance, how a particular policy effort was imaginable or unimaginable at a particular time in the minds of particular actors. This perspective also accommodates an understanding of the potential for resistance to such policies at particular historical junctures. In sum, a focus on structures, media and process provides the analytical tools needed to develop a precise understanding of history, anticipate future tensions and conflicts, and better pin-point strategic opportunities when and where they emerge.

For example, the essential role played by technologies, organizations and institutions (including the state) in contemporary structural transformations in the global political economy intrinsically involve efforts to forge and maintain consent as to what kinds of political and economic policies are feasible and desirable. The neo-liberal World Order being constructed is a far more tenuous development than what recent analyses emphasizing the 'inevitability' of globalization and the transformative magic of new technologies would have us believe. As developed in this book, and stressed in its final chapter, these media of structural change and consensus building have been and will remain the sites of contradiction and struggle. Technologies, organizations and institutions process such struggles and contradictions in their own ways – what I refer to as their historically constructed 'biases' – and the structural and cultural implications of such mediations will reflect these pre-established capacities and dispositions. As such, the American state, as a core and biased medium of domestic and global political, economic and cultural developments, stands as an institution through which political action and structural reform can modify the outcome of contradictions and struggles.

## 2.5 CONCLUSIONS

The state plays a crucial role in shaping the social-economic conditions through which capitalism develops. It is not a static entity: *it is a living but relatively inflexible institution, painfully reinventing itself in response to changing historical conditions and dominant social-economic interests.* In relation to DBS and international information and communication developments, *the American state has been a complex mediator – 'complex' in that the response of its personnel at any given time is biased by pre-existing structural conditions that subsequently may be reformed.*

The orderly functioning of the international political economy involves the predominance of general assumptions or shared mythologies as to what is feasible and infeasible, realistic and unrealistic, imaginable and unimaginable. This can occur when a fraction of capital or conjunction of powerful vested interests come to dominate an existing or emerging hegemonic bloc. Through its economic and ideational predominance – both facilitated through the capacity to reform or control core institutions (including nation states), organizations and technologies (such as DBS) – a hegemonic development strategy can be pursued. This economic effort and ideational perspective then can be universalized into a shared common sense. To some extent, the present study traces the problematic emergence of a particular fraction of capital – those corporations directly involved in or dependent upon emerging information and communication commodity activities.[41]

Thinking about the American state in the way prescribed in this chapter compels the development of a comprehensive understanding of the structural biases affecting human thought and its historical underpinnings. This involves taking some significant steps beyond what the cultural imperialism paradigm now provides, especially given its vague notions of systemically generated, elite-dominated, largely unproblematic (and monolithic) state-corporate structures. Ultimately, what the work of Schiller and others lacks is a nuanced and empirically precise understanding of agency. By examining the history of the American state and DBS developments, the complexities and contradictions of intra-state and inter-corporate activities *within the core of the hegemon itself*, a more sophisticated theorisation can be developed. Using Cox and the work of other critical students of IPE, the following chapters redress Schiller's essential limitations while, in the process, also elaborating on what remains lacking in Gramscian approaches – a theorization of the role of culture in general and knowledge in particular in hegemonic orders and counter-hegemonic projects. These and other points are discussed in what follows, beginning with a largely empirical analysis of early US tele-satellite developments and the public and private sector structures forged in relation to their history.

## NOTES

1  MacBride et al., *Many Voices, One World*. International Commission for the Study of Communication Problems (Paris: UNESCO, 1984) p. 193.
2  Luiz Felipe de Seixas Correa, 'Direct Satellite Broadcasting and the Third World', *Columbia Journal of Transnational Law*, 13 (1974) 73.
3.  Herbert I. Schiller, *Communication and Cultural Domination* (New York: M.E. Sharpe, 1976), p. 9.
4.  *Ibid.* pp. 64–5.
5  Herbert I. Schiller, 'Not Yet the Post-Imperialist Era', in *Critical Studies in Mass Communications* Vol., 8(1) (March 1991) 14.
6  The centrality of elite networks linking government, military and corporate communication interests is first articulated in Schiller, *Mass Communications and American Empire*. For example, see pp. 55–9.
7  *Ibid.*, p. 61.
8  *Ibid.*, p. 62.
9  *Ibid.*, pp. 82–3.

10    *Ibid.*, esp. pp. 68-70. On p. 80, Schiller writes that 'Each new electronic development widens the perimeter of American influence, and the indivisibility of military and commercial activity operates to promote even greater expansion.' Exceptions to this apparently unproblematic perspective include the work of Vincent Mosco, 'Who Makes US Government Policy in World Communications?' *Journal of Communication*, 29 (1) (Winter 1979) 158–64.

11    Representative examples can be found in Jorg Becker, Goran Hedebro and Leena Paldan (eds) *Communication and Domination, Essays in Honor of Herbert I. Schiller* (Norwood: Ablex, 1986)

12    A comprehensive critique on the purported effects of cultural imperialism has been produced by John Tomlinson, *Cultural Imperialism, A Critical Introduction* (Baltimore: The Johns Hopkins University Press, 1991).

13    *Ibid.*, p. 7.

14    The term 'media imperialism' has been used, sometimes interchangeably with 'cultural imperialism.' The former is often used by liberal or non-'critical' writers. A core reason for this is that the broader context of domination informing the Marxist or more critical scholar, and the role of the mass media in this more holistic conceptualization, is not accepted a priori. Moreover, empirical efforts to quantify mass media penetration constitutes a far more straightforward proposition than attempts to evaluate the quantitative *and* qualitative implications of a complex of 'cultural' domination. See Chin-Chuan Lee, *Media Imperialism Reconsidered* (Beverly Hills: Sage, 1979).

15    An 'invasion' of consumerist practices and values is often portrayed in the context of an external force disrupting the cultural harmony present in a previously unsullied society. The MacBride Commission report and other NWICO studies reflects this kind of cultural protectionism based on the assumed 'naturalness' or righteousness of existing nation states as cultural entitities. For a critique of this 'invasion' approach, see Tomlinson, *Cultural Imperialism*, esp. pp. 23–4, and David Morley, 'Where the Global Meets the Local: Notes from the Sitting-Room', in Morley, *Television, Audiences and Cultural Studies* (London, Routledge, 1992) ch.13.

16    Edward A. Comor, 'Introduction', in Comor (ed.), *The Global Political Economy of Communication: Hegemony, Telecommunication and the Information Economy* (London and New York: Macmillan and St Martin's Press, 1994) esp. pp. 6–10.

17    Robert W. Cox, 'Multilateralism and the World Order', in Cox (with Timothy J. Sinclair), *Approaches to World Order* (Cambridge: Cambridge University Press, 1996) p. 517.

18    Stephen Gill, *American Hegemony and the Trilateral Commission* (Cambridge: Cambridge University Press, 1990), p. 118.

19    Cox, ' 'Multilateralism and the World Order', pp. 517–18.

20    In relation to the individual, the term 'culture' is used in the following pages to mean 'a general state or habit of the mind,' while for a community it will be used in references to 'the whole way of life, material, intellectual, and spiritual': Raymond Williams, 'Culture and Civilization', in Paul Edwards (ed.), *The Encyclopedia of Philosophy*, vol. 2 (New York: Macmillan and The Free Press, 1967) p. 273.

40        *Communication, Commerce and Power*

21    On this general perspective, see Paul Levinson, *Mind at Large: Knowing in the Technological Age* (Greenwich, Conn. JAI Press, 1988).
22    Ian Parker, 'Myth, Telecommunication and the Emerging Global Informational Order: The Political Economy of Transitions', in Comor (ed.), *The Global Political Economy of Communication*, p. 47.
23    Susan Strange, *States and Markets* (London: Pinter Publishers, 1988) p. 25.
24    *Ibid.*, p. 115.
25    *Ibid.*, see esp. pp. 126–31.
26    *Ibid.*, p. 118.
27    Robert W. Cox, *Production, Power, and World Order: Social Forces in the Making of History* (New York: Columbia University Press, 1987) p. 2.
28    See L. David Ritchie, 'Another Turn of the Information Revolution, Relevance, Technology, and the Information Society', *Communication Research* 18 (3) (June 1991) 412–27.
29    Stephen Gill, 'Globalisation, Market Civilisation, and Disciplinary Neo-liberalism', *Millennium*, 24 (3) (Winter 1995) 422.
30    Theda Skocpol, 'Bringing the State Back In: Strategies of Analysis in Current Research', in Peter B. Evans, Dietrich Rueschemeyer and Theda Skocpol (eds.), *Bringing the State Back In* (Cambridge: Cambridge University Press, 1985) p. 9.
31    *Ibid.*, p. 11.
32    Robert W. Cox, *Production, Power, and World Order*, p. 6. Cox defines 'historical structures' as the 'persistent social practices, made by collective human activity and transformed through collective human activity' – p. 4. By the term 'state structure,' Cox means 'both the machinery of government and enforcement (where power lies among the policy-elaborating and enforcement agencies...) and the historic bloc on which the state rests' – p. 254.
33    *Ibid.*, p. 6.
34    Craig N. Murphy, *International Organization and Industrial Change, Global Governance since 1840* (Cambridge: Polity Press, 1994) pp. 27–8.
35    *Cox, Production, Power, and World Order*, p. 410, fn. 10.
36    *Ibid.*, p. 254.
37    Ibid., pp. 399–400.
38    See David Harvey, *The Condition of Postmodernity* (Oxford: Basil Blackwell, 1990) esp. pp. 121–97.
39    Robert W. Cox, 'The Global Political Economy and Social Choice', in Cox, *Approaches to World* Order, p. 193.
40    *Ibid.*
41    Among the preconditions for this fraction's success are the following: its ability to unite various interests both through its willingness to make compromises and provide economic and ideational leadership; its compatibility with other domestic and international political and economic interests and growth strategies; and, fundamentally, its essential compatibility with predominant productive capitalist activities. See Rene Bugge Bertramsen, 'From the Capitalist State to the Political Economy', in Bertramsen, Jens Peter Frolund Thomsen and Jacob Torfing (eds), *State, Economy and Society* (London: Unwin Hyman, 1991) p. 112.

# 3 Telesatellite Policy and DBS, 1962–1984

The history of the Direct Broadcast Satellite (DBS) in the United States from 1962 to 1984 involves a paradox. The year 1962 was the one in which the Communications Satellite Act was passed. By 1984 most of America's first DBS license holders either had failed to establish viable domestic systems or had given up their direct broadcasting plans altogether. It also was the year in which the United States withdrew from UNESCO – then the most troublesome and perhaps also the most vulnerable of UN agencies opposing US foreign communication policy.

The paradox of US policy over these years most visibly involved ongoing schisms in the relationship between public sector investments in the development of DBS on the one hand, and the efforts of public sector agencies to derail its commercial application on the other. Without government funding, mostly through National Aeronautics and Space Administration (NASA) research and development contracts, direct broadcasting probably would not have become technologically feasible when it did – in the mid–1970s. Yet, as Delbert D. Smith recognized in 1976, the 'capabilities of direct broadcast satellites are so countervailant to vested interests and represent such a spectrum of controversial applications' that efforts to develop DBS services were repeatedly suffocated over the course of this formative period. [12]

NASA's mandate was to fund the preliminary development of non-commercial outer space technologies. It had relative independence (along with the Department of Defense) in the allocation of these contracts. There was, at first, a limited threat posed by aerospace manufacturers interested in developing DBS technologies in relation to the interests of AT&T and Comsat. These were significant factors facilitating the preliminary development of direct broadcasting. In this effort, aerospace companies such as Hughes Aircraft and Fairchild Industries had early access to public sector research and funding. But the DBS prototype ATS-F system was never put into commercial service. Instead, this first direct broadcast satellite was used in a much-publicized series of educational television experiments for the

Indian government beginning in 1974. Despite its successful application overseas and warnings from some senior policy officials that DBS developments should be encouraged in light of the emerging plans of foreign countries to develop their own capabilities, powerful elements of the US private sector and key American state agencies blocked the domestic use of DBS until the early 1980s.[3]


## 3.1  FORMATIVE TELESATELLITE DEVELOPMENTS

In 1955, President Eisenhower endorsed a National Academy of Sciences (NAS) proposal, in conjunction with the Department of Defense, to design and launch an experimental vehicle capable of collecting geophysical data from above the earth's atmosphere by the end of 1958. It was not until the launch of the Sputnik satellite by the Soviet Union in October 1957, however, that American efforts to develop satellites were directed substantially beyond post–1945 work involving long-range weapons systems.[4] As a result of the positive publicity Sputnik generated for Soviet science and engineering, and the fact that this experimental satellite was technologically superior to the NAS/DoD proposal, the international leadership held by US science and thus also its dominant international military position were publicly questioned.[5] One significant American response was the formation of NASA in July 1958.[6] Congress limited NASA activities to military-related research and development and to funding private sector projects.[7] Underlying this mandate was the assumption that although the public sector should play a leading role in experimental research, it should not be directly involved in commercial satellite applications. In other words, government's role in the United States was to 'lead the way' in order to establish the foundations for subsequent private sector activities.[8]

The first 'true' telecommunication satellite launched by the United States (that is, a satellite that receives a signal from earth and then transmits it back) was called Echo I. It was placed into orbit by NASA in August 1960. But despite this achievement, private sector interests leveled frequent complaints against NASA. Telecommunication and aerospace companies demanded that government research programs be more directly focused on private sector applications.[9] Moreover, in April 1961, the successful launch of the world's first manned spacecraft by the Soviet Union stimulated a significant growth in US government allocations to American corporations for their development of space-related technologies.[10] One funding recipient was Hughes Aircraft. As with AT&T and the Radio Corporation of America (RCA), Hughes submitted proposals for research contracts involving the development of telesatellites in 1959 and 1960. In 1961, NASA announced its partnership with AT&T in the development of the Telstar series of experimental satellites, beginning with the launch of Telstar I in July 1962.[11] RCA, with NASA, developed and placed into orbit the Relay satellite series beginning in December of that same year.[12] Both Telstar and Relay were elliptical orbit systems. Because these satellites circled the earth approximately once every 2 hours and 40-minutes, a large number of vehicles had to be launched so that at least one could maintain contact with two earth stations at any given time. Moreover, because of their ongoing movement in relation to a fixed point on earth, large and expensive tracking equipment had to be used to maintain ground-station to satellite communications.

These and related weaknesses of elliptical systems provided Hughes with an opportunity to develop what was, in the early 1960s, the purely theoretical idea of placing a satellite in a geostationary orbit (GSO). In contrast to elliptical systems, a satellite in a GSO would maintain a fixed position in relation to a location on earth. In 1961, the DoD had conducted a series of failed laboratory GSO tests called the Advent program. Apparently because these failures suggested to NASA officials that a GSO system was, at best, a long-term proposition, Hughes failed to generate the same large-scale support for its funding proposals as had the proponents of elliptical systems. But beyond the theoretical nature of the GSO, AT&T initially opposed its development due to the inherent conflicts that such a system posed for established common carrier interests.

Hughes research into the technological feasibility of a GSO system began in 1959. In February 1962, Hughes laboratory experiments encouraged NASA to pay for the construction of a small synchronous satellite that could be launched using contemporary rocket technologies.[13] The DoD shared in the research information generated by this experiment in exchange for the use of its international ground-station facilities.[14] In February 1963, the world's first GSO satellite, called Syncom, was launched. The third Syncom satellite, Syncom III, was placed into orbit not coincidentally in time to transmit television signals from the Tokyo Olympic Games to the United States.

Almost a year prior to the launch of Syncom I, Hughes Vice President Allen E. Pucket explained to a Senate subcommittee that the key advantages of an advanced type of GSO system in relation to existing AT&T and RCA elliptical systems included the potential to transmit a signal to one-third of the earth's surface. This, explained Pucket, 'gives us more than just a cable in the sky; it gives us, in effect, a network in the sky':

> If, for example, we choose to use a satellite of this sort as a TV transponder, we might be transmitting TV signals from a single station on the earth to the satellite which would then be repeated and transmitted back into this beam and cover all the area.[15]

Pucket also told Congress that the stationary characteristics of a GSO satellite would significantly lower the costs associated with both the many ground receivers required to track elliptical satellites and with the relatively complex trunking systems needed to distribute the signals on the ground. Moreover, world-wide coverage was conceivable using just three high-altitude satellites, while elliptical systems would require between 20 and 100 low-orbiting vehicles to do the same thing 'depending on who makes the calculations and how optimistic one is.'[16] In a subsequent hearing, the head of the Hughes Syncom project, C. Gordon Murphy, suggested that the US government should reassess its financial support for research related to AT&T's and RCA's elliptical systems. Once these systems are put in place, warned Murphy, their high overhead costs would impel the FCC 'to maintain a system of international telephone and television rates that will be high enough to permit the recovery of the... [original] investment through the tariffs charged.' Murphy argued that it was in the public interest 'to wait and see whether Syncom will work before proceeding with any system.'[17]

Unfortunately for Hughes, US policies shaping the development of these new technologies involved far more than these kinds of cost-based calculations. The AT&T telephone monopoly, due to the terrestrial cable-based characteristics of its system, initially favored the development of elliptical satellites because they constituted the best 'fit' in terms of its own telecommunication infrastructure. Because AT&T controlled America's point-to-point telephone transmissions through its ownership of switching facilities, microwave relay stations and cable lines, the establishment of relatively low-power elliptical systems would compel broadcasters and other satellite users to remain dependent on the AT&T ensemble of terrestrial services. In 1962, AT&T owned about 80 per cent of all transoceanic cables to and from the United States, it held an absolute monopoly over all domestic US long-distance telephone calls, and about 80 percent of the local US telephone market was under its control.[18] In sum, the GSO alternative – beyond its technological uncertainties – entailed the *potential* of excluding significant components of the AT&T infrastructure altogether. AT&T executives thus became champions of the kind of telesatellite system they assumed would minimize competitive incursions.[19]

At the same Congressional hearing in which C. Gordon Murphy promoted the Hughes Syncom project, the Director of Research and Engineering for the Department of Defense argued that because the 'business' of the DoD 'is to look to the future and try to hedge our bets' *both* kinds of technologies should be developed as quickly as possible.[20] Moreover, given that the DoD spent US$1 billion on telecommunications in 1962 alone, and due to its overwhelming reliance on relatively high-cost cable-based systems that are 'distance-sensitive,' the DoD considered the rapid development and implementation of various telesatellite systems to be both a cost-savings and a security priority.[21]

Beyond these military interests and beyond the commercial aspirations of a select number of US corporations, the emergence of the Telstar system generated an interest in the political implications of telesatellites. According to the 1962 Congressional testimony of the Assistant Secretary of State for Economic Affairs, G. Griffith Johnson, while telephone service developments were widely recognized to be the most important commercial application of these new technologies, from a general foreign policy perspective, 'I am sure that the possibilities offered for the international broadcast of television programs will loom the most important.'[22] In reference to the Soviet space program and the perception that its success had damaged America's international reputation, the Chairman of the same Congressional hearing, Representative Ken Hechler, remarked that 'the average man in the street in nations around the world would ... be inspired' by the first international telesatellite television transmission in history.[23] Indeed, with this propaganda dimension in mind, the United States Information Agency (USIA) commissioned a Gallup poll to trace the reactions of the British public to Telstar. A representative of the USIA told Congress that 'half or more of the total British public rated the new satellite a "very good" scientific achievement ... and indicated that their opinion of scientific development in the United States has gone up as a result of Telstar.'[24]

Preoccupied with the development of telesatellites in relation to technological achievements in the Soviet Union, the formative regulatory arrangements that constituted the framework in which these were to be pursued were subjected to remarkably little Congressional scrutiny. In May 1961, the FCC released a report stating that emerging telesatellite applications should remain within its jurisdictional sphere using those rules and regulations already governing the activities of common carriers. This approach constituted the *de facto* exclusion from the regulatory process of manufacturers like Hughes Aircraft. Five months later, the FCC issued another report proposing the establishment of a government-sanctioned corporation charged with the responsibility of developing, operating and managing a single telesatellite system for overseas communications. Private sector carriers, dominated by AT&T, would lease circuits from this so-called 'carriers's carrier.' The new entity also would be run by the established carriers with some of its directors appointed by the US President. By 1962, neither Congressional legislators nor even State Department officials could agree on the extent to which the private sector should control this proposed monopoly. Nor was there ready agreement on what private sector entities should be allowed to take part.[25] Nevertheless, by the end of August 1962, the Communications Satellite Act became federal law and Comsat (the Communications Satellite Corporation) was established as the instrument through which a commercial telesatellite system would be developed for American overseas communications.[26] The Act charged the FCC with the responsibility of formulating and enforcing the rules and regulations to carry out its provisions.[27]

A small number of Democratic Party Congressmen led the only sustained resistance to the commercial monopoly implications of Comsat. Driving legislation through, however, was both the urgency of telesatellite developments in the minds of White House personnel and the lobbying efforts of established domestic common carriers.[28] Throughout this period, AT&T officials claimed that telesatellite systems were far too expensive in relation to established terrestrial services for investments to be made toward their construction for domestic use only. The overhead costs of establishing an international telesatellite system, it was argued, could be justified, however, if the common carriers already handling overseas telephone communications controlled the new technology *without competition*. As such, executives representing AT&T argued that Comsat stock should be controlled by established US-based international common carriers only – namely, AT&T.

The US Department of Justice (DoJ), while cautious, did not formally oppose this prospective monopoly. In 1961, Lee Loevinger, the head of the DoJ, recognized that control of Comsat by the common carriers would, however, generate a 'natural reluctance... [among the carriers] to take speedy action which would make... [their] facilities obsolete.' Loevinger compared the formation of Comsat to the history of US road transportation:

> Suppose that in the early days in the development of motor transportation service we had decreed that all motor transportation should be owned by railroads. I think it is self-evident that we would not have quite the same system of motor transportation we... have today.[29]

In response to this general concern – particularly in light of the potentially revolutionary impact of satellite technologies on the telecommunications industry – AT&T Vice President James E. Dingman claimed that the telesatellite would *never* challenge the predominance of cable systems. At best, said Dingman, outer space platforms 'will merely provide the means by which broadband microwave techniques employed for continental communications can be extended across the oceans to supplement existing... facilities.'[30] Nevertheless, given the American government's general interest in the development of telesatellites, the organizational and technical expertise required, the experience that Comsat's management would need in its dealings with foreign entities, and the massive overhead costs involved, Dingman argued that the new corporation could only succeed if placed under the control of AT&T. Moreover, if non-carriers (such as aerospace companies) were allowed to participate, delays and economic inefficiencies would be inevitable as a result of the imposition of competing interests.[31]

Members of Congress opposing the Satellite Communications Act argued that Comsat would become the tool of AT&T, enabling the domestic monopoly to control international telesatellite developments 'to suit its purposes.'[32] As later established in the Act, however, one half of the new corporation was to be owned by US common carriers and the other half by the public – although the carriers could purchase up to 20 per cent of these shares. Six Comsat board members were to be representatives of FCC recognized carriers, six were to be elected by public shareholders, and three were to be Presidential appointees. At the request of Comsat, NASA launch facilities and other services, including research and development funds, were made available to the new monopoly on a cost reimbursement basis.[33]

The Kennedy administration's publicly stated justification for this arrangement included its desire to avoid the potentially wasteful duplication of costly satellite and ground-station facilities; the desirability of establishing a system whose components were technologically compatible; and the more political desire to establish eventually the 'fruitful exchange of communication between all countries' in order to 'avoid destructive competition' between different countries tied to different 'political blocs.'[34] However, Comsat was also established as the vehicle through which US interests could directly guide the development of a future international telesatellite system. As discussed below, the predominance of AT&T and smaller common carriers in Comsat was to become a significant bottleneck in DBS developments *and* in the conception and implementation of US foreign communication policy in general. Again, the overwhelming priority at the time of Comsat's creation was the rapid development of American technological (and hence military) capabilities in relation to the Soviet Union. Less crucial, but also present, was the fear of potential space-based Soviet propaganda activities. In 1962, for instance, Senator Wayne Morse told Secretary of State Dean Rusk, 'Russia in the not too distant future will be in competition with us in exporting her enslaver philosophy of communism through the satellite communications system.'[35]

In the end, Congress, the DoJ, the FCC and the White House accepted the claims of common carriers that the text of the Satellite Communications Act prevented Comsat from eventually controlling prospective domestic telesatellite services if, indeed, these were ever to be developed. Congress and the Kennedy administration also accepted the carriers's arguments that they would have to be the unchallenged leaders in commercial telesatellite developments as a byproduct of their existing expertise and capital holdings. One reason for the legislature's final acceptance of these assertions involved the presence of a gap in knowledge. As Senator John Pastore put it in 1962, specifically on the subject of proceeding with the development of the AT&T elliptical Telstar system:

I am not a technician or a scientist, I am a member of Congress who listens to the experts. We have been assured by those who are proficient, conversant and knowledgeable in this particular field that our objective will be realized by a low-altitude [elliptical] system.... It must be done expeditiously in order for us to win the race and triumph in this particular field before our adversaries [based in the USSR] do.[36]

As mentioned above, DoJ officials, apparently aware of the support of both the administration and the FCC for the carrier-dominated Comsat proposal, also accepted the conditions of Comsat's creation. Rather than its preliminary support of the aerospace companies' 'right' to own part of Comsat, the DoJ eventually came to support the vague language of the Communications Satellite Act that apparently gave non-carriers the right to participate.[37] However, four years later, when the ABC television network applied to the FCC to launch its own domestic telesatellite,[38] Comsat officials argued that the Communications Satellite Act gave their corporation a monopoly over *domestic* telesatellite systems.[39] Moreover, claims that the capital required to develop and launch international telesatellites could only be generated through the predominance of common carrier investments became increasingly dubious when public demand for Comsat stock pushed its initial shares up from $20 to a high of $78 in 1967. But most importantly, common carrier claims that their expertise and capital investment would compel the progressive development of telesatellite systems made little sense when evaluated in relation to the carriers' other (and much larger) vested interests. For example, AT&T's original investment of $58 million in Comsat was not only insignificant in relation to its terrestrial investments (a single transatlantic cable would cost just as much), but the profits from its control over domestic television transmission services alone totalled $65 million in 1966.[40]

Fortunately for Comsat and the common carriers, in need of overseas entities to communicate with, other advanced industrialized countries soon became interested in participating in US-initiated telesatellite developments. In 1964, Comsat became the American signatory to the International Telecommunications Satellite Organization (Intelsat) cooperative. While the original Intelsat membership was dominated by mostly European public sector telecommunication authorities (the PTTs),[41] the American common carrier-dominated Comsat was guaranteed no less than 50.6 per cent of voting shares in the new organization. These shares were to be distributed in accordance with the respective capital investments made by its members.

Comsat thus became the managing entity of Intelsat.[42] European interests actively pursued this arrangement in order to maintain some influence on what they recognized to be mutually beneficial developments. They also supported Comsat's vision of telesatellites being developed to *complement* existing cable-based infrastructures. Both Comsat and European PTTs hoped to use Intelsat in ways that would *protect* most existing terrestrial-based services and related manufacturing interests. However, while AT&T shared this interest in relation to domestic developments (while also monopolizing whatever domestic telesatellite developments were to take place), it *also* considered the telesatellite to be an ideal technology through which it could outflank long-standing international undersea cable infrastructures then mostly controlled by West European interests.[43]

In sum, NASA and DoD contracts to the US private sector involving rocketry and telecommunications facilitated the rapid development of telesatellites soon after the successful launch of Sputnik. While DoD officials made use of Soviet space achievements to express their concerns regarding future US military power capacities, electronics, computer and telecommunication equipment manufacturers all understood that the space race could substantially increase their receipt of short-term government procurements and long-term domestic and international sales. As for the established common carriers – dominated by AT&T – telesatellite developments were seen to be beneficial *if* they complemented existing facilities. Because telesatellites had the potential to circumvent or even replace significant components of this infrastructure, carriers sought to control the pace and direction of these developments through, for instance, their dominant position in Comsat.

The general success of the common carriers and their retarding influence on initial GSO system developments in part reflected the general absence of an elaborated appreciation of the hegemonic power potentials of telesatellites among US public sector officials.[44] As media through which some form of state or private sector-led cultural power could be applied, US officials – including representatives of the USIA – understood that telesatellites could become important propaganda platforms. But rather than endorsing the development of international public or private sector broadcasting services through telesatellites, foreign policy officials were more concerned with establishing America's world-wide leadership in new technologies (not necessarily synonymous goals). As discussed below, within five years of the formation of Comsat, the technological capabilities of DBS became much discussed but were rarely addressed in terms of their cultural-power implications. By 1967, DBS instead was considered to be a potentially useful medium through which to deliver mass education programs *largely designed by developing countries* to LDCs, or it was seen as a potentially threatening state propaganda vehicle if developed and used by the Soviet Union. Less common but nevertheless present was the view that DBS constituted a potentially disruptive technology in terms of its impact on the stability and predictability of domestic and foreign public opinion, possibly undermining aspects of traditional behind-closed-doors diplomatic practices and, more generally, complicating established foreign policy activities.

Early telesatellite developments in general, and those involving DBS in particular, were not influenced by American state policies involving prospective cultural-power applications. In fact, quite the opposite perspective was expressed by the USIA in 1967. As one official testified to Congress, private sector control over tele-satellites and their use as commercial media could provide 'little control' by the US government 'over what we [Americans] send out.' As a result, according to Wilson Dizard, 'we often send out the second rate, the irrelevant things that don't count, in terms of... problems with... developing countries, all countries.' Dizard regretfully concluded that the emerging status of commercial interests in international communications constitute part of the 'price we pay for freedom.'[45]

The urgency of the US response to Soviet space achievements and the dominance of *status quo* common carrier interests pushed forward the creation of Comsat. Moreover, because of its majority control of Intelsat, American carriers directly shaped the formative development of international telesatellite systems. These circumstances placed these interests in an extraordinarily powerful position which, as discussed later in this chapter, enabled them to retard preliminary DBS developments. By the late 1960s, Comsat and Intelsat were generally viewed by American officials to be little more than world-wide extensions of the AT&T domestic monopoly and, as such, their regulation involved a seemingly straightforward geographic extension of FCC oversight responsibilities. However, as pursued in the next section, while 'the US government... easily outplayed the USSR on the world telephone/communications stage,... [it] had a much more difficult and indecisive struggle with its home telephone monopoly AT&T.'[46]

## 3.2   THE OPPORTUNITY AND THREAT OF
TELESATELLITE TECHNOLOGY

In 1965, David Sarnoff, the Chairman of RCA, predicted that by 1975 it would be 'technically feasible to broadcast directly into the home from synchronous satellites.' Not only would this prospective system require only one satellite 'to beam [television] programs to the entire US and north into Canada,' but the scale of savings involved would make educational programing directly available to most less developed countries.[47]

At the time of Sarnoff's speech, RCA executives were preparing a proposal to build an experimental DBS system called Vista. RCA executives argued that by making use of available but underapplied UHF frequencies, direct broadcast satellites could become operational with little or no need to pursue the politically and technically complicated reassignment of existing television frequencies.[48] In 1965, NASA signed separate contracts with RCA and General Electric to conduct laboratory studies on the feasibility of DBS radio broadcasting. One year later, favorable results generated general agreement among aerospace engineers that a DBS television system was not only theoretically feasible, but provided with the necessary resources direct broadcasting could be fully operational as early as 1971.[49]

As it was generally conceptualized, a DBS system would involve a ground station that processes and radiates a signal to a relatively high-power satellite located in geostationary orbit. The uplink transmission would then be converted into the frequency needed for the downlink. This would involve satellite components called transponders.[50] A significant limitation involving transponders, however, was (and still is) their mass. As a general rule of thumb, the more powerful the satellite, the greater its mass, and thus the more costly it is to place into orbit. Because of this, the only launch system in the late 1960s capable of placing a DBS into geostationary orbit was the expensive Saturn 5 rocket, designed primarily for the Apollo moon missions.[51] After the signal's frequency is converted within the transponder, it would be amplified for the earthbound transmission using a device called a travelling wave tube amplifier. For this phase, an antenna capable of focusing the signal in the form of a beam would be needed to prevent the signal from becoming too dissipated. This is especially important for a DBS signal that would be received by a relatively small reception dish. Also, because of their small size, these ground receivers would require the transponder to generate relatively power-ful signals.[52]

The implications of this prospective technology – most notably its reduction in both transmission costs per receiver and terrestrial infra-structure requirements – generated widespread opposition, most voci-ferously (and predictably) from AT&T, Comsat and established American broadcasting interests. In 1965, Hughes Aircraft officials, recognizing that their construction of a mass audience DBS system would be too controversial, submitted a proposal to NASA for funding to support the development of a medium-power DBS system specifically designed for use by educational institutions. NASA initially rejected the proposal without explanation but subsequently formed joint experiments with Hughes in what was called the Applications Technology Satellite (ATS). ATS–3, launched in 1967, constituted the first applied quasi-DBS experiment. Hughes executives, aware of the resistance of Comsat and other domestic interests to its commercial application, publicized these developments to be little more than precursors for equipment sales to LDCs.[53]

Comsat claimed that the participation of NASA in these DBS experiments contravened the space agency's mandate. Specifically, NASA supposedly was not permitted, directly or indirectly, to fund prospective private sector broadcasting activities. The National Association of Broadcasters (NAB), representing US television net-works and local stations, provided additional arguments against DBS funding. From this period, the NAB consistently portrayed DBS as potentially undermining both local broadcasting and the economic viability of community programing. Other companies opposed to public sector support for DBS included fledgling cable television services. Their arguments were more direct, recognizing DBS as a potential threat to the successful development of their industry. More-over, some Congressmen again expressed concern that telesatellites – especially DBS – could become influential propaganda tools in the hands of 'unfriendly' nation states. By 1967, DBS proponents (mostly representatives of aerospace companies) acknowledged that regardless of its economic and technological efficiencies, little if any opportunity existed for direct broadcasting to become *acceptable* in relation to predominant private sector interests. NASA nevertheless continued to fund preliminary DBS research, providing mostly small-scale laborat-ory contracts to Hughes Aircraft, General Dynamics, General Electric and TRW Systems.[54]

In the late 1960s, some members of Congress argued that DBS one day would become 'the most widely used and influential... medium of communication... for the advancement of mass education, and the fostering of economic and social change in developing countries.'[55] For the first time, direct broadcasting was directly associated with the use of the American mass media as a means to influence the perspectives of foreign publics. According to a report prepared in 1967 for Congress, 'modern communications... [can be used to advance] our international objectives.... For example, we have not yet succeeded in making our national experience and achievements relevant to the aspirations for a better life of some two-thirds of the human race.'[56]

Similar observations were made two years later in Congressional hearings and in a House of Representatives Foreign Affairs subcommittee report.[57] But rather than representing a growing awareness among American officials of the cultural-power implications of DBS, the issue was only raised in relation to the development of the ATS experimental DBS system and its forthcoming application by the government of India. Although plans for this had begun in 1967, these educational television transmissions were not initiated until 1974 when 5,000 communities located throughout India received signals.[58] By this time, however, the ATS experiment was more than just a response to the long-standing marginalization of DBS among predominant US telecommunication interests. In 1974, the Indian experiment also constituted a response to the growing foreign resistance to US foreign policy efforts involving communications (see Chapter 4).

By the end of the 1960s, DBS, despite its technological and commercial underdevelopment, already had become 'the most viable point of contention' for LDCs seeking to organize a response to more general development issues.[59] Domestically, DBS remained a threat to AT&T and the NAB. However, the new Nixon administration – attempting to counter more general foreign opposition to the United States – sought to promote DBS as a tool for Third World development needs while simultaneously redressing the concerns of domestic DBS opponents by limiting its application.[60] Through NASA and its legislated mandate to conduct and support research toward the general advancement of knowledge concerning outer space, the US executive quite possibly sought to deflect domestic anti-DBS lobbying while appeasing pro-DBS aerospace interests.

By the end of the 1960s, the economic efficiencies and potential cultural-power applications provided by DBS remained altogether secondary to US policy in relation to predominant communication interests. During this decade, not even officials in the USIA were interested in prospective DBS radio applications as a method either of reducing expenditures through their replacement of costly short-wave transmission facilities or as a means of overriding the signal-jamming efforts of foreign governments.[61] Over the course of these years, the focus of US foreign communication policy generally was limited to maintaining America's scientific and technological leadership, the internationalization of the AT&T monopoly, and little more.[62] Established private and public sector interests dominated the institutional parameters in which telesatellites and US foreign communication policy developed. Rather than their direct control over state policy, powerful vested interests (especially AT&T and the DoD) directed history most effectively through their dominant roles in constructing the core institutional, organizational and technological mediators that in turn shaped the day-to-day imaginings of what policy officials believed to be possible and impossible, feasible and infeasible.

## 3.3   TOWARD 'OPEN SKIES' AND THE POLITICAL FEASIBILITY OF DBS

In response to Comsat, and the distance-sensitive rates charged by the AT&T-dominated domestic television transmission system, the ABC television network filed an application with the FCC to develop its own distribution telesatellite in March 1966.[63] This initiative marked the beginning of a political struggle that eventually led to the end of the Comsat monopoly.[64] In response to the ABC application, the FCC initiated formal hearings to determine whether it should proceed to license new telesatellite systems and, if so, how this should be pursued. During these proceedings, the development of the GSO and its impact on existing policy became a key issue. The Communications Satellite Act of 1962 was drafted at a time when only an elliptical orbit and the Telstar system were technologically feasible. In 1962, the scale and cost of this type of system made Comsat appear to many to be the most economically viable of options. However, with the emergence of GSO technologies, cost efficient alternatives to a single shared system became viable.[65]

A formative development in the eventual re-regulation of telesatellites and in shaping more general US foreign communication policy was a federal task force on telecommunication policy established by the Johnson administration.[66] Chaired by the Department of State Undersecretary for Political Affairs, Eugene V. Rostow, the commonly called Rostow Report was completed in December 1968. Although Rostow's official assignment had been to recommend how public sector satellite technology could best be applied by the American private sector, the scope of his final report addressed much broader issues.

The most tangible outcome of the Rostow Report was the establishment of the Office of Telecommunications Policy (OTP) in 1970. The OTP was an executive branch office with headquarters in the White House. Its mission was to address and represent the President on all questions concerning US communication policy, both domestic and international. Given this extraordinarily broad mandate, OTP officials participated directly in FCC proceedings and legislative lobbying activities. By 1977, due in large part to a Carter administration promise to cut White House staff and spending, the opposition of commercial and public broadcasters to OTP support for the emerging cable television industry, and past activities involving efforts by President Nixon to curb negative media coverage of his administration,[67] the office was moved out of the White House and into the Department of Commerce and renamed the National Telecommunications and Information Administration (NTIA). The new NTIA's mandate was modified from that of its predecessor by focusing it more toward domestic telecommunications.

On domestic telesatellite policy, the Rostow task force concluded that because it was unlikely that substantial cost savings could be achieved in the short term by substituting telesatellite systems for existing terrestrial facilities, the 'balanced' development of the existing cable and microwave-based (AT&T dominated) system with complementary, multipurpose satellites constituted the best policy for the United States 'with Comsat playing the leading role.'[68] These and other Rostow conclusions were not, however, the unadulterated products of a far-reaching and somehow objective deliberation. Instead, the task force unilaterally extended its mandate in an effort to construct some kind of sector-wide *rapprochement* in light of the ongoing dominance of AT&T in domestic developments.[69] As for DBS, Rostow reported that 'The high cost and disruptive effects of direct satellite-to-home broadcasting make it unpromising, at least in the near term.'[70]

Even in 1968, the assumptions made in this one sentence were dubious. Although the task force reported that the overhead costs of a DBS system would be 'inordinately expensive' in relation to existing 'cable or over-the-air broadcast techniques,' Rostow did not provide detailed cost figures for these established systems.[71] In addition to this assumption, Rostow considered DBS to be a threat to the ability of local broadcasters to expand 'opportunities for local expression' due to direct broadcasting's 'highly centralized control over transmission and program origination.'[72] Whereas this latter point might well have been taken seriously if the US public sector had ever displayed a serious concern for localism before or after the report,[73] the former point is made even more questionable by Rostow's recognition that cable companies already received a monthly fee for cable services from subscribers to pay-down their overhead costs while no mention is made of a similar option being possible for prospective DBS operators.[74] One explanation for representing these assumptions as if they were facts probably involved the affiliations of Rostow's private sector participants. While representatives from AT&T and CBS were invited to work with the task force, the Rostow Report lacked official input from the early leader in DBS developments – Hughes Aircraft.

Rostow's general support of the US telesatellite *status quo* was not favorably received by the succeeding Nixon administration. One month before the establishment of its Office of Telecommunications Policy in January 1970, the Nixon White House issued a memorandum to the FCC urging the Commission to adopt a more 'open market' approach. According to this memo, '*any* financially qualified public or private entity... should be permitted to establish and operate domestic satellite facilities for its own needs.'[75] Three months later, Dean Burch, the Nixon-appointed FCC Chairman, initiated the Commission's so-called Open Skies policy.[76] This involved Burch's well-known belief that the FCC, despite the Comsat home-to-overseas monopoly, always had possessed the exclusive authority to authorize any entity to own and/or operate a domestic telesatellite system.[77] By 1972, the FCC was evaluating several applications.[78] However, after reviewing these, the Commission ruled that the terms of its authorization of a telesatellite license should be restricted in order to avoid 'fragmenting the market... to such an extent that most carrier entrants would fail to come even remotely close to covering costs.'[79] The OTP responded by threatening to seek Congressional legislation supporting its Open Skies policy while the Department of Justice also opposed the FCC's position on the stated grounds that more competition, it was assumed, would encourage technological innovation.[80]

In the general absence of a leading state agency possessing the clear capacity to compel this policy shift, the task of locating its historic development requires some analysis of more general contextual forces, including technological change and the particular characteristics of capitalist activities at the time. Beginning in the late 1960s, the expansion of wideband transmission capacities made telesatellites attractive vehicles through which state and corporate computer systems could be interlinked over great distances. This general development of long-distance capabilities using a technology whose costs were not distance-sensitive, at transmission speeds far exceeding available terrestrial capacities, and with the ability to serve almost any location on earth, generated a growing private sector and military demand for new telesatellite technologies. This rising demand compelled an accompanying advancement in technologies specifically designed to facilitate the interconnection of computers over such systems. Largely because of the predominance of telephone traffic, the international common carrier infrastructure was based on analogue transmission technologies and related mechanical switching facilities. As such, the new large-scale demand for vast and rapid computer data transmission capacities provided telesatellite proponents with an important means of compelling the FCC to liberalize the field of telecommunications. Telecommunication technologies and policies emerged to accommodate the capacities of emerging computer systems, and computer technologies and policies emerged to accommodate the capacities of telecommunications. Most importantly, these developments transcended traditional communication policy processes through the unprecedented inclusion not only of computer companies but also of large corporations interested in the capabilities and efficiencies that the marriage of computers and telecommunications could provide. In other words, FCC deliberations concerning telesatellites increasingly involved far wider interests than those represented by officials at the DoD, Comsat, AT&T, the NAB and the aerospace companies.[81]

The Open Skies policy established in 1972 eventually involved acceptance by the FCC of all qualified telesatellite applications, based on technical feasibility and antitrust criteria alone. Additional restrictions, however, were placed on proposals from both Comsat and AT&T. The latter, for instance, was barred from participating in new telesatellite developments for three years in order to provide other companies with an opportunity to become established.[82] By this time, AT&T executives recognized that their rarely discussed but universally known quest to control a domestic telesatellite monopoly by means of a state sanctioned arrangement was over. Beginning in the early 1970s, fortified by their dominant market position, AT&T officials themselves became leading advocates of an Open Skies approach to the regulation of domestic telesatellites.[83]

In establishing the Rostow task force, President Johnson stated that 'The communications satellite knows no geographic boundary ... [and] owes allegiance to no single language or political philosophy. Man now has it within his power to speak directly to his fellow man in all nations.'[84] But despite this rhetoric, policy initiatives that would enable the development and application of DBS or quasi-DBS technologies, or policies designed to stimulate US private sector ventures in telesatellite broadcasting, remained altogether absent in Rostow's final report. Established common carriers and domestic broadcasting interests instead managed to curb the development of competitive telesatellite services until the Open Skies policy emerged in the early 1970s. As both communication *and* computer-based technologies developed, TNC activities became increasingly dependent on telecommunications. As such, the Open Skies policy itself became an issue of growing concern for a broad range of private sector interests not directly involved in the telecommunications business. Public sector officials were pressured to promote a more competitive marketplace among communication and information service providers based largely on the assumed cost savings and innovations that would result. Moreover, as TNCs became increasingly dependent on telecommunications and electronic data flows in their day-to-day *international* operations, US government officials were encouraged to export this relatively competitive market regulatory approach. While the forces underlying these developments and their implications are directly addressed in later chapters, again it is important to make the general point that the Open Skies policy was formulated with little or no recognition that new communication technologies could be applied to service some kind of international cultural-power strategy. Instead, TNCs such as IBM and General Motors became increasingly influential participants in the development of foreign communication policy as both technological innovators and large-scale telecommunications users.[85] According to Jill Hills, once these and other large business users became directly involved in policy developments concerning equipment and services, 'the two fed off each other':

the liberalisation of equipment increasing the demand for the liberalisation of transmission and the liberalisation of transmission increasing the demand for the liberalisation of equipment. Alliances formed between large users, equipment manufacturers and computer service companies in opposition to AT&T.[86]

Nevertheless, by 1980, four of the eight companies that had been granted telesatellite licenses by the FCC in 1972 had abandoned their projects and had collectively lost approximately $576 million.[87] Those companies that successfully established telesatellite systems in the 1970s – RCA and Western Union – found that persistent technological difficulties and AT&T's ongoing control over local networks and interconnection facilities provided them with little or no real opportunity to compete in the telephone services market. The most significant of their technological problems involved the inability to provide two-way voice communications exclusively over telesatellite transponders due to the presence of voice echoes. As such, until the development of an echo-cancelling technology, telesatellites practically could only be used in one-way communications, such as the transmission of a television signal.[88] As an unexpected result of these shortcomings, long-distance television signals enjoyed excess transmission capacities. This capacity glut unexpectedly stimulated the rapid development of US cable television services beginning with the Home Box Office (HBO) movie channel. By the end of 1979, twenty of the twenty-four RCA Satcom I system transponders distributed cable television programing to cable distributors located throughout the country.[89] This largely accidental impact on the US cable television industry, the entrenched anti-competitive interests of the NAB, and the remarkable growth of in-home videotape technologies beginning at the end of the 1970s, coalesced in the early 1980s to retard the economic feasibility of America's first DBS services.

## 3.4  THE RISE AND FALL OF DOMESTIC DBS: 1980–1984

In 1980, the first telesatellite to make use of Ku band frequencies was a company jointly owned by IBM, Comsat and Aetna Life Insurance, called Satellite Business Systems (SBS). The SBS venture hoped to provide customers with integrated intra-corporate computer and voice telecommunications through the use of relatively sophisticated roof-top receivers. Opposition by both AT&T – which recognized its potential large-scale revenue losses resulting from this type of service – and other computer manufacturers (who feared the perpetual dominance of IBM hardware)[90] succeeded in having the introduction of SBS services delayed on antitrust grounds for almost five years until federal courts finally permitted its operation. Having invested approximately $1.26 billion in its new telesatellite system while failing to attain its anticipated customer base, SBS narrowed its service offerings to intra-corporate telephone services only. Nevertheless, SBS established the first competitive challenge to AT&T's national long-distance monopoly.[91] Significant for DBS, however, was the successful establishment of commercial Ku band applications. As discussed below, one of SBS's parent companies, Comsat, subsequently filed America's first DBS license application with the FCC.

Comsat officials recognized that a DBS service in the United States was a risky proposition. In addition to the high overhead costs involved in establishing such a system,[92] millions of household consumers would have to be convinced to pay several hundred dollars for a reception unit accommodating just four or five new television channels. The rapid growth in the early 1980s of cable distribution services in urban centers, the emergence of alternative microwave relay services in rural areas, the initial use of large backyard dishes mounted to receive telesatellite signals intended for cable redistribution companies, and the introduction of household VCR technologies collectively made DBS an unlikely economic success at that time.[93] Nevertheless, Comsat estimated that the potential benefits of establishing a continental television system (at a fraction of the set-up costs of terrestrial-based networks) justified the risk. It would cost approximately $683.6 million to put its DBS project into operation by 1986.[94] Its initial plan involved the use four high-power telesatellites to provide North Americans with transmissions using a 2 or 3 foot reception dish. As project costs rose and other difficulties developed, Comsat modified its plans several times.[95]

As discussed in Chapter 4, the ITU's World Administrative Radio Conference (WARC) had set aside parts of the Ku band for DBS services in 1971. In 1977, however, when nation-state officials met again to allocate specific geostationary orbital positions, US officials convinced most of its regional neighbors (in North, Central and South America) that these allocations should be delayed until technological advancements enabled (presumably private sector) officials to make more 'rational' evaluations as to how best the resource should be exploited. Thus, in 1977, the United States orchestrated a postponement of WARC assignments for Greenland and the Americas (referred to as Region 2) until 1983. However, these six years provided both the cable television and VCR industries with the time required to become established forces in the US market. In 1976, 33.2 per cent of US television households were passed by cable television lines, and just over half of these homes subscribed. By 1980, 45.7 per cent were passed and 55 per cent of these subscribed. By 1985, cable television lines passed 76.2 per cent of all American homes and, of these, 56.7 per cent subscribed.[96] The use of videotape recorders grew even more rapidly. In 1975, the in-home use of VCRs was virtually non-existent. By 1980, 1.1 per cent of US homes had a videotape machine. In 1985, this total had increased to 20.8 per cent.[97] When the FCC received its first DBS license application from Comsat subsidiary Satellite Television Corporation (STC) in late 1980, ITU geostationary orbit allocations for DBS systems thus had not yet been negotiated. The NAB immediately filed its opposition to the STC proposal. Its official argument was that because GSO allocations would not be made until 1983, FCC approval of any DBS system was premature and would constitute an unfair head-start in relation to other prospective direct broadcasters.[98] In response, the FCC invited other DBS applications, and by the end of 1981 it had accepted both the STC plan and eight others.[99]

In light of the STC proposal, RCA and Western Union executives believed that they were compelled to file for DBS licenses in order to protect aspects of their telesatellite businesses *in case* the new distribution technology was successful. The CBS plan, while also in large part a risk-aversion investment (involving the protection of its television network), was also promoted by its executives as a vehicle through which the network could develop high definition television (HDTV) services.[100] On the whole, most of these plans were driven by the conviction that because of the telesatellite resources and expertise held by Comsat, its initiation of a North American DBS system *in itself* necessitated a response. Control over the scarce GSO and frequency allocations available for direct broadcasting – requiring a degree of ongoing capital investment in order to maintain a FCC license – thus made strategic sense at the time in anticipation that the STC gamble could one day pay off.

A relatively small company called United Satellite Communications Incorporated (USCI), leasing transponders on the medium power Canadian Anik C–2 satellite, surprised the original license holders by establishing the first North American DBS-type service just four months after the 1983 WARC regional allocations.[101] Within six months, USCI was unable to secure a $40 million bank loan and was forced to shut down. Given the limited power generated by Anik C–2 (and thus a minimum 4-foot reception dish required to receive its signals); the provision of only three of its five promised channels; and its ability to acquire only 9,000 subscribers, the USCI venture lost approximately $53 million.[102] By October 1984, only four prospective DBS services remained registered with the FCC. The three applicants that had appeared most capable of mounting a successful DBS service (apart from STC) – RCA, Western Union and CBS – by this time had all withdrawn. By the end of 1984, citing the competitive strength of the cable television industry and the high cost of acquiring popular programing, STC officials also canceled their plans. As Jeremy Tunstall summarizes, 'the 1983–84 disaster for DBS was on such a scale as to somewhat depress the entire business of space satellites.'[103]

## 3.5  CONCLUSIONS

The early development or underdevelopment of DBS technologies was dominated by powerful domestic and international, private and public sector, terrestrial telecommunications interests. Rather than an awareness and application of some form of cultural power influencing US policy, the more than two decades reviewed in this chapter reveal a history reflecting not only the early marginal status of DBS but even the presence of some disdain toward commercial mass media exports in general. In 1962, some of the Democratic Senators opposing the Communications Satellite Act argued that rather than fearing the Soviet propaganda potentials represented by telesatellites, the exploitation of the international airwaves by corporate interests should be of at least equal concern.[104] Even the notion of telesatellites being used to serve the propaganda interests of American state agencies was consistently rejected, despite a general recognition of the potential technological and economic advantages of a DBS system. Apparently, the only force that would have compelled US officials to pursue the public or private sector development and application of direct broadcast technologies aggressively would have been the use of DBS by the Soviet Union. As noted in 1967 by the *Bulletin of the Atomic Scientists*:

> We can expect that within a few years the Russians will begin stationing communications satellites..., permitting the beaming of television pictures to South Asia, Africa, and Latin America.

*At that time,* one can anticipate a sudden awakening of American interest in the communications satellites as educational and propaganda tools in the developing parts of the world.[105]

Despite its potential propaganda applications; its anticipated technological and economic advantages; the emerging recognition, in the words of one State Department official in 1976, that 'The commercial export of information has a significant market potential';[106] and the growing politicization of international institutions through LDC references to the 'threat' of direct broadcasting, US foreign communication policy officials generally remained uninterested.

These formative years were directly shaped by two overarching interests. The first expressed the need to redress the much publicized technological challenge mounted by the Soviet Union. The second was an expression of the interests held by established telecommunications companies, dominated by AT&T. These forces – the former primarily driven by international security concerns and the latter by business interests favoring the telecommunication states quo – delayed first GSO and later DBS developments. Due to the priority needs of both the Department of Defense and the fixed costs represented in the AT&T monopoly, large-scale public sector investments into telesatellites initially were predicated on the needs of these vested interests.

Again, remarkable in their absence were concerns about the cultural-power implications of telesatellites. Not only were such considerations altogether secondary in this early period, but Congressional acceptance of the new Comsat monopoly also involved a related lack of knowledge about the capabilities of new telesatellite systems. Comsat was not just the product of entrenched interests dominating formative debate, Congressional officials were to some extent reliant on the 'expert' views of the very officials representing this *status quo.* In other words, the newness and technological and economic complexities featured in the hurried Communications Satellite Act debate were not counter-balanced by the perspectives of critical public or private sector agents – mostly because such agents either did not yet exist or their arguments necessarily relied on unproved theorizations regarding the viability and relative cost-effectiveness of GSO systems. Similarly, the structural framework in which the cultural-power implications of telesatellites could be fully assessed was also underdeveloped.

Although these early structures directly shaped the form and scope of the Communications Satellite Act, the US military's need for ongoing technological developments, coupled with demands by private sector interests that they directly benefit from these expenditures, set a contradictory process in motion. Despite the overwhelming reliance on AT&T technologies, DoD and NASA contracts continued to fund Hughes, RCA and other corporations in GSO and subsequent DBS-related developments. AT&T interests seemingly were secured through the construction of the Comsat monopoly and the recognition by the FCC that telesatellite developments were the regulatory domain of the common carriers. However, allocations to manufacturers provided the seed money required to furnish the DoD and an expanding range of corporations with new satellite-related technologies and alternative services. Although the Soviet threat helped forge the AT&T/Comsat monopoly, the same threat compelled the American state to finance challenges to that monopoly – challenges that first came about through GSO and rocketry advancements and were subsequently developed through the attempt by television networks to bypass the AT&T domestic system.

With these challenges, the NAB emerged to lead domestic corporate resistance to the kind of direct-to-home broadcasting developments proposed by Sarnoff and others. Prospective DBS systems threatened not just the economic viability of the television networks, they could be used to undermine the capacity of local television and radio broadcasters in order to exploit local markets. Just as GSO developments in 1962 constituted a high-risk and unwarranted expenditure in the minds of AT&T executives, according to the rhetoric of the NAB in the late 1960s, DBS purportedly had the potential to undermine the 'democratic fabric' of community-based broadcasting. Of course behind such transparent arguments were monopoly or oligopoly interests, legitimized by the American state through the Rostow Commission and other agents and their pursuit of a rather biased *rapprochement*. The new Nixon White House, carrying less of this institutional baggage and spurred on by the emerging interests of IBM and other non-carrier entities seeking to benefit from newly converged telecommunication and computer technologies, possessed enough political power and private sector support at least to challenge the AT&T/Comsat monolith.

Both the introduction of the Open Skies policy and the broadening use by businesses of communication and computer technologies stimulated the subsequent direct involvement of an expanding range of private and, subsequently, public sector agents in the making of communication policy. These interests, how they were expressed through government offices, and how these pressures and mediations in turn reshaped state foreign policy structures and outcomes are questions that will be pursued in the next chapter. By examining these developments, Chapter 4 begins the task of specifying how American state structures affected and were affected by private sector and intra-state forces.

## NOTES

1  Delbert D. Smith, *Communication via Satellite: A Vision in Retrospect* (Leyden: A.W. Sijthoff, 1976) p. 255.
2  For instance, in 1972 FCC commissioner Robert E. Lee argued in favor of this development in a series of public speeches. See 'Lee Cites Need Now to Start Shaping Ground Rules for Direct Satellites', in *Broadcasting* (27 August 1973) 38.
3  Following the Second World War, the US military initiated classified feasibility studies on the potential applications of earth-orbiting satellites. But largely due to the absence of clear research objectives, coordinated inter-agency planning and an overriding interest in ballistic missile developments, the only significant advancement made by the mid–1950s involved launch vehicles. As for the social implications of telesatellite technologies, the Rand Corporation in 1949 organized the first national conference on the subject. One conference conclusion was the assumption that 'the paramount utility of a satellite probably resides in its potentialities as an instrument for the achievement of political/psychological goals,' Delbert D. Smith, *Communication via Satellite*, pp. 18–19 and 29.
4  See excerpts from US Senate, Committee on Aeronautical and Space Sciences, Staff Report, 'The Background of United States Involvement,' in Lloyd D. Musolf (ed.), *Communications Satellites in Political Orbit* (San Francisco: Chandler, 1968) p. 13.
5  Sputnik's technological superiority was made most apparent by the fact that its mass was nine times greater than the proposed American satellite and its orbit reached twice the altitude of the NAS/DoD plan.
6  NASA was to become the largest and most active civilian space science research agency in the world, although all its research related to US defense would be the responsibility of the DoD. Other American responses to Sputnik are summarized in Heather Hudson, *Communication Satellites: Their Development and Impact* (New York: Free Press, 1990) pp. 14–15.
7  'National Aeronautics and Space Act of 1958.' Public Law 85–568, 85th Cong., 72 Stat. 426, 29 July 1958. See discussion in Smith, *Communication via Satellite*, pp. 41–60.
8  *Ibid.*, p. 63.

9    *Ibid.*, pp. 64–71.

10   Hudson, *Communication Satellites*, p. 17.

11   On 23 July 1962, the world's first transatlantic television broadcast was conducted in public. The primary reason for this display of US technology was its assumed propaganda value for American science and innovation. See US Congress. House. Committee on Science and Astronautics. Hearings on 'Commercial Communications Satellites.' 87th Cong., 2nd sess., 18 September 1962, p. 153.

12   Hudson, *Communication Satellites*, p. 18.

13   According to Delbert Smith, 'Hughes was ready to abandon its project in 1961 if NASA would not add its sponsorship' – Smith, *Communication via Satellite*, p. 88.

14   US Congress. Senate. Committee on the Judiciary. Subcommittee on Antitrust and Monopoly. Hearings on 'Antitrust Problems of the Space Satellite Communications System.' 87th Cong., 2nd sess., 12 April 1962, pp. 412–17.

15   Pucket testimony in *ibid.*, p. 421.

16   *Ibid.*, p. 425. Cost calculations were provided by the Program Manager of Syncom, C. Gordon Murphy, to another Congressional hearing held in 1962. In comparing the construction, launch, and ground-station investments required for a world-wide elliptical satellite system and a GSO system, Murphy's 'bottom line' was that the former would cost approximately US $80 million annually and the latter would cost about $30 million. See House Hearings on 'Commercial Communications Satellites,' 1962, pp. 5–6.

17   Murphy in *ibid.*, p. 7.

18   Jeremy Tunstall, *Communications Deregulation, The Unleashing of America's Communications Industry* (Oxford: Basil Blackwell, 1986) p. 65.

19   Lawrence Lessing, 'Cinderella in the Sky,' *Fortune*, LXXVI (5) (October 1967) 196.

20   Eugene G. Fubini quoted in House Hearings on 'Commercial Communications Satellites,' 1962, p. 117.

21   *Ibid.*, p. 116. Unlike cable and other terrestrial systems, per unit satellite transmission costs are not affected by distance. In other words, telesatellite transmission costs do not go up as the distance between communicators increases (and vice versa). Terrestrial telecommunication system costs thus are said to be distance-sensitive while non-terrestrial systems, in relative terms, are not.

22   G. Griffith Johnson testimony in *ibid.*, pp. 141–2.

23   Rep. Hechler quoted in *ibid.*, p. 141. Representatives at this hearing also raised questions concerning the propaganda implications of satellite television broadcasting. In reply to the prospect of a four-hour Fidel Castro speech being broadcast around the world, Hechler speculated that it 'would probably do us more good than harm.' With less humor, Rep. James G. Fulton responded by observing that 'The question is who it does good to. The question there is whether the good or the bad is to the United States or to the poor countries of Africa and the unenlightened natives who might hear it' – *ibid.*, p. 150.

24    Robert Mayer Evans, Special Assistant to the Director of the US
      Information Agency, testimony in *ibid.*, p. 153. In 1962, the USIA
      produced pamphlets, magazines, books, films and shortwave radio
      broadcasts promoting US space achievements. See p. 160.
25    Hudson, *Communication Satellites*, pp. 24–5.
26    Communications Satellite Act of 1962, 47 USC 704–44. This Act was
      passed eleven months after President Kennedy's announcement that the
      United States would put a man on the moon by 1970. According to
      Kennedy advisor McGeorge Bundy, Comsat was conceived 'for the
      purpose of taking and holding a position of leadership . . . in the field
      of international commercial satellite service.' Quoted in Herbert I.
      Schiller, *Mass Communications and American Empire*, 1st edn, p. 131.
27    Robert S. Magnant, *Domestic Satellite: An FCC Giant Step* (Boulder,
      Col.: Westview Press, 1977) p. 74.
28    Jeremy Tunstall, *Communications Deregulation*, p. 66.
29    US Congress. Senate. Select Committee on Small Business. Subcommit-
      tee on Monopoly. Hearings on 'Space Satellite Communications,' 87th
      Cong., 1st sess., 2, 3, 4, 9, 10 and 11 August 1961, p. 52.
30    Dingman quoted in *ibid.*, p. 251.
31    Michael E. Kinsley, *Outer Space and Inner Sanctums: Government,
      Business, and Satellite Communication* (New York: John Wiley & Sons,
      1976) p. 10.
32    Senator Russell Long, speaking on 18 June 1962, quoted in *ibid.*, p. 12.
33    Jonathan F. Galloway, *The Politics and Technology of Satellite Commu-
      nications* (Toronto: Lexington Books, 1972) p. 90.
34    Hudson, *Communication Satellites*, p. 27.
35    US Congress. Senate. Committee on Foreign Relations 'Hearings on the
      Communications Satellite Act of 1962,' 87th Cong., 2nd sess., 3, 6, 7, 8
      and 9 August, 1962, p. 188.
36    Pastore quoted in Michael E. Kinsley, *Outer Space and Inner Sanctums*,
      p. 135.
37    Robert S. Magnant, *Domestic Satellite*, p. 64.
38    Hughes Aircraft, seeking prospective markets, originally approached
      ABC with the concept of a 'national network in the sky'. See *ibid.*, p. 91.
39    The reader will recall the assurances made by common carriers during
      the Congressional hearings preceding the Communications Satellite Act
      of 1962 that the legislation would provide Comsat with a monopoly
      over overseas telesatellite communications *only*.
40    Kinsley, *Outer Space and Inner Sanctums*, pp. 17–21.
41    PTTs are the dominant agents in most nation-state telecommunication
      systems. Controlling their own domestic cable-based networks, PTTs
      today not only manage most distribution activities but together consti-
      tute the world's largest equipment market and control most available
      telecommunication research and development funds. European govern-
      ments generally have taken somewhat uncoordinated and/or reluctant
      steps to privatize PTT activities.
42    While US officials had originally envisioned that Comsat would estab-
      lish bilateral communication agreements with foreign nation states,
      European countries – through their formation of the European

Conference of Posts and Telecommunications Administrations (CEPT) in 1962 (partly in response to Comsat) – instead pushed for the formation of Intelsat. The Soviet Union rejected participation largely because of the prospect of American dominance. See Hudson, *Communication Satellites*, pp. 28–32.

43    Dan Schiller, *Telematics and Government* (Norwood, NJ: Ablex, 1982) p. 171. This interest in ending the dominance of mostly British-owned transoceanic cable systems also was a long-stated goal of US public sector officials. In 1945, James Lawrence Fly (Chairman of the FCC), referring to the United Kingdom's ownership of much of the world's cables (and thus its control over their use), stated that '[a]mong the artificial restraints to the free development of commerce throughout the world none is more irksome and less justifiable than the control of communication facilities by one country'. Quoted in Herbert I. Schiller, 'Genesis of the Free Flow of Information Principles' in A. Mattelart and S. Seiglaub (eds), *Communication and Class Struggle*, Vol. 1 (New York. International General, 1979) p. 346.

44    See US Congress. House. Committee on Foreign Affairs. Subcommittee on International Organizations and Movements. Hearings on 'Modern Communications and Foreign Policy.' 90th Cong., 1st sess., 8 and 9 February 1967.

45    Wilson P. Dizard, Office of Policy and Research, US Information Agency, quoted in *ibid.*, p. 67.

46    Tunstall, *Communications Deregulation*, pp. 64–5.

47    Sarnoff quoted in Lessing, 'Cinderella in the Sky,' p. 196.

48    Lessing, 'Cinderella in the Sky,' p. 196.

49    *Ibid.*, p. 198.

50    The main reason why this conversion is necessary involves the immediate proximity of the satellite's receiving and transmitting antennas. In many systems, the reception and the transmission units are one and the same. By using different frequencies, interference between the reception signal and the transmission signal can be minimalized. See D.J. Flint, 'Satellite Transponders' in B.G. Evans (ed.), *Satellite Communication Systems* (London: Peter Peregrinus, 1991) esp. pp. 237–8.

51    Lessing, 'Cinderella in the Sky,' p. 198.

52    The use of a small ground receiver was considered to have been very important as it significantly increased the number of people able to receive transmissions and, subsequently, the variety and success of potential DBS services. At the 1977 World Administrative Radio Conference (WARC–77) – a regulatory entity of the ITU – high-power DBS systems were allocated a frequency range in what is called the Ku band (11.7 to 12.7 GHz). The use of this band is impractical for less powerful satellites. In large part, the Ku band assignment also reflected, in the late 1970s, the capacity to mass-produce receivers for home consumers in developed countries and the 'basic' communication needs of LDCs. See Mark Williamson, 'Broadcasting by Satellite: Some Technical Considerations', in Ralph Negrine (ed.), *Satellite Broadcasting*, (London: Routledge, 1988) p. 38.

In general, the physical limitations of satellite transmissions involve two core factors: *first*, the power of the radio-wave signal; and, *second*, the bandwidth available for transmission. In North, Central and South America, high-power DBS positions now have available 500 MHz of the Ku band (12.2–12.7 GHz) for downlink transmissions. This bandwidth may be subdivided into 'channels' – perhaps 24 MHz per channel. Again, depending on the needs of the user, space on this channel again can be subdivided. A standard television signal, for instance, now requires at least 6 MHz of bandwidth. In digital form, the uncompressed data rate (bps) needed to transmit the standard North American NTSC television signal is 90 million bps, whereas a high definition television (HDTV) transmission requires over 200 million bps. Other uncompressed data rates, in order of bps requirements, are as follows: video teleconferencing – from 64,000 to 1.5 million bps; telephone voice services – 64,000 bps; electronic mail – from 1,200 to 64,000 bps; and for a digital alarm system – 100 bps. Walter S. Baer, 'New Communications Technologies and Services,' in Paula R. Newberg (ed.), *New Directions in Telecommunications Policy*, vol.2 (Durham, NC: Duke University Press, 1989) p. 162.

53  Lessing, 'Cinderella in the Sky,' pp. 131 and 201–2.
54  *Ibid.*, p. 198.
55  Dante R. Fascell, 'Modern Communications and Foreign Policy.' Report by the US House of Representatives Committee on Foreign Affairs (unpublished: 13 June 1967) p. 3R.
56  *Ibid.*, p. 5R.
57  See US Congress. House. Committee on Foreign Affairs. Subcommittee on National Security Policy and Scientific Developments. Hearings on 'Satellite Broadcasting: Implications for Foreign Policy.' 91st Cong., 1st sess., 13, 14, 15, 22 May 1969.
58  For more on this experiment (referred to as SITE – Satellite Instructional Television Experiment) and subsequent developments, see *ibid.*, pp. 14–18; Vijay Menon, 'The Case of India,' in Meheroo Jussawalla, Tadayuki Okuma and Toshihiro Araki (eds), *Information Technology and Global Interdependence* (New York: Greenwood Press, 1989) pp. 281–5; and P.C. Chatterji, *Broadcasting in India* (New Delhi: Sage, 1991) pp. 126–33.
59  Larry Martinez, *Communication Satellites: Power Politics in Space* (Dedham, Mass.: Artech House, 1985) p. 30.
60  'Satellite Broadcasting: Implications for Foreign Policy,' Report tabled in Hearings before US Congress, 13 May 1969, pp. 3R–6R. Also, personal interview with John Sigmund, Senior Economist, Division of Service Industries, International Trade Administration, US Department of Commerce, 10 September 1992, Washington, DC.
61  See US Congress. House. Committee on Foreign Affairs. Subcommittee on National Security Policy and Scientific Developments. Hearings on 'Foreign Policy Implications of Satellite Communications,' 91st Cong., 2nd sess., 23, 28, 30 April 1970, pp. 69–71. Also, Hearings on 'Satellite Broadcasting: Implications for Foreign Policy,' pp. 138–40.
62  See testimony by Richard N. Gardner, President Kennedy's former Deputy Assistant Secretary of State for International Organization

Affairs, in Hearings on 'Satellite Broadcasting: Implications for Foreign Policy,' pp. 64–5.

63  In 1966, AT&T charged ABC $12 million annually for its microwave distribution services. ABC estimated that a telesatellite system designed for its particular needs could save $5 million over a five-year period. See Smith, *Communication via Satellite*, p. 158. According to Heather Hudson, because of these minimal savings, 'ABC may have been using its satellite option merely to put pressure on AT&T, by threatening defection if AT&T increased its rates' – Hudson, *Communication Satellites*, p. 40.

64  In 1974, as a result of what was commonly called the 'Open Skies' policy, Western Union launched the first competitive domestic telesatellite. By 1984, seven US companies operated domestic telesatellite systems.

65  Building on the earlier ABC application, in 1969 CBS television officials proposed the formation of a domestic telesatellite system owned and operated by all three television networks.

66  *President's Task Force on Communications Policy, Final Report*, (Washington, DC: US Government Printing Office, 7 December 1968); herein referred to as 'Rostow Report'.

67  For example, in 1972 (the year of the Watergate break-in and Presidential election) Nixon directed John Mitchell to file antitrust suits against the three television networks through the DoJ. These had been prepared in 1970 and were apparently applied two years later only as a result of the broadcasters' 'negative/anti-Nixon' news reports. Two months before election day, the head of the OTP, Clay Whitehead, delivered a speech in San Francisco that was commonly interpreted as another threat. Whitehead claimed that an OTP study supported the demands of the American Screen Actors' Guild that ABC, NBC and CBS should be compelled by the FCC to spend more money on original productions rather than airing reruns. The message to the networks was clear: modify negative coverage of White House activities or face higher costs and legal skirmishes. Tunstall, *Communications Deregulation*, p. 208.

68  Lyndon B. Johnson, 'Message from the President of the US: Recommendations Relative to World Communications' (14 August 1967), reprinted in Rostow Report, Appendix A, p. 3.

69  Kinsley, *Outer Space and Inner Sanctums*, p. 150.

70  Rostow Report, chap. 7, p. 32.

71  *Ibid.*, p. 33. Lloyd Musolf estimated in 1968 that a domestic DBS system with roughly similar capacities would cost half as much as the GSO-terrestrial hybrid system proposed by Comsat in 1966. See Musolf (ed.), *Communications Satellites in Political Orbit*, p. 148.

72  Rostow Report, chap. 7, p. 33.

73  For examples, see Barry Cole and Mal Oettinger, *Reluctant Regulators, The FCC and the Broadcast Audience* (Reading, Mass.: Addison-Wesley, 1978), chap. 10.

74  Rostow Report, chap. 7, pp. 36–9.

75    White House Memorandum to Dean Burch, Chairman FCC, 23 January 1970. Quoted in Kinsley, *Outer Space and Inner Sanctums*, p. 157 (emphasis added).

76    Burch was a well-known ideologue in favor of private enterprise. Opponents to his FCC appointment called him 'rash' and a 'reckless intellectual hipshooter,' among other things. Unnamed sources quoted in Magnant, *Domestic Satellite*, p. 160.

77    Hudson, *Communication Satellites*, pp. 46–7. According to Burch, the 'public interest' is served by actions that 'create a prevailing climate in which the widest possible range and variety of services are provided to the public by the greatest practical number of independent entities, each one seeking to satisfy public wants in its own way.' From Dean Burch, 'Public Utility Regulation: In Pursuit of the Public Interest', *Public Utilities Fortnightly* (September 1973) 70.

78 ·  Details on these proposals are available in Smith, *Communication via Satellite*, pp. 168–72.

79    FCC recommendations quoted in Kinsley, *Outer Space and Inner Sanctums*, p. 176.

80    Smith, *Communication via Satellite*, p. 175.

81    See Magnant, *Domestic Satellite*, pp. 112–40.

82    Jill Hills, *Deregulating Telecoms, Competition and Control in the US, Japan and Britain* (London: Frances Pinter, 1986) p. 61. In response to the emergence of the Open Skies approach, AT&T Chairman John D. deButts assured shareholders that '[in the words] of our first president,... "We have established and organized the business, and we do not propose to have it taken from us".' Quoted in Magnant, *Domestic Satellite*, p. 186; also see pp. 170–1.

83    Kinsley, *Outer Space and Inner Sanctums*, pp. 154–5.

84    'Message from the President of the US' to House of Representatives, 90th Cong., 1st sess., August 1967, p. 4.

85    Interview with Jean Pruitt, Associate Administrator for International Affairs, NTIA, 4 March 1994, Washington, DC.

86    Jill Hills, *Deregulating Telecoms*, p. 50.

87    *Ibid.*, p. 62.

88    Also, of course, a telephone transmission could use terrestrial facilities for one way of its communication.

89    Tunstall, *Communications Deregulation*, p. 72.

90    These opponents often cited IBM's strategy of locking customers into its technical standards, thereby establishing an end-to-end hardware, information and communication monopoly. See Magnant, *Domestic Satellite*, pp. 229–37.

91    On the cost advantages of non-terrestrial telephone services for large business users, see Dan Schiller, *Telematics and Government*, p. 50.

92    In the early 1980s, publicly discussed cost estimates of establishing a DBS system ranged from approximately US $200 million to $1 billion. Tunstall, *Communications Deregulation*, p. 76.

93    *Ibid.*, pp. 73–4.

94    Comsat's authority enabled it to secure a $400 million line of credit from Chase Manhattan Bank despite the risky nature of the venture.

James Chieh Hsiung, 'Status and Implications of Federal Regulation of Direct Broadcast Satellite' (unpublished PhD dissertation: Bowling Green State University, 1984) pp. 128–9.

95  *Ibid.*, pp. 130–1. Also, personal interview with Michael Alpert, President, Michael Alpert and Associates, 2 September 1992, Washington, DC.

96  Figures in Florence Setzer and Jonathan Levy, *Broadcast Television in a Multichannel Marketplace*. Working Paper No.26 (Washington, DC: FCC Office of Plans and Policy, 1991) p. 68.

97  Figures in *Ibid.*, p. 106.

98  For more details on the opposition of domestic broadcasters to DBS, see testimony of Vincent T. Wasilewski, President of the National Association of Broadcasters, in US Congress. House. Committee on Energy and Commerce. Subcommittee on Telecommunications, Consumer Protection, and Finance. Hearings on 'Satellite Communications/Direct Broadcast Satellites,' 97th Cong., 1st sess., 13 December 1981, pp. 207–20.

99  The other initial DBS license holders were CBS, Direct Broadcast Satellite Corporation, Focus Broadcast Satellite Corporation, Graphic Scanning, RCA, USSB, Video Satellite Systems. and Western Union.

100  Tunstall, *Communications Deregulation*, pp. 74–5. Also, interview with Michael Alpert.

101  Major investors in USCI included General Instruments and Prudential Insurance. The USCI coverage area was restricted to the US Northeast, providing mostly movies for a $150 installation charge plus a monthly subscription fee of $40. Hudson, *Communication Satellites*, p. 74.

102  Tunstall, *Communications Deregulation*, p. 73.

103  *Ibid.*, pp. 76.

104  Kinsley, *Outer Space and Inner Sanctums*, p. 3.

105  'Communications Satellites: An Introduction,' *Bulletin of the Atomic Scientists*, 23 (April 1967) 3 (emphases added).

106  Samuel Lewis, Assistant Secretary for International Organization Affairs, Department of State, testimony in US Congress. House. Committee on International Relations. Subcommittee on International Organizations. Hearings on 'UNESCO: Challenges and Opportunities for the United States,' 94th Congr., 2nd sess., 14 June 1976, p. 3.

# 4 Foreign Communication Policy and DBS: 1962–1984

State support for DBS research, including the active participation of NASA and the Department of Defense in the Applications Technology Satellite (ATS) experiments, coupled with ongoing government support for USIA and CIA propaganda activities, generated a degree of mistrust among officials of foreign states toward the American stated disinterest in DBS. By the mid-1970s, direct broadcasting was seen by many LDCs both to be a boon and a threat to their development aspirations. A DBS system could be applied in the manner of the ATS educational television trial, yet it could also be used for Northern-defined commercial or political ends. The latter appeared more likely given the large-scale costs involved in establishing a DBS system. These costs also inhibited any one LDC from pursuing DBS developments without foreign assistance.[1]

The international debate concerning direct broadcasting began in the late 1960s and, importantly, involved broader questions than DBS alone. The more pressing contextual issue concerned LDC-based challenges to the legality of free flow of information applications. Long before any US-based entity planned to implement a commercial DBS system, LDCs – mostly through UN-based agencies – refuted American arguments that transnational transmissions conducted without the prior consent of receiving countries constituted a 'right' under existing principles of international law. While American propaganda activities for the most part were tolerated by US public and private sector interests – indicating at least some domestic acceptance of the use of cultural power by the American state – no serious plan to implement a USIA or a CIA direct broadcasting service emerged. Beyond LDCs' stated distrust of publicly known US private or public sector plans involving direct broadcast technologies (or lack thereof), during the 1970s the DBS conflict emerged to become a front-line issue in a more significant North–South conflict.

The technological potential of US interests to develop and apply direct broadcasting was used mostly by Third World officials as a rallying point through which more general North–South information and communication disparities were addressed. It was the development of DBS as an *issue*, rather than any concrete plan to apply it, that made direct broadcasting a significant foreign policy concern for US officials. The emerging economic importance of information-based activities and the growing reliance of US-based corporations on transnational communications both came into conflict with LDC demands for a New World Information and Communication Order (NWICO). The DBS issue in the context of US structural capacities thus became the site of a larger political-economic conflict. Developing countries effectively made use of one-nation-one-vote UN agencies – some of which, ironically, in 1945 the United States had promoted as organizations through which American post-war interests could be mediated and legitimized.

## 4.1  US PROPAGANDA BROADCASTING

Propaganda broadcasting has been a component of US foreign policy since the end of the 1930s. Institutionalized after the Second World War, American state efforts to influence foreign opinions and perspectives have been tolerated by US mass-media interests largely because the former has operated with the goal of either supporting the latter's commercial aspirations or because state agencies only operated in areas where private sector opportunities for profit were negligible.[2]

Shortwave radio broadcasts sponsored by the American state – whether presenting the 'official' foreign policy of the United States through, for example, the Voice of America (VoA), or seeking to roll back communism through the more overtly propagandistic Radio Free Europe (RFE) and Radio Liberty (RL) services – have been operating since 1945 to support general and specific foreign policy objectives. The ambitions of these radio services have been restrained for more than just commercial reasons. Department of State officials, for instance, have consistently resisted mass propaganda activities due to their potentially negative impact on both the work of American diplomats and the problems that these official information services could have on foreign interpretations of US policy.[3] Historically, some members of Congress have considered shortwave radio services to be the indirect servants of the executive branch.[4] This perspective has been based largely on the President's constitutional supremacy in foreign relations and the general absence of a professional civil service able to counter-balance his political agenda in agencies such as the USIA. These apprehensions were reaffirmed under the Nixon administration when USIA Director James Keogh placed restrictions on the VoA's coverage of Congressional Watergate hearings.[5] But despite such instances, the American state has engaged in and apparently will continue to be involved in propaganda activities. Why then, given the potential economic efficiencies and cultural-power capacities associated with DBS, were direct broadcasting technologies never developed or applied by the USIA or other agencies?

In 1958, with a forty-person staff and a $3-million budget, an International Television Service (ITV) was created in the USIA. During the early years of Comsat, USIA officials anticipated that an international television broadcasting service using telesatellites eventually would become an established part of American propaganda operations. With world-wide distribution ambitions in mind, ITV began to develop appropriate in-house production facilities.[6] In the 1960s, as anticipated, ITV production and distribution activities became increasingly important components of USIA overseas broadcasting.[7] This boom was directly associated with the more general US foreign policy commitment to the 'modernization' of LDCs. According to Robert Elder, television was widely recognized as an efficient means for mass education, able 'to bring societies from tribalism to a sense of unity.' This association, in turn, stimulated a 'government-wide consideration of new uses of television in international communication.'[8] By 1966, 2,082 foreign-owned television stations located in ninety-four countries broadcast some USIA programing.[9]

In the late 1960s, the CIA-funded (and to some extent directed) Radio Free Europe (RFE) and Radio Liberty (RL) East European and Soviet-targeted shortwave services raised the idea of developing and using DBS technologies. In early 1967, John Richardson Jr of the National Committee for a Free Europe (then the front organization financing RFE and RL) told a Congressional subcommittee that direct broadcasting constituted a positive development. Given that a DBS signal would be extremely difficult to block, and that the only way to stop a direct broadcast transmission would be to destroy the satellite in orbit, Richardson believed that Soviet Union officials would have no choice but to accept both direct broadcasting and its implications regarding the free flow of information. Whether Soviet officials resisted DBS transmissions or accepted them, Richardson thought the general result would be that 'their own publics would distrust them more than they did before.'[10] Two years later, however, it became apparent that the development of DBS for American state broadcasting services would not proceed. In a Congressional hearing, the recently replaced VoA Director Leonard H. Marks resisted the urgings of legislators to prognosticate on future US direct broadcast applications while, during the same period, the VoA publicly called DBS technologically not feasible for at least another decade.[11] This latter point, however, was an assertion that contradicted both the Congressional testimony of private sector engineers and NASA presentations on the ATS project (scheduled to be launched in just five years).[12] Again, in 1970, USIA officials stated that they had little interest in DBS because of ongoing 'technological' and 'economic' barriers.[13]

It is doubtful that these officials were being altogether truthful. Leonard Marks, for instance, as a member of the Comsat board of directors prior to his posting at the USIA in 1965, had direct knowledge of the role that political will played in the development or derailment of new telesatellite technologies.[14] The seeming irrationality of not pursuing DBS applications became more apparent over the course of the 1970s when, increasingly, a premium was placed on the economic efficiency and centralized management of state broadcasting services. Whereas the VoA's news operations had always been located in Washington, DC, in 1975 the RFE and RL newsrooms were consolidated into offices located in Munich in order to reduce costs and coordinate activities better.[15] More generally, according to the 1973 report by the Presidential Commission on International Radio Broadcasting, titled *The Right to Know*, the short-term costs associated with effective propaganda activities were seen to be minimal in relation to the potential savings that cultural-power applications could provide in terms of potentially unnecessary Cold War military expenditures.[16]

In sum, the refusal of US propaganda agencies to pursue DBS during these formative years demonstrated their unwillingness to interfere with established private sector telecommunications and mass-media interests. Given the (at best) tentative support for state broadcasting activities from the State Department and Congress, direct broadcasting represented a potential domestic political minefield which USIA and CIA officials seem to have thought best to avoid – at least until the Soviet Union initiated such broadcasts.[17]

## 4.2   THE FREE FLOW OF INFORMATION AND INTERNATIONAL LAW

Because international law constitutes a means of regulating relations among nation states, it necessarily develops with, and is dependent on, relations between nation states through bilateral and multilateral agreements. These inter-state obligations generally constitute what is referred to as 'conventional' international law. 'Customary' international law, on the other hand, is based on the general norms of inter-state relations involving common practice and mutual acceptance.[18] Thus, for common law to be established, not only must a well-established practice be in place, but also a universal recognition of its legality needs to be present [19] The most fundamental principle of international law is the sovereignty of the nation state. As such, the domestic actions of governments are legally limited only by established international laws and recognized practices. This means that a nation state may not break its obligations to another on the grounds that domestic laws take precedence. Put differently, where a conventional or customary legal obligation is not present, the nation state is theoretically free to exercise its sovereignty within its territories. Questions concerning the obligations of nation states to facilitate or resist transnational DBS transmissions, from an idealistic legal perspective, therefore can be evaluated in terms of the existence or absence of treaty commitments, international conventions, or of the presence of customary law.[20]

The predecessor to the International Telecommunications Union – the International Telegraph Union – was established in 1865 by twenty European countries. Its mandate was to coordinate the technical aspects of transnational telegraph activities. The ITU thus constituted the first *de facto* international law-making institution. Its membership now includes all members of the United Nations and its activities still involve mostly regulatory and technical issues concerning transnational telecommunications.[21] In 1959, when the ITU first allocated frequency bands for remote-controlled vehicles in outer space, it established a jurisdictional precedent in international space law. Today, this precedent is exercised through the Union's allocation of DBS frequencies and other activities.[22]

Until recently, with the exception of the League of Nations Treaty of 1936, no international agreement has explicitly limited nation-state sovereignty over foreign communication transmissions nor has any such agreement formally limited that sovereignty.[23] Issues concerning the interference of signals, however, have been and continue to be managed through the ITU's regulation of the radio-wave spectrum, frequencies and technological standards. To put it generally, customary international law now facilitates the legal transmission and reception of radio waves while also recognizing ITU jurisdiction over the technical parameters of their utilization. Where conventional agreements are lacking, it is necessary to draw on other legal sources to clarify conflicts in transnational communication. International institutions such as the ITU and the UN provide forums through which conventional and customary law are developed. For example, when deliberations in the UN produce a convention or treaty, these become legally *relevant* for all member countries. However, only treaties are legally *binding*. Declarations and resolutions, on the other hand, are directly relevant only once they become part of a customary legal tradition.

Article 19 of the 1948 Universal Declaration of Human Rights, for instance, states that 'Everyone has the right to freedom of opinion and expression; this right includes freedom to hold opinions without interference and to seek, receive and impart information and ideas through any media and regardless of frontiers.' Although this establishes the right to send information across nation-state borders, Article 29 of the same Declaration modifies Article 19 as a result of its acknowledgement that only states can provide such rights.[24] Individuals (that is, people, corporations, unions and so on) therefore enjoy the right to send and receive information but within the legal parameters prescribed by nation states. The important question here is what legal obligation these provisions have on countries and the organizations and individuals in them. Unless accompanied by complementary and unambiguous international agreements, the Universal Declaration of Human Rights, *like all declarations and resolutions*, is not necessarily applicable unless accompanied by a conventional agreement.[25]

In 1961, the United Nations General Assembly recognized the ITU as the forum in which the regulatory development of telesatellites should be pursued.[26] Already in 1962, questions concerning the use of telesatellites for propaganda purposes were raised by the Soviet Union. Soviet delegates to the UN proposed a resolution stating that 'the use of outer space for propagating war, national or racial hatred or enmity between nations shall be prohibited.'[27] One year later, the Brazilian delegation echoed this proposal using language more in keeping with the technical terminology used in the ITU. The phrase 'harmful interference,' for instance, was emphasized and the Brazilians called for consultations between nation states to prevent the entry of unwanted satellite signals.[28] In 1963, an Extraordinary Administrative Radio Conference was convened by the ITU in response to the formation of Comsat and the immediate need to allocate frequency bands for space communications. With Soviet support, the US delegation received frequency allocations from the ITU for the experimental development of telesatellites.[29] Increasingly, however, telesatellite issues were considered to be broadly 'political' rather than narrowly 'technical.' For example, until the prospective feasibility of DBS technology was widely acknowledged, transnational satellite communications had been coordinated by the ITU on a largely *ad hoc* basis, and as such the introduction of new satellite services through the administration of ITU engineers primarily involved the protection of existing frequency assignments. With DBS, however, both the political ramifications of the technology and its relatively high research, development and implementation costs compelled ITU officials to move toward a *planned* use of the radio-wave spectrum.[30] Instead of first-come first-serve allocations, the *prospect* of DBS (and the ITU's responsibility to promote universal telecommunication developments, among other factors) led the Union to adopt a long-term planning regime. This shift in approach involved far more political intrigue than past decisions based largely on the short-term calculations of engineers.

In 1964, following a report by the UN Scientific and Technical Subcommittee of the Conference on the Peaceful Uses of Outer Space (COPUOS), which concluded that DBS transmissions would be technologically feasible within ten years, the UN Secretariat put the COPUOS in charge of all prospective DBS issues. One year later, the Brazilian delegate to an Outer Space Committee Working Group to Organize a UN Conference on Outer Space recommended that 'the question of the cultural and political impact of television programs transmitted by artificial satellites' should be put on the conference agenda.[31] By 1966, requests by the United Arab Republic (UAR), Mexico and Chile resulted in the COPUOS commissioning a broad-based study on the implications of space communications. An open political conflict ensued, involving delegations from countries as diverse as the Soviet Union, the UAR and France, all pushing for a formal UN recognition that DBS activities require the accompanying development of a regulatory regime reaching beyond the mostly technical boundaries of the ITU. The United States often stood alone in resisting these developments, emphasizing the economic risks involved in establishing an international legal regime *before* outstanding technical questions concerning DBS capabilities were resolved. During this period, questions concerning DBS were almost always raised in the context of more general uses of outer space. American officials, aware that commercial direct broadcasting plans were not being aggressively pursued by US corporations, resisted any agreement that potentially would have limited either the future development of DBS or related technologies. Given this limited domestic interest, US suggestions that DBS issues be set aside for further study at this stage were generally accepted in UN committees as a means of *not* precluding anything.[32]

As discussed in Chapter 3, by 1967 the capacity to develop a transnational DBS system was widely recognized, especially through the promotional activities of Hughes Aircraft and its efforts to sell .direct broadcasting as an educational medium for LDCs. Moreover, the establishment of Comsat and US leadership in Intelsat, in addition to the emerging involvement of NASA and the US Department of Defense in the ATS satellite experiments, generated much publicity and concern among UN delegations previously uninterested in the seemingly distant technological applications of DBS[33]. A Czechoslovakian delegate to the Outer Space Committee in 1967 suggested, for the first time, that prospective regulations governing the use of DBS should include 'principles that...[the] transmission must serve the interests of international peace and security and must respect the sovereign equality of all states.'[34]

In 1968, the COPUOS established a DBS Working Group in response to a widespread belief that a DBS-type system could be operational by the early 1970s. As David Blatherwick points out,

> The establishment of the Working Group was a turning point and a success for the proponents of [DBS] regulation. It provided a dedicated platform, it institutionalized the issue and ensured its inscription on the international agenda, and it obliged states hitherto neutral to develop a position and declare themselves.[35]

Over the course of the 1960s, therefore, the international forum for issues concerning DBS expanded beyond the ITU into the UN. In effect, this development served to politicize further what the United States in particular had preferred would remain largely technical issues concerning allocations and standards. As the only international, inter-state organization *exclusively* concerned with outer-space issues, the COPUOS stood as an important early medium in the emerging DBS debate. Preliminary US-based DBS developments and expert predictions that direct broadcasting applications were close at hand generated 'a sense of urgency' at least within the COPUOS.[36] Its DBS Working Group was particularly concerned with how direct broadcasting might affect developing countries. Specifically, the Working Group set out to study how to insure that all states could gain access to DBS systems; how to insure that DBS would be used for the development needs of LDCs; and how to insure that DBS would be used for peaceful purposes only.[37] Because of its status, agreements stemming from the COPUOS potentially would have a significant impact on the development of customary international law concerning the principles of the free flow of information in general and DBS in particular.

In 1970, the delegation representing France in the COPUOS DBS Working Group proposed the adoption of legal principles – normally the first step in the formation of an international treaty – that would require DBS broadcasts to take place under conditions respecting 'the sovereignty of States that do not wish their territory to be covered by... [DBS] broadcasts.'[38] Although specific issues concerning international copyright, advertising, right of reply, the impact of DBS on domestic film and television industries, and others were discussed, the Working Group eventually was dissolved having failed in its efforts to reach even the most general consensus. Again, US officials were opposed to *any* potentially precedent-setting agreement restricting DBS activities. American delegates insisted that such regulations were premature and contravened the principles of the free flow of information found in Article 19 of the Universal Declaration of Human Rights.[39] The working paper submitted by the US delegation, rather than taking part in a discussion of how prospective DBS systems might be used, instead limited its attention to those mostly technical issues that remained unresolved (namely, how space telecommunications can best be integrated with terrestrial systems, the technical requirements to develop interference-free transmissions and so forth).[40] Throughout the COPUOS DBS Working Group's deliberations, concluded in 1970, US officials refused to address directly the concerns raised by other delegations as to the prospective regulation of what DBS systems might one day transmit. At an international colloquium on space law, held in 1973, the Deputy General Counsel of the USIA, F.S. Ruddy, responded to his government's emerging isolation regarding its free flow principles by claiming that the American constitutional protection of 'free speech' prohibited US state officials from participating in any international agreement limiting 'the right to free expression.'[41]

Given the general lack of interest shown among most US public and private sector officials in the commercial or propaganda-based development of DBS, what were the substantive reasons for this official American resistance to the international regulation of direct broadcast applications? US officials had no interest in the establishment of *any* legal precedent that could restrict the future ability of its private or public sector to exploit the GSO and the radio frequency spectrum fully. Given that an international agreement on how these resources are put to use is an essential precondition to the stability and reliability of telesatellite applications, and the emerging recognition that secure international telecommunications were becoming more and more the essential prerequisites to international commercial and military operations, the direct broadcasting issue – despite the absence of foreseeable plans by core US interests to apply DBS – constituted a direct challenge to future American power capacities. Moreover, as will be discussed below, the international legal debates that centered on the DBS issue, and the institutional prominence of the UN and the ITU in mediating them, facilitated a remarkable assertion of collective power by mostly less developed countries against the aspirations of relatively developed nations in general and the United States in particular. At least until the 1980s, unsolicited transnational US-based DBS developments and other unilateral assertions of American cultural power generally were sublimated in foreign policy to the maintenance of *status quo* relations. Rather than analyzing the DBS issue in terms of DBS capabilities and DBS interests alone, therefore, the actions of US and foreign officials can only be fully understood by keeping these contextual power issues in mind.

While legalistic conflicts over free flow principles versus prior consent/state sovereignty rights remained unresolved, satellite broadcasting technologies were being developed at a rate requiring some form of ITU rule-making in order to prevent the possibility of chaos emerging over the airwaves. In 1971, the Union's World Administrative Radio Conference on Space Telecommunications (WARC-ST) established a process for countries to register frequencies that require protection from prospective DBS signal interference. WARC-ST defined a 'broadcasting satellite service' (such as DBS) as a 'radiocommunication service in which signals transmitted or retransmitted by space stations are intended for direct reception by the general public.'[42] The ITU also established a distinction between what it still calls 'fixed satellite services' (FSS) and 'broadcasting satellite services' (BSS). BSS is the ITU's formal term for DBS. Unlike the intended distribution of signals directly to end receivers (namely, households), as with BSS/DBS, a FSS system – also known as point-to-point as opposed to point-to-multipoint broadcasting – involves the transmission of signals to a single or limited number of fixed receivers (namely, a cable television operator). WARC-ST also allocated parts of the Ku band for BSS/DBS transmissions. Finally, WARC-ST adopted a procedure to deal with inter-state conflicts concerning unwanted (but inevitable) spillover signals. The Conference agreed, through Regulation 428A, that *'all technical means available shall be used to reduce, to the maximum extent practicable, the radiation over the territory of other countries unless an agreement has been previously reached with such countries.'*[43]

Some nation states considered Regulation 428A to be a *de facto* prior consent agreement. Some, like the Soviet Union, also argued that it should be expanded to include explicitly broadcasting from telesatellites direct to household receivers. US officials counter-argued that Regulation 428A constituted nothing more than a technical agreement. As such, it could not be used as the basis for establishing prior consent (nor nation-state sovereignty over the free flow of information) as a principle of international law. Representatives from Canada and Sweden, however, considered Regulation 428A to be an agreement regulating unwanted DBS transmissions. US officials responded by pointing out that 428A was relevant in questions involving *unintentional* signal spillover only.[44] Stephen Doyle, the US representative to the COPUOS Working Group on DBS, argued that the Regulation, in conjunction with other ITU regulations, relate only to radio-frequency coordination and potential interference problems.[45] In other words, the US interpretation of 428A was that it constituted little more than an agreement that DBS activities should take place over frequencies that would not, if possible, interfere with existing domestic broadcasts. In effect, however, this interpretation meant that

> in countries where television is hardly existent ... 428A would in no way inhibit the broadcasting country, since the receiving countries' channels would be unlikely to be in full use by domestic broad casting, and thus there would be no problem of interference.[46]

In 1972, the Soviet Union presented a draft convention to the UN General Assembly reiterating its official position on DBS. Four points were emphasized:

- state sovereignty as a supreme principle;
- transmissions into another country without prior consent must be prohibited;
- countries in which the transmission systems are located are legally responsible for those transmissions; and
- the right to counteract illegal transmissions both in one's own country and in outer space entails the right to use any means available.[47]

The US delegation again responded with assurances that while no plan existed in either the American public or private sectors to launch a commercial or state-controlled DBS service, rather than restricting future developments through prior consent regulations, the UN instead should encourage its potentially beneficial utilization.[48] Following this debate, the Soviets submitted a final draft to the General Assembly. After removing the prior consent provision, the UN General Assembly passed the Soviet resolution, titled 'Convention on Principles Governing the Use by States of Artificial Satellites for Direct Television Broadcasting,' with just one dissenting vote – that of the United States.[49]

But again, unlike a treaty, resolutions alone do not constitute international law. Among the five UN space-related treaties,[50] only the Outer Space Treaty (OST) is directly relevant to DBS. Although the OST does not mention DBS by name, its preamble refers to UN General Assembly Resolution 110(II). This particular Resolution condemns 'propaganda designed or likely to provoke or encourage any threat to peace.' And although treaty preambles unlike treaty comments are not in themselves binding, Article 31 of the Vienna Convention on the Law of Treaties, adopted in 1969, states that the preamble constitutes a source of information as to the *intent* of treaty signatories.[51] Nevertheless, it remains unclear what is meant by 'propaganda.'[52]

Article I of the OST states that the use of outer space must be pursued 'for the benefit and in the interests of all countries.' However, this paragraph also indicates that equality of *access* rather than just *use* is essential. Article II states that outer space is not susceptible to appropriations by nation states. Indirectly, therefore, the OST prescribes that the geosynchronous orbit is to be treated like any other limited and shared natural resource. In sum, however, the OST is too vague a treaty on which to determine the legal status of DBS transmissions entering a country without prior consent.[53]

## 4.3  US RESPONSES TO THE FREE FLOW IMBROGLIO

In the 1970s, US public and private sector free flow advocates, recognizing the need for substantive legal arguments beyond references to Article 19 of the Universal Declaration of Human Rights and the Constitution of the United States, initiated domestic research through foundation grants, law school study programs, and more directly through the US Department of State. In February 1974, for instance, the State Department sponsored a conference in Virginia titled 'The Free Exchange of Information and Ideas and the Integrity of National Cultures.' Its 'Draft Work Statement' addressed four questions to be dealt with by invited academics, lawyers and bureaucrats:

1 How well established in principle and in practice internationally is the right to receive and impart information across national borders?;
2 Does the right to receive information and ideas apply more to certain types of information and ideas than to others? For example, is the right of a citizen of any country to receive cosmetics advertising from abroad equivalent to his or her right to receive debates by the United Nations Security Council?
3 Does the practice of governments that impose controls on the volume of imported information material, such as films and television programs, violate the principle of 'free flow'?
4 What validity is there to the argument of some governments that they must control foreign media that are assumed to have an intense impact, such as television, as contrasted with media that have less impact, such as shortwave radio?[54]

Even when some of the more extreme opinions in response to these questions are excluded,[55] the conference and other such forums produced little agreement as to the legality of the free flow principle relative to prior consent. But despite this, with no alternative argument in hand, US officials continued to resist international prior consent agreements using the free flow principle as their baseline argument. In 1975, a study prepared for the US Senate Foreign Relations Committee on DBS developments, updated in 1977, reaffirmed this strategy.[56] Significantly, however, this study concluded that a free flow policy promoted through diplomacy and legal argument alone would *not* yield desired results. The report states that,

> At the present time, attention to the international communications implications of direct satellite broadcasting appears to be limited to consideration of the immediate political/legal question of an international convention regulating such activity....
>
> The US lead in the development of telecommunications technology, and the role that US communications systems and products play in the international transfer of information constitute foreign resources of great significance. *Recognition of this advantage might be the starting point for the consideration of a comprehensive, or an incremental US Government policy on international mass communications.*[57]

By the end of the 1970s, public officials concerned with America's capacity to shape future international telecommunications developments apparently had come to recognize that general US power resources should be applied in efforts either to resist free flow restrictions or to promote desired reforms. However, a coordinated and comprehensive method of putting such resources to use – including cultural-power applications – was not readily available. Perhaps not coincidentally, American officials at this time began to consider DBS to be an important technology in terms of its potential *economic* implications, despite the ongoing absence of more than marginal domestic private sector interest. In the Senate DBS study, for example, the general absence of domestic DBS activities in relation to emerging development plans overseas (namely, in Japan and Western Europe) became an issue of some concern. According to the report, 'the current lack of private commercial interest in the United States in the technology persists,' and as such 'Congress might consider whether or not to follow the recent advice of the National Academy of Sciences and authorize NASA to resume its own development program in this potentially important medium.'[58] The Senate report goes on to recommend that public sector support should be pursued through the development of domestic direct broadcasting educational and health-care services – areas in which domestic private sector resistance to direct state involvement would be relatively low.[59]

Also in 1977, WARC-77 – held to allocate DBS frequencies, power levels and GSO assignments – formally restricted countries from appropriating those orbital positions or frequency channels not assigned to them or without the permission of the country holding the assignment. These assignments were facilitated by dividing the world into three DBS service areas: Region 1 (including Europe, the Soviet Union and Africa); Region 2 (Greenland and the Americas); and Region 3 (Asia, Australia and New Zealand). Geostationary orbital slots, each capable of accommodating more than one satellite, were allocated 6 degrees apart to prevent signal interference. US and Canadian delegates to WARC-77 considered these decisions to be premature and unnecessarily restrictive given the likelihood of significant technological advancements. As a result of their complaints, the Region 2 allocation meeting was delayed until 1983.[60] Nevertheless, the WARC-77 allocation planning process implicitly reaffirmed the supremacy of prior consent. Delegates from France and Sweden, however, left the conference seeking a more explicit and universal recognition of prior consent as an undebatable legal principle.[61] WARC-77 failed to define the term 'unavoidable spillover'[62] and the ITU did not suggest a process through which one country could deal with the unwanted signals generated by another.[63]

Taken together, WARC-ST and WARC-77 made transnational DBS legally permissible as long as, first, it took place on a frequency channel legally held by or legally provided for use to the transmitting country; and second, it could not be reasonably limited to the intended receiving country.

In 1982, a draft resolution was presented in the COPUOS by officials representing Brazil.[64] While reiterating much of what previous UN resolutions had said, this resolution included a section explicitly supporting the principle of prior consent. For the first time in the history of the COPUOS, the resolution was passed by majority vote rather than a consensus agreement. This undermining of the consensus procedure in COPUOS itself was significant. The consensus procedure had been established in 1961 in order to appease the Soviet Union which, at the time, insisted that the COPUOS and its subcommittees should act only through unanimous agreement. The United States disagreed and supported the majority rule procedures practiced in the General Assembly. With the COPUOS resolution supporting the necessity of a prior consent agreement on DBS transmissions, US officials suddenly became strong advocates of the consensus standard because they recognized that, on issues involving the free flow principle, it would lose most majority-based votes.[65]

On 10 December 1982, the Brazilian COPUOS resolution was adopted by the General Assembly under the title 'Principles Governing the Use by States of Artificial Earth Satellites for International Direct Television Broadcasting' (UN Resolution No. 37/92).[66] Article 1, paragraph 1 of the Resolution states that 'activities in the field of international direct television broadcasting by satellite should be carried out *in a manner compatible with the sovereign Rights of States*.'[67]

In the 1980s, the international forum most politicised through the free flow–prior consent debate was the United Nations Educational, Scientific and Cultural Organization (UNESCO). Article 1, paragraph 2, of UNESCO's founding constitution declared that the organization should 'recommend such international agreements as may be necessary to promote the free flow of ideas by word or image.' However, European delegates insisted that this free flow commitment should be pursued only in accordance with the more general UNESCO mandate which committed the agency to promote international 'peace and security.' Moreover, the reference to 'international agreements' in Article 1, paragraph 2, assumes the supremacy of the principle of national sovereignty. In other words, UNESCO's constitution contains a commitment to the free flow of information in a context that respects the more fundamental principles of international law – including the supremacy of the nation state.[68]

As mentioned in Chapter 2, the struggle between free flow and prior consent emerged in the context of the crisis of Fordism and the related crisis of US hegemony. The response involved innovation in production, distribution, exchange and consumption activities directly involving communications and information technologies. This crisis and the American-based corporate response to it implied a struggle to control the media – institutions, organizations and technologies – through which new capitalist activities and complementary social relations could be forged. International legal debates concerning DBS, of course, were significant for prospective direct broadcast and related communications developments, but for students of international political economy they were more significant in terms of a larger struggle involving control over how key institutions – such as the UN and the ITU – would mediate future struggles. US efforts to control these and other such historical nodal points generally did not reflect the pressing and immediate needs of US private and public sector interests. US efforts more importantly reflected the perceived long-term needs of an American state seeking to redress hegemonic decline. State officials pursued free flow principles on behalf of mostly domestic capitalists – especially the emerging and expanding information and communication sector – but did so as biased mediators working within the parameters of complex policy and cultural structures.


## 4.4   DBS, UNESCO AND THE NWICO

Ironically, US efforts to promote an international free flow of information confronted their most concerted opposition in UNESCO. From its inception, the role of UNESCO in relation to US foreign communication policy has been significant in that its institutional mandate involved issues explicitly concerning cultural-power aspects of American hegemony. In 1945, US officials sought to expand US 'Open Door' relations with the world.[69] International institutions, including the UN, constituted essential nodal points in this effort, and UNESCO was considered to be a potentially important agent for generating international stability and market access overseas for US commercial interests. In sum, through its apparently neutral offices and activities, UNESCO was established to stimulate liberal economic and political values. Given the predominant position of the United States in the post-war international economy, UNESCO's cultural mandate, it was believed, could serve to benefit both American state and post-war capitalist interests.[70]

Until the Soviet Union joined UNESCO in 1954, the US ideal of the free flow of information was opposed among its members only by West European countries interested in defending their international news media corporations from US-based competitors. As technological change, post-colonial movements and the Cold War became predominant forces influencing international affairs, UNESCO gradually emerged as a medium through which relatively 'powerless' countries could organize against the 'powerful' directly and transnational corporate activities indirectly. Since its inception, American state officials had worked to influence the perspectives and activities of UNESCO personnel. But by the mid-1970s, the CIA both monitored these officials and were directly involved in financing hundreds of information and news programs (including the propaganda radio operations discussed above) that were created in efforts to counter the broadcasts of communist states and what were viewed as subversive,

UNESCO-funded activities.[71] The turning point for US–UNESCO relations, according to William Preston, Jr, came in 1965 with the launch of the first Intelsat satellite. Less developed countries, according to Preston, which had been 'closing somewhat the disparities of media power, found themselves suddenly and totally outdistanced.'[72]

UNESCO's Space Communications Conference of 1965 produced a report that, in light of Intelsat's unprecedented telesatellite capabilities, called for a shift in emphasis from the techniques of communication to a concern with content.[73] From this date forward, an increasing number of US officials recognized UNESCO to be a threat to US interests. Outside the United States, Third World nationalist and anti-imperialist movements challenged the interests and activities of the American state and US-based corporations. Domestically, anticommunist conservatives, elements of the news media, and corporations seeking a stable transnational business environment, formed an informal anti-UNESCO coalition.[74] During this period, the US Congress issued threats to those UN agencies that appeared intent on undermining the 'common-sense' assumptions underlying US foreign policy.[75] But behind the pro-and anti-free flow rhetoric, the reform demands issued by UNESCO and other UN agencies involved the formation of international institutions and organizations that First World countries could not readily control. Underlying this LDC-based mobilization in one-country-one-vote international forums was the more general demand for, as Senator George McGovern put it in reference to foreign challenges to the free flow of information, 'a bigger slice of the pie.'[76]

The most significant danger issue for the anti-UNESCO coalition was the prospective implementation of a New World Information and Communication Order as developed in UNESCO and affirmed through the UN General Assembly. Three general goals characterized this LDC-led proposal. First, the NWICO movement sought to challenge the dominant international position of Western mass media in terms of content, bias and technological development. Second, the NWICO sought to equalize nation-state access to radio spectrum frequencies and considered these to be shared natural resources that should not be allocated on the basis of economic exploitation capabilities. And third, the NWICO sought to redress predominantly one-way information flows out of the developed world into the less developed. This third goal directly and positively influenced UNESCO support for the universal adoption of prior consent principles over the free flow of information.

The historical context in which the NWICO emerged is revealing. In the early 1970s, both the US decision to undermine the Bretton Woods fixed exchange system[77] and the assertion of economic power by OPEC stimulated the unification of somewhat disparate LDCs – some seeking the alleviation of poverty, and others pursuing development policies aimed at escaping the Third World altogether – under the general quest to establish a so-called New International Economic Order (NIEO). Its proponents sought an international system featuring Keynesian-type global economic mechanisms. In the early 1980s, however, with the collapse of the power of OPEC, West European states became far less interested in accommodating NIEO reforms. Moreover, the recession experienced in the United States in the mid-1980s greatly reduced, at least for a few years, First World demands for LDC products, including oil. Interest rates reached post-1945 highs and Third World debt payments – mostly contracted in the 1970s – became dangerously unmanageable. Both the NIEO and the NWICO thus affirmed general efforts to redress deepening North–South dependency patterns, particularly in light of growing US budget deficits and subsequent Congressional cuts to America's UN and foreign aid support payments. In the 1980s, the US government, while reforming its own welfare state, had little interest in efforts to develop a kind of global Keynesianism. Importantly, *neither the NIEO nor the NWICO threatened the ongoing survival of international capitalism* – in fact, it can be argued that such reforms to the system constituted (and still constitute) essential components in capitalism's long-term stability.[78]

The election of Jimmy Carter in 1976 generated a re-evaluation among American state officials on how best to counteract the NWICO. A shared view among White House and State Department personnel that a hard-line anti-UNESCO policy likely would fuel the alienation of LDCs and that this, in turn, would only result in escalating threats to more pressing US policy interests (especially in relation to the desire of the Carter administration to promote a relaxation in US–Soviet relations) guided US-UNESCO policy for the rest of the decade. In 1977, Senator McGovern, through the Senate Foreign Relations Committee, recognized the existence of an international information imbalance and the need to provide LDCs assistance in efforts to develop their communication infrastructures. McGovern argued that both 'the information sector' and more general 'international communications and information' activities were of 'grave import' to the future power capacities of the United States.

'Throughout the world,' said the Senator, 'there is a growing corps of government officials who seek control of communications as a key lever to be used against the West.' McGovern directed his colleagues to pay attention to 'narrowly defined technical questions concerning direct broadcasts from satellites' raised in WARC-77 and subsequent ITU and UN conferences that could produce 'a seriously damaging blow to the concept of free flow of information across world borders.'[79]

In 1980, at a UNESCO General Conference in Belgrade, the United States responded to a recommendation made by UNESCO's International Commission for the Study of Communication Problems (the MacBride Commission) to establish a kind of Marshall Plan for LDC telecommunications.[80] A new US-sponsored UNESCO organization – the International Program for the Development of Communications (IPDC) – was to be established. It would involve no corporate money and a majority of its membership would come from LDCs. American officials considered the IPDC to be an essential counter-move to the Third World drift toward a NWICO and the Soviet Union's apparently rising influence in LDCs through, among other things, its technological assistance programs. By attracting more moderate states back to the 'practical non-ideological approach' offered by the United States, Carter administration officials believed that not only could the rapidly growing US telecommunication equipment sector benefit from rising overseas demands but also that apparently 'ideological' UNESCO activities could be transformed into a 'concrete development opportunity.'[81]

Nevertheless, US-based news media organizations and conservative think-tanks (especially the Institute for Contemporary Studies, founded by Caspar Weinberger and Edwin Meese III, and the Heritage Foundation) remained active in opposing UNESCO. In 1980, the election of Ronald Reagan provided these interests with a neoconservative White House that, from the start, was determined to curb LDC opposition through unilateral US action if necessary.[82] Rather than a policy designed to hold the line on LDC demands and Soviet influence, the new administration proceeded to demand their immediate retreat. UN agencies, such as UNESCO, were to be brought to heel.

UNESCO – described by some conservative policy analysts as 'the Grenada of international organizations'[83] – was explicitly targeted to be made an example of for all UN agencies.[84] In December 1983, the US officially announced its intent to withdraw from UNESCO in one year. Appointed to represent the US at UNESCO conferences over this period of reckoning was Edward P. Hennelly, Heritage Foundation member and a Vice President of the Mobil Oil Corporation. After attending his first UNESCO meeting and subsequent negotiations with UNESCO officials, Hennelly surprised Reagan by recommending that because significant progress had been made in his talks the United States should retain its membership. American allies, including Israel, also wanted the United States to remain in UNESCO, as did the USIA and even the CIA.[85] Nevertheless, the US withdrawal was to proceed as scheduled. According to a confidential State Department memorandum, dated 13 December 1987, arguments that the US absence would create an international void in valuable cultural, educational and scientific exchanges were dismissed by the administration. As its author writes, 'given the fact that neither culture, commerce, nor world science can proceed meaningfully without the participation of US nationals and American institutions, cooperative [alternative] arrangements ... will surely be activated – and on a healthy non-ideological basis.'[86]

In July 1984, less than five months before its scheduled withdrawal, State Department officials sent UNESCO Director General Amadou-Mahtar M'Bow a letter specifying the precise terms for a US policy change. These included proposals that were tantamount to a US veto over all UNESCO budget allocations and policies. The goal, said the letter, was to ensure that UNESCO would never again sanction 'uncritical and simplistic approaches to disarmament, economic theorizing, and global standard-setting' and would never again become a 'partisan participant in existing quarrels' such as the debate on the free flow of information versus prior consent.[87]

With the US withdrawal from UNESCO in December 1984, it appeared as though US efforts to *compel* international institutions and nation states to accept the precedence of free flow over prior consent principles had failed. However, this 'failure' may well have constituted a calculated first step in a more general effort to redefine the institutional terrain on which a larger hegemonic struggle was taking place. It became apparent in the 1980s that US officials preferred the absence of agreement when faced with alternative agreements involving prior consent. Rapidly developing technological capacities and the emerging neo-liberal market interests of transnational corporate actors took precedence over any potential compromise of free flow principles.

Again, the historical context in which this US challenge to LDCs took place goes some way in explaining the aggressive nature of the

American counter-offensive. Emerging out of the relative economic, military and political decline of the United States, and fueled by 'sunbelt'-inspired neo-liberalism, the so-called New Cold War in the 1980s constituted an attempted reassertion of post-1945 US hegemonic might.[88] The assumed location in which America's eroding power could most readily be redressed was the Third World. The Soviet Union was represented as the force underlying LDC resistance movements. The Reagan Doctrine – the strategy of arming right-wing proxies and pro-Western insurgents to engage in the disruption or overthrow of socialist LDC governments – sought not only to discipline the international left, it also sought to undermine the perceived gains of the Soviet Union in international affairs.[89] As Fred Halliday summarizes, 'The Second Cold War was neither an accident, nor the product of some neat conspiracy: it reflected ... decisions taken by people in power with limited control over world events.'[90]

The Reagan Doctrine was promoted as a struggle for 'freedom' – an ideal that the White House religiously pursued in efforts to establish secure capitalist market economies. In this effort, 'basic principles, political as well as legal and moral, on which the international system is based' were selectively repudiated.[91] Such an aggressive turn in US foreign policy was justified during a brief period in which Reagan administration officials vilified the Soviet Union as 'the evil empire.'[92] The US attack on the NWICO and virtually every international organization supporting it were components of this New Cold War offensive.

## 4.5   CONCLUSIONS

The claims made by some US officials, as early as 1969, that DBS was impractical due to ongoing technological and economic barriers ring hollow in light of the role played by the American state in directly shaping the history of domestic and international telesatellites. If DBS remained 'ten years away' in 1970, and again in 1975, and again in 1980, the policy preferences and subsequent regulations affecting direct broadcasting developments were to blame, not the intellectual abilities of engineers nor the dictates of a mythological free market. Despite established but limited US cultural-power applications, despite the relative efficiency and probable effectiveness of DBS technologies, and despite the emergence of direct broadcasting as the formative international issue of free flow versus prior consent/national sovereignty, DBS itself remained a technology of only marginal interest to most American officials. Moreover, given the presence of the NWICO and other assertions of collective and national power among LDCs, foreign communication policy officials had little incentive to push forward a working transnational DBS system. Before Reagan took office, foreign communication policy had been characterized by a cautious assertion of free flow principles. After 1980, communication policy goals were as aggressively pursued as any other component of the Reagan administration's New Cold War.

The crisis period in foreign communication policy that emerged in the 1980s, and the history of American intra-state policy conflicts, again reveal the cultural imperialism paradigm to be too simplistic. For example, the tendency of Schiller and others to characterize US conflicts with both the UN and the ITU as a clash of largely homogeneous interests tends to gloss over a more complex history. While neither the UN nor the ITU acted as passive institutions mediating conflicts concerning free flow versus prior consent interests, neither were the unified proponents of some kind of counter-hegemonic world order. The US–UNESCO conflict, for instance, more accurately involved the efforts of LDCs (and others) to reach a compromise on free flow versus prior consent in order to maintain some amount of policy-making autonomy in relation to capitalist developments. For the Reagan administration, however, any such compromise was unacceptable given the crisis then facing the American political economy and the commitment of the executive branch to define it in a freedom-versus-communism context. While US-based TNCs and the White House were compelled to apply a take-no-prisoners approach, as Theodore H. Von Laue has argued, UN agencies pursued little more than a kind of 'anti-Western [means of] Westernization.'[93]

In 1984, UNESCO, the so-called Grenada of international agencies, became the primary target of US efforts to discipline international institutions and organizations. This did not constitute the sudden development of a well-conceived free flow reform plan among American state officials. Not only was a free flow–prior consent compromise unacceptable to the Reagan White House, the very existence of *potentially* oppositional international institutions could no longer be tolerated. While ignoring the advice of State Department and FCC personnel, and even recommendations from its own appointees to UNESCO, the administration's withdrawal – inspired by its New Cold War ideology – produced little more than a strategic vacuum. Rather than the outcome of some sort of seamless web of state-corporate interests (as the cultural imperialism paradigm might suggest), the subsequent ascendancy of the services-as-trade issue was largely the result of private sector interests filling a vacuum generated by what were, for the most part, incidental but contextually inspired developments.[94]

This foreign communication policy crisis, to some extent, was rooted in the Communications Satellite Act of 1962 and the context in which this piece of legislation was formulated and applied. The priority status of US military and technological capacities in relation to the Soviet Union compelled the rather blinkered construction of the common carrier-controlled Comsat corporation.[95] The subsequent role played by AT&T in retarding telesatellite advancements that threatened its bottom line – including DBS – was facilitated by the similar terrestrial cable-based interests of European PTTs as expressed through Intelsat. Beyond the subsequent erection of hurdles and barriers to DBS, these conditions established AT&T and Comsat as the *de facto* leaders of American foreign communication policy. No public agency was able to challenge this leadership position. As shown in Chapter 3, the AT&T/Comsat monopoly, followed by the dominant influence of the NAB in broadcasting, blocked the commercial development of DBS until the 1980s. LDCs, however, had used the 'threat' of DBS as an ideological focal point through which to organize against the free flow of information and more general Western communication and information dominance. Contrary to the assumptions of Schiller and others, the principal agents shaping US policy were not proponents of transnational DBS systems. Rather than LDCs, UNESCO or the ITU, arguably the most formative barrier to a conscious and/or systemic form of US cultural imperialism were domestic vested interests and related American state structures. US agents in charge of international propaganda – officials in the USIA and CIA – played a supporting or secondary role to the relatively diplomatic priorities of the State Department and the economic interests of dominant and emerging corporations.

By the end of the 1970s, the strategic priorities brought forth through US corporate leadership in new communication and computer technology applications – underlining the growing importance of forging a secure international regime favoring the free flow of information – ran up against a formidable barrier. The immediate barricade was not the resistance of the LDCs through UN organizations; it was the structural capacities of the American state itself. In the early 1980s, it was institutionally beyond the abilities of the State

Department, the FCC or even a special Presidential appointee, either to compel the rest of the world to accept free flow over prior-consent principles or to reform foreign opinions as to the purported benefits of the former. Not only was no one clearly in charge of US foreign communication policy; the capacity of American state agencies – even if temporarily coordinated – to enforce the universal obedience of free flow principles (assuming they would one day be accepted) did not exist.

In relation to the crisis facing US hegemony, *the struggles outlined in this chapter reflect the need to control the institutional, organizational and technological media through which a consensual world order is generated or maintained.* By the middle of the 1980s, American officials recognized that the conflict between free flow of information and prior consent, as it had been played out in such international media, was essentially unresolvable. Neither the reform nor the destruction of dominant mediators could themselves lead to a stable world in keeping with the needs of emerging information and communication interests. A *new* medium had to be constructed – one that could lead to an enforceable free flow regime and perhaps even revisions in the cultural context in which foreign governments make policies affecting information and communication commodity developments. The domestic conditions in which this realization took place are addressed in the next chapter, which focuses on the agents and structures of US foreign communication policy in the 1980s.

## NOTES

1    Nandariri Jasentuliyana, 'Direct Satellite Broadcasting and the Third World,' *Columbia Journal of Transnational Law*, 13 (1974) 68–70.
2    Jeremy Tunstall, *The Media Are American* (New York: Columbia University Press, 1977) p. 222. In fact, after 1945 US officials compelled Marshall Aid recipients to import set quotas of Hollywood films. Foreign aid grants often included American state subsidies to LDCs for the purchase of US books and other mass-media products. The USIA was established in 1954 in part to stimulate international consumer interest in a broad range of American exports through its general promotion of a middle-class American lifestyle. See Tunstall, pp. 223–9, and Robert E. Elder, *The Information Machine, the United States Information Agency and American Foreign Policy* (Syracuse, NY: Syracuse University Press, 1968) p. 36.
3    Elder, *The Information Machine*, p. 39.
4    Tunstall, *The Media Are American*, p. 222.

5     Keogh explained that foreign audiences could interpret these hearings as a conspiratorial attempt by Congress to overthrow the President. Because he believed that this impression could lead to international destabilization, Keogh directed USIA personnel to focus on the 'positive' aspects of the Watergate affair. Rather than approaching the story with the 'cynicism' of the private sector news media, Keogh explained that because bugging was a normal means of governing in communist regimes, an emphasis on the 'pluralism' of American political institutions constituted a preferable approach. See 'Lowering the Voice,' *Newsweek* (9 July 1973) 60–1, and Donald R. Browne, *International Radio Broadcasting* (New York: Praeger, 1982) p. 143.

6     In 1963, ITV moved into new Washington, DC offices which included the most modern of production facilities. Elder, *The Information Machine*, pp. 234–5.

7     *Ibid.*, p. 9.

8     *Ibid.*, p. 20.

9     *Ibid.*, p. 9.

10    Richardson testimony in hearings on 'Modern Communications and Foreign Policy,' p. 77.

11    Hearings on 'Satellite Broadcasting: Implications for Foreign Policy,' pp. 138–40.

12    See *ibid.*, pp. 14–47.

13    Hearings on 'Foreign Policy Implications of Satellite Communications,' pp. 69–71.

14    Elder, *The Information Machine*, p. 12.

15    Browne, *International Radio Broadcasting*, p. 143.

16    Presidential Commission on International Radio Broadcasting, *The Right to Know* (Washington, DC: US Government Printing Office, 1973) p. 56.

17    Without documentary evidence, this conclusion is the speculative product of both logical reflection and a general absence of counter-proposals by many of the American state officials interviewed for this book.

18    Leo Gross, 'Some International Law Aspects of the Freedom of Information and the Right to Communicate', in Kaarle Nordenstreng and Herbert I. Schiller (eds), *National Sovereignty and International Communication* (Norwood, NJ: Ablex, 1979) pp. 196–97.

19    I.H.Ph. Diederiks-Verschoor, *An Introduction to Space Law* (Deventer and Boston: Kluwer Law and Taxation Publishers, 1993) p. 11.

20    Leo Gross, 'Some International Law Aspects of the Freedom of Information and the Right to Communicate,' p. 200.

21    The ITU has evolved into a largely autonomous UN agency, with headquarters in Geneva. Its aims and purposes were made explicit at its 1947 Atlantic City Conference. They are as follows: to maintain and extend international cooperation for the improvement and rational use of telecommunications; to promote the development of technical facilities and their most efficient operation with a view to improving the efficiency of telecommunication services, increasing their usefulness and making them so far as possible generally available to the public; and to harmonize the actions of nations in the attainment of those common

ends. See Jean-Luc Renaud, 'The Role of the International Telecommunications Union: Conflict, Resolution and the Industrialized Countries,' in Kenneth Dyson and Peter Humphreys (eds), *The Political Economy of Communications* (London: Routledge, 1990) p. 38.

22    Although the ITU has no enforcement mechanism, its regulations have enjoyed a remarkable history of near-universal acceptance. In large part, this has been due to the ability of the Union both to arbitrate conflict and to modify the intellectual framework within which conflicts take place. Because ITU membership is conditional on membership of the UN, expulsion from the UN can be used as a significant sanction against non-compliance. At least one legal scholar has argued that 'the growing and often inescapable dependence of states on participation in activities of global and indivisible concern, where the principle sanction is exclusion from participation of those states that refuse to comply with universally accepted standards' probably constitutes a sufficient although an as yet untested enforcement mechanism for international organizations such as the ITU. See Charles Henry Alexandrowicz, *The Law of Global Communications* (New York: Columbia University Press, 1971) p. 157. More fundamentally, Marika Natasha Taishoff argues that

'since all countries' interests are best served by consultation and coordination in order to avoid interference, the ITU's efforts have frequently been fruitful. The more intractable problem resides not in the ITU and its powers, or lack thereof, but in the state of the art of technological developments.' (Taishoff, *State Responsibility and the Direct Broadcast Satellite* [London: Francis Pinter, 1987] p. 160)

23    Recent developments in the European Union, for instance, and international trade agreements have explicitly limited sovereignty and have established enforceable controls over nation states in relation to foreign communications.

24    Article 29 contains three points: *first*, 'Everyone has duties to the community in which alone the free and full development of his personality is possible'; *second*, 'In the exercise of his rights and freedoms, everyone shall be subject only to such limitations as are determined by law solely for the purpose of securing due recognition and respect for the rights and freedoms of others and of meeting the just requirements of morality, public order and the general welfare in a democratic society'; and *third*, 'These rights and freedoms may in no case be exercised contrary to the purposes and principles of the United Nations.'

25    Leo Gross, 'Some International Law Aspects of the Freedom of Information and the Right to Communicate', pp. 201–2.

26    General Assembly Resolution 1721 (XVI) of 1961 in *Official Records*, Supplement No.17, UN Doc. A/5100 (1961).

27    General Assembly Resolution 1963 (XVIII) of 1962 in *Official Records*, Supplement No.15, UN Doc. A/5515 (1963).

28    M. Lesueur Stewart, *To See the World, the Global Dimension in International Direct Television Broadcasting by Satellite* (Dordrecht: Martinus Nijhoff Publishers, 1991) p. 11.

29 See David E.S. Blatherwick, *The International Politics of Telecommunications* (Berkeley, Cal.: Institute of International Studies, 1987) pp. 37–8.

30 James Edwin Bailey III, 'Current and Future Legal Uses of Direct Broadcast Satellites in International Law,' *Louisiana Law Review*, 45(3) (1985) 707.

31 Quoted in Benno Signitzer, *Regulation of Direct Broadcasting from Satellites, the UN Involvement* (New York: Praeger, 1976) p. 27. In the end, the issue was not placed on the agenda.

32 *Ibid.*, p. 33.

33 Lawrence Lessing, 'Cinderella in the Sky,' *Fortune*, LXXVI (5) (October 1967). Also, Signitzer, *Regulation of Direct Broadcasting from Satellites*, p. 33.

34 United Nations Document A/AC.105/C.2/SR.80 (1967) p. 15.

35 See David E.S. Blatherwick, *The International Politics of Telecommunications*, p. 40.

36 Signitzer, *Regulation of Direct Broadcasting from Satellites*, p. 31.

37 See United Nations Document A/AC.105/PV.55 (1968) pp. 62–70.

38 United Nations, Conference on the Peaceful Uses of Outer Space, 'Report of the Working Group on Direct Broadcast Satellites on its Third Session.' 25 May 1970. Reprinted in Annex V of United Nations Document A/AC.105/83 (25 May 1970) p. 29. The French delegation argued that DBS constituted 'a technique for the dissemination of thought which is so powerful that it can, depending upon the use made of it, exalt or trample upon this very freedom [i.e., freedom of thought].' Quoted in M. Lesueur Stewart, *To See the World*, p. 65.

39 Blatherwick, *The International Politics of Telecommunications*, p. 40.

40 Signitzer, *Regulation of Direct Broadcasting from Satellites*, p. 36.

41 From Ruddy's paper presented at the Sixteenth Colloquium on Outer Space Law (International Institute of Space Law, 1973) quoted in Sara Fletcher Luther, *The United States and the Direct Broadcast Satellite* (New York: Oxford University Press, 1988) p. 89.

42 This definition goes on to point out that 'the term reception shall encompass both individual reception and community reception.' The term 'radiocommunication' includes television and data transmissions. See Article 84AP, Spa 2 in World Administrative Radio Conference for Space Telecommunications, *Final Acts* (Geneva: International Telecommunications Union, 1971) p. 41.

43 Article 428A, Spa 2 SS 2A in *ibid.*, p. 117 (emphases added).

44 Luther, *The United States and the Direct Broadcast Satellite*, pp. 101–02.

45 Kathryn M. Queeney, *Direct Broadcast Satellites and the United Nations* (The Netherlands: Sijthoff & Noordhoff, 1978) pp. 152–3.

46 Luther, *The United States and the Direct Broadcast Satellite*, p. 103.

47 The Soviet draft convention was attached to a letter from the Soviet Foreign Affairs Minister André Gromyko to the UN Secretary-General, dated 8 August 1972. UN Doc. A/8771 (9 August 1972).

48 Signitzer, *Regulation of Direct Broadcasting from Satellites*, p. 55.

49 General Assembly Resolution 2916 (XXVII) of 9 November 1972 in UN Doc. A/8771, p. 4 *et seq.* (1972). 102 votes were cast in favor of the

resolution and seven countries abstained – Central African Republic, Fiji, Gabon, Israel, Lesotho, Nicaragua and Tunisia.

50   These are the Outer Space Treaty of 1967, the Moon Treaty of 1979, the Rescue and Return Treaty of 1968, the Treaty on the Registration of Objects Launched into Outer Space of 1975, and the Liability Treaty of 1972.

51   Bailey III, 'Current and Future Legal Uses of Direct Broadcast Satellites in International Law,' pp. 703–4.

52   On the definitional problems of propaganda, see Taishoff, *State Responsibility and the Direct Broadcast Satellite*, pp. 31–5; and Jon T. Powell, 'Towards a Negotiable Definition of Propaganda for International Agreements Related to Direct Broadcast Satellites,' *Law and Contemporary Problems*, 45(1) (Winter 1982) 3–35.

53   Bailey III, 'Current and Future Legal Uses of Direct Broadcast Satellites in International Law,' pp. 704–6.

54   Quoted in Luther, *The United States and the Direct Broadcast Satellite*, p. 89.

55   In *ibid.*, Luther considers the then acting head of the American Society of International Law, John L. Hargrove, to have presented the most extreme pro-free flow position at the 1974 State Department conference. The gist of Hargrove's argument was that the principle of nation-state sovereignty is not absolute where state authorities are not deemed to be representatives of the nation. On what bases and by whom such an evaluation is to be made were not made clear by Hargrove. See pp. 90–1.

56   Joel H. Woldman, 'The View Ahead: Direct Satellite Broadcasting and International Communications.' Report to the United States Senate. Committee on Foreign Relations. Reprinted in United States Congress. Senate. Committee on Foreign Relations. Subcommittee on International Operations. Hearings on 'The Role and Control of International Communications and Information,' 95th Cong., 1st sess., June 1977, pp. 38–54.

57   *Ibid.*, pp. 50 and 53–4 (emphases added).

58   *Ibid.*, p. 50. On the NAS recommendation, see Craig Covault, 'NASA Urged to Study Satcom Program,' *Aviation Week & Space Technology*, 106 (14 March 1977) 41–2.

59   Woldman, 'The View Ahead: Direct Satellite Broadcasting and International Communications,' p. 53.

60   A Department of Commerce report released prior to these Region 2 negotiations made the US position clear: 'We should adhere to current policies that favor allocation on the basis of efficiency and established need, while assuring that the needs of future users will be effectively met.' – US Department of Commerce, 'Long-Range Goals in International Telecommunications and Information, An Outline of United States Policy.' Published in Kenneth W. Leeson, *International Communications* (Amsterdam: Elsevier Science Publishers, 1984) p. 19.

61   David I. Fisher, *Prior Consent to International Direct Broadcast Satellite Broadcasting* (Dordrecht: Martinus Nijhoff Publishers, 1990) p. 26. While the French and other Western delegations feared the potentially damaging impact of externally based broadcasters on existing domestic

television and radio infrastructures, the Swedes (and others) also were concerned with the need to establish universally accepted regulations in light of the potential for instability and conflict stemming from the collapse of existing regimes governing telecommunication applications. See Signitzer, *Regulation of Direct Broadcasting from Satellites*, pp. 29 and 51. Also Belinda Canton and Herbert S. Dordick, 'Information Strategies and International Trade Policy,' *Transnational Data Report*, V (6) (September 1982) 311–12.

62  The degree to which a country was in compliance with this provision was to be determined by the ITU's International Frequency Registration Board, although the technical basis for this determination was not established.

63  Taishoff, *State Responsibility and the Direct Broadcast Satellite*, p. 161.

64  Brazil was one of the few developing countries actively pursuing the development of its own telesatellite system in conjunction with a more general-high-technology industrial strategy. As such, it held a vested interest in limiting immediate international advancements by established computer and telesatellite interests. The Brazilian draft resolution in the COPUOS was especially timely given the recent entry of IBM in the US telecommunication services market through SBS. See Signitzer, *Regulation of Direct Broadcasting from Satellites*, p. 16, and Canton and Dordick, 'Information Strategies and International Trade Policy,' pp. 310–11.

65  Luther, *The United States and the Direct Broadcast Satellite*, pp. 111–12.

66  See UN Document A/37/PV.100 (10 December 1982) in United Nations *Plenary Meetings*, vol. III (New York: United Nations, 1986) p. 1661. The General Assembly vote saw 107 nation-state delegates raise hands in favor, thirteen in opposition, and another thirteen in abstention. Those opposing or abstaining were almost exclusively First World countries. The United States voted against the resolution.

67  Emphases added. Subsequent UN activities involving DBS have been relatively non-contentious, involving, for example, studies on educational applications. See Blatherwick, *The International Politics of Telecommunications*, p. 49.

68  Wolfgang Kleinwachter, 'Freedom or Responsibility Versus Freedom and Responsibility,' in Jorg Becker et al. (eds), *Communication and Domination*, p. 136.

69  William Appleman Williams, *The Tragedy of American Diplomacy* (New York: Dell Publishing, 1982) esp. pp. 229–43.

70  On the history of UNESCO–US relations, see William Preston, Jr, Edward S. Herman and Herbert I Schiller, *Hope & Folly, the United States and UNESCO 1945–1985* (Minneapolis: University of Minnesota Press, 1989) pp. 5–202. Also see Mark F. Imber, *The USA,ILO, UNESCO and IAEA, Politicization and Withdrawal in the Specialized Agencies* (Houndmills: Macmillan, 1989), chap. 6.

71  Preston et al., *Hope & Folly*, pp. 60–75.

72  *Ibid.*, p. 100.

73  Kaarle Nordenstreng, *The Mass Media Declaration of UNESCO* (Norwood, NJ: Ablex, 1984) p. 14.

74    The challenge mounted by UNESCO to the 'common sense' of free flow of information and First Amendment principles constituted not only a potential threat to US hegemony but, more fundamentally, a threat to the profit-making capacities of transnational media and marketing interests. In 1973, the US-based World Press Freedom Committee was formed with the mandate to resist *any* UNESCO proposal that in some way could limit the 'freedom' and 'independence' of Western mass-media corporations. This marked the beginning of a series of US news reports on the 'radicalism,' 'bureaucratic incompetence' and 'anti-Americanism' of UNESCO.

75    See, for example, United States Congress. House, Committee on International Relations. Subcommittee on International Organization. hearings on 'UNESCO: Challenges and Opportunities for the United States,' 94th Cong., 2nd Sess., 14 June 1976.

76    George McGovern, 'The Role and Control of International Communications and Information.' Report to the US Senate Committee on Foreign Relations, Subcommittee on International Operations (Washington, DC: US Government Printing Office, 1977) p. v.

77    The substitution of the gold–dollar linkage with a floating exchange rate introduced largely unforeseen bouts of instability and uncertainty in international monetary relations.

78    Craig N. Murphy, *International Organization and Industrial Change* (Cambridge: Polity Press, 1994) pp. 248–59.

79    George McGovern, 'The Role and Control of International Communications and Information,' p. vi.

80    Emerging out of the Commission was the MacBride Report. It based its questions, research and recommendations on the assumption that communication policy cannot be developed without simultaneously addressing economic, cultural, educational and technological issues. US officials generally considered such complex interconnections to obfuscate and distort the essentially 'neutral' and 'righteous' free flow of information principle. See Rafael Roncagliolo, 'New Information Order in Latin America: A Taxonomy for National Communication Policies,' in Jorg Becker et al. (eds), *Communication and Domination*, pp. 168–76.

81    Sarah Goddard Powell, Deputy Assistant Secretary for Human Rights and Social Affairs, US Department of State, quoted in Preston et al., *Hope & Folly*, p. 129.

82    David Stockman, Reagan's first Director of the Office of Management and Budget (OMB), wrote a position paper during the Carter-Reagan transition period recommending that the United States withdraw from UNESCO due to its 'pro PLO policies, and its support for measures limiting the free flow of information.' Quoted in Seymour Maxwell Finger, 'Reform or Withdrawal,' *Foreign Service Journal*, 61(6) (June 1984) 20.

83    Personal interview with Diana Dougan, Senior Advisor and Chair of the International Communications Studies Program, Center for Strategic and International Studies, 3 September 1992, Washington, DC.

84    From 1981 to 1983, the Reagan administration launched a news media attack on UNESCO. In the fall of 1981, President Reagan accused UNESCO of turning 'its back on the high purposes ... [it] was originally

intended to serve' and said that the NWICO represented the antithesis to a world characterized by 'a broad and rich diversity of opinion.' Quoted in Preston et al. (eds), *Hope & Folly*, p. 157.

Although Reagan's first budget eliminated all US funds to UNESCO, this was modified through Congress to provide it with minimal appropriations, including just US $100,000 for the IPDC. Despite the administration's intent to withdraw, the State Department filed obligatory reports on UNESCO to Congress that repeatedly cleared it of suspected financial, administrative or ideological wrongdoings. In its 1983 report, the State Department argued that 'US interests are generally well served by UNESCO programs which are, for the most part, non-political and which can most effectively be pursued through international cooperation.' In the section titled 'US Goals and Objectives,' the report considers UNESCO to be 'a major forum for US multilateral diplomacy' where 'US values and methods' can be promoted, 'particularly in the Third World.' Report quoted in *ibid.*, pp. 164–5.

85   *Ibid.*, p. 171.
86   Memorandum authored by Gregory Newell, the Reagan-appointed Assistant Secretary of State for International Organization Affairs. Quoted in *ibid.*, p. 172.
87   Quoted in *ibid.*, p. 181.
88   On American neo-liberalism, see James R. Kurth, 'The United States and Western Europe in the Reagan Era,' in Morris H. Morley (ed.), *Crisis and Confrontation, Ronald Reagan's Foreign Policy* (Totowa, NJ: Rowman & Littlefield, 1988) pp. 65–6.
89   Larry Pratt, 'The Reagan Doctrine and the Third World,' in Ralph Miliband, Leo Panitch and John Saville (eds), *Socialist Register 1987* Lodon: Merlin Press, 1987) pp. 63–4.
90   Fred Halliday, *The Making of the Second Cold War* (London: Verso, 1983) p. 23.
91   Pratt, 'The Reagan Doctrine and the Third World,' in Miliband et al. (eds), *Socialist Register 1987*, p. 92.
92.   Jeff McMahan, *Reagan and the World, Imperial Policy in the New Cold War* (New York: Monthly Review Press, 1985) p. 224.
93   Von Laue quoted in Murphy, *International Organization and Industrial Change*, p. 242.
94   For example, see the text of the board of directors of the US Chamber of Commerce, March 1983, 'Findings and Recommendations Regarding the Flow of Information Across National Borders,' published in 'Information Flow Vital to Global Economy,' *Transnational Data Report*, VI (5) (July/August 1983) 239–42.
95   As James Webb of NASA and Secretary of Defense Robert McNamara stated in a joint memorandum written in 1961, 'Our attainments are a major element in the international competition between the Soviet system and our own. The...'civilian' projects such as lunar and planetary exploration are, in this sense, part of the battle along the fluid front of the cold war.' – Memorandum to President Kennedy quoted in Michael E. Kinsley, *Outer Space and Inner Sanctums; Government, Business, and Satellite Communication* (New York: John Wiley & Sons, 1976) p. 2.

# 5 DBS and the Structure of US Policy Making

In 1967, the Chairman of the House of Representatives Committee on Foreign Affairs, Dante R. Fascell, wrote that during 'the coming decade, television promises to become the most widely used and influential mass medium of communication' capable of fostering 'economic and social change in developing nations.' Direct broadcast satellites, Fascell predicted, would spearhead this movement largely as a result of the capacity of DBS to transcend the 'physical' and 'political boundaries' that traditionally have constituted the primary 'barriers to the flow of communications.'[1]

Two years later, in a report issued by the same House of Representatives committee, the development of international telesatellite broadcasting was directly associated with the 'vital interest' of the United States. The reasons were the perceived importance of maintaining America's world leadership in communications technology; its position as world leader in the promotion of the free flow of information; and through both of these, the importance of having a direct role in shaping what impact such new technologies would have on the international order. But largely due to the structural characteristics of the American state, most clearly expressed in the tendency of US officials to focus on case-by-case issues, the ability of the public sector to lead or even coordinate various private sector interests generally has been absent.[2] From the late 1960s, occasional Congressional hearings reviewed the prospects and implications of DBS while members of Congress and federal officials repeatedly bemoaned the absence of a well-coordinated foreign communication policy.[3] Joel Woldman's Senate study on direct broadcasting, cited in Chapter 4, considered DBS to be an important new technology in extending the domination of US-based private sector mass-media products in overseas markets. However, the potential foreign backlash that could arise from this dominance, expressed through the potential imposition of foreign trade barriers to a broad range of American products could, according to Woldman, lead to 'diplomatic, as well as economic problems.'[4] As such, the 1975 Senate report concluded that

Whatever changes the media experience in the years ahead, there would appear to be a clear need for long-range consideration of an international communications role for the United States which takes into account the predictable development of the new communications technology [DBS]. Somewhere in the upper reaches of the US government... an attempt might be made to anticipate some of the problems which these technological changes may bring.[5]

## 5.1   POLICY AGENTS AND THE FRAGMENTED CHARACTER OF US POLICY

The structural conditions necessary for the formulation of a policy involving DBS-related cultural-power applications have been absent. Foreign opposition to US DBS applications have had little direct effect on the thinking and policies of American state officials. Instead, in a bureaucratic environment that is structurally antagonistic to sustained policy efforts, public or private sector direct broadcasting developments had remarkably little chance of being successful in the United States.

Richard N. Gardner, the Assistant Secretary of State for International Organization Affairs during the period in which Comsat was conceived, told a Congressional hearing in 1969 that he had experienced great frustration in his attempts to link America's early telesatellite development policies with the general goal of what he called the strengthening of 'common values in our shrinking world.' In his efforts to promote this, Gardner explained that 'I could not get the responsible leaders of the US government sufficiently concerned with this dimension' to any degree approaching their overwhelming interest in the 'short-term political advantages' of telesatellite developments.[6]

As discussed in Chapter 4, telesatellite communications involving television broadcasts transmitted direct to homes across nation-state borders involve not only a broad range of issues and institutions but also a number of questions concerning the uses of outer space, transborder information flows, and related issues involving national sovereignty. Moreover, international institutions specifically mandated to deal with these – such as the ITU and the UN – have remained underdeveloped in the scope of their policies and enforcement capabilities. As such, without the sustained efforts of domestic corporations seeking to establish a transnational DBS service, American state officials have had little incentive to forge and execute a specific policy concerning direct broadcasting apart from *ad hoc* responses to foreign concerns regarding DBS in its context as a free flow issue.

The United States has never had a single agency or department responsible for the formulation or implementation of its foreign communication policy. Instead, depending on the specific issue, its context and the timing of its formulation, a range of political and bureaucratic actors – including Congressional committees, the White House, the Department of Commerce, the Federal Communications Commission, the United States Information Agency, the State Department and others – may be involved to various and largely unspecified degrees. This fragmentation of responsibility should not be of any great surprise. In part it is a reflection of the predominance of day-to-day communication activities in the American private sector involving communication and information producers, users and service providers. In part reflecting the relative decline of AT&T, Comsat and other predominant agents, in the 1980s communication policy issues usually involved a broad range of actors holding particular vested interests. In part as a result of this, government agencies and departments at best aspired to mediate rather than coordinate or lead private sector activities.

Despite the occasional acknowledgement by senior US policy officials of the role that DBS could play in stimulating future international technological convergence developments, US policy has 'often... [taken] the form of a shopping list of negotiated objectives advocated by competing interest groups.'[7] But rather than characterizing the federal bureaucracy as merely the passive conduit of such interests, the structural conditions in which they are received and delineated have directly shaped policy outputs. The US Constitution, for example, compels the separation of powers between the executive, legislative and judicial branches of government. For foreign communication policy developments – given the increasingly intimate relationship among domestic corporate activities and international communications – the constitutional supremacy of the executive branch in foreign policy has generated predictable intra-state conflicts.[8] Moreover, private sector dominance over a broad range of communication and information activities has been institutionalized in judicial interpretations of the First Amendment.[9] As such, an 'activist' state has been inhibited while inter-agency (and to some extent intra-agency) conflict has been commonplace due, to some degree, to the often enormous economic stakes involved in most communication policy decisions.[10] Additional factors shaping policy-making structures include the political nature of key civil service executive branch appointments and related problems involving relatively under-qualified appointees. All of these factors have contributed to the ongoing predominance of influential lobbyists in the American public sector – a phenomenon that itself was exacerbated by efforts of the Reagan administration to 'deregulate' domestic and international communications.

As for foreign policy specifically concerning telesatellites, it was only in the early 1980s that the impact of the decade-old Open Skies policy became widely felt. Also at this time, AT&T's domestic activities were radically re-regulated and, as a result, the focal point of US relations with international institutions and foreign telecommunication entities was substantially decentralized out of the hands of Comsat and AT&T executives. In the early 1980s, for example, while the Department of State was responsible for coordinating US private sector applications to Intelsat in order to establish new international telesatellite systems (the step that followed the approval of such projects by the FCC), the often vigorous opposition mounted by Comsat derailed most proposals.[11]

A comparative review of the responsibilities of key US foreign communication policy agencies provides a basic understanding of why intra-state policy-making activities have been historically fragmented and, at times, conflictual.

The Communications Act of 1934 formally mandated the FCC to regulate international communications involving traffic going into or out of the United States through the Commission's approval of required facilities, its allocation of frequencies, its licensing of specific services, and its setting of domestic tariff and rate structures. The FCC also was mandated to participate in US government negotiations with foreign countries and organizations when these involved or affected domestic services.[12]

Domestic DBS systems, because of the continental scope of their prospective transmissions, constitute virtually *de facto* transnational systems. Indeed, US-based companies such as DirecTV consider Canada to be a 'natural' extension of the American market.[13] Since first formally addressing the DBS issue in the early 1980s, the FCC has limited its oversight to four tasks: first, define, assign and enforce appropriate frequency bands for domestic services; second, establish the right of one license holder to transfer his or her license to someone else; third, set out-of-band emission standards to prevent interference with non-DBS services; and, fourth, license blocks of frequencies rather than individual channels. Also significant are the regulatory tasks FCC officials have *not* pursued. These include a refusal to set the technical standards for DBS transmissions; a refusal to apply cross-media ownership restrictions on DBS; a refusal to regulate the ownership of DBS reception equipment; a refusal to regulate program content; and a refusal to regulate the types of services offered, their availability or price.[14] Current FCC regulations prohibit foreign nationals controlling domestic DBS services. Moreover, DBS applicants must satisfy an annual 'due diligence' requirement involving the contracting/construction of the satellite within one year of receiving a FCC license. Only then does the FCC make GSO and frequency assignments.

The assumption underlying this generally hands-off approach is that market forces will enable entrepreneurs to satisfy consumer preferences at the lowest possible price.[15] More than just an attempt to promote the development of DBS systems as competitive entities, the FCC's hands-off approach can also be understood to be a matter of regulatory convenience.[16]

As discussed earlier, the USIA conducts a range of communication activities, including international radio and television broadcasting. Its official mandate includes the task of strengthening 'foreign understanding between the United States and other countries.'[17] More specifically, the USIA is responsible for advising the President, the Secretary of State and other officials on foreign public opinion regarding current and prospective US policies; cooperating with the US private sector to enhance American 'information and cultural efforts' overseas; assisting in efforts to extend the free flow of information; and for countering 'attempts to distort the objectives and policies of the United States' by foreign governments and mass media.[18] But despite this comprehensive mandate, the role of its cultural-power responsibilities have rarely been coordinated with other agencies during the policy-making process.[19]

As previously mentioned, the White House Office of Telecommunications Policy was succeeded in 1977 by the National Telecommunications and Information Administration located in the Department of Commerce. While the NTIA's mandate was modified from that of its predecessor by formally directing (but not restricting) it to responsibilities involving domestic telecommunications, the spillover of domestic into foreign affairs (and vice versa) has led its personnel to focus increasingly on international policy.

Executive Order 12046, issued in 1978, provides the NTIA with a range of responsibilities. These include its role as the President's principle advisor on telecommunications; its role, with the State Department and other agencies, in developing plans, policies and programes dealing with international telecommunications, including the responsibility of the Secretary of Commerce to coordinate the 'economic, technical, operational and related preparations for United States participation in international telecommunications conferences and negotiations'; and its responsibility to make recommendations concerning the impact of digital convergence developments.[20] This Executive Order also mandates the Secretary of Commerce to 'provide advice and assistance to the Secretary of State on international tele-communications policies...in support of the Secretary of State's .responsibility for the conduct of foreign affairs.'[21]

Because the Secretary of State is largely responsible for the coordination and supervision of all foreign relations, the Department of State is mandated to advise other relevant agencies on foreign communication issues. Moreover, the Secretary of State, as the President's principal foreign policy advisor, is in charge of coordinating and supervising foreign communication policies on specific issues in relation to other US government departments and agencies. Executive Order 12046 reaffirmed this role. It states that

> the Secretary of State shall exercise primary authority for the conduct of foreign policy, including the determination of United States positions and the conduct of United States participation in negotiations with foreign governments and international bodies.

It also states that

> 'In exercising this responsibility the Secretary of State shall coordinate with other agencies as appropriate, and in particular, shall give full consideration to the Federal Communications Commission's regulatory and policy responsibility in this area.[22]

As will be discussed in Chapter 6, since the mid-1980s the government agency that has become the hub of US foreign communication policy activities is the Office of the United States Trade Representative (USTR). The United States Trade Representative is a Cabinet-level official charged with the responsibility of coordinating and administering US trade policy.[23] This has involved the USTR in an extraordinarily broad range of activities, including the negotiation of new international services, telecommunications and intellectual property rights agreements. However, in mandating the USTR to take the lead in these and other issues, Executive Order 12188 (see note 23) *did not* formally modify FCC, Commerce Department or State Department responsibilities in related foreign policy matters.

These agencies constitute only the most prevalent policy participants. Others of note include the Department of Defense, NASA, the CIA, the National Security Agency (NSA), and the Senior Interagency Group for International Communications and Information Policy (SIG). The latter is a Cabinet-level committee on which represen-tatives from a range of federal agencies sit. In 1984, this SIG delivered a fifty-page report to the National Security Council (NSC) on foreign communication policy – the *first* inter-agency attempt to define, in a comprehensive manner, the problems facing American foreign communication policy.[24]

In 1983 and 1984 – the two years leading up to the US withdrawal from UNESCO – the emerging crisis facing free flow of information interests in the face of defiant LDCs stimulated a significant executive-led effort to coordinate American policy. However, given the presence of established policy interests (such as the State Department's responsibility for diplomacy, the Commerce Department's responsibility for trade, and the FCC's responsibility for domestic policy), the reforms introduced by the Reagan administration generated little more than intra-state conflict. In retrospect, as explained below, this period (and failure) constituted a watershed in US foreign communication policy. From this time forward, the free flow of information as an *approach* to international reform was transcended by the funneling of communication issues onto America's international trade agenda.

## 5.2   THE US POLICY PROCESS AND WARC-79

In the 1979 the World Administrative Radio Conference (WARC) held in Geneva, for the first time since the 1950s, the ITU sought a comprehensive revision of international Radio Regulations. Given that the 1970s had been a period of mounting anti-US obstinacy in one-country-one-vote international institutions, and that a widening range of corporate interests would be directly affected by the outcome of the conference, American state officials invested an extraordinary amount of preparatory work. According to Michael Stoil:

> Adverse actions by the conference could potentially have prevented expansion of AM radio broadcasting in the US, delayed development of critical electronic warfare equipment, reduced the effectiveness of the Voice of America, scuttled [potential] US proposals for direct broadcasting satellites.... Interest in WARC among suppliers and users of telecommunication services and equipment was understandably high, and participation in US preconference activities was unusually high.... Some commentators warned that radical lesser-developed countries would use the concept of the New World Information [and Communication] Order to rally support against benefits enjoyed by the technically-advanced countries in the existing Radio Regulations.[25]

Although the State Department Office of International Communications Policy (OICP) – later reformed and enlarged into the Bureau of International Communications and Information Policy – was put in charge of the US delegation in 1976 because of its official responsibility for foreign relations concerning communications, within a year President Carter opted to appoint a special ambassador to coordinate the US effort. Two reasons were given. First, the OICP was deemed to be too small and lacking in the resources needed to prepare for the conference. Second, because the State Department was not responsible for implementing domestic communications policy, other agencies possessing this expertise and holding established relationships with key private sector interests were seen to be more desirable pre-WARC coordinators. Preliminary preparations for WARC-79 were made by President Nixon's Office of Telecommunications Policy. Under Carter, the OTP's successor, the NTIA, became the lead agency. However, due to the direct responsibility held by the Federal Communications Commission for domestic issues, FCC officials argued that they should take charge of the WARC preparations in consultation with the Department of State. When, in 1977, Carter attempted an inter-agency compromise by naming Glenn Robinson (a law professor and a former FCC Commissioner) as the WARC-79 chair and the US ambassador-designate for the conference, while also naming three vice-chairs – one representative from the NTIA, one from the FCC, and one from the State Department – the result instead was a continuance of past problems stemming from confused responsibilities and conflicting interests.[26]

Examples of these took place in 1978. Chairman Robinson limited FCC participation in WARC-79 preparations to the coordination of US private sector interests. Robinson also limited the role of the NTIA to coordinating various federal government radio-spectrum demands. In this action, the Chair sought to limit the practice of competing corporate and public sector interests pitting the FCC against the Commerce Department and Commerce against the Commission. But despite this attempt, powerful and well-organized corporate and state interests tended to dominate the preparatory activities of the US delegation. The Department of Defense, for instance, successfully compelled Robinson to accept its assertion that DoD frequency needs transcended those of other public *and* private sector interests by *denying* the Chair's requests for substantiating evidence, due, according to Defense officials, to the 'classified' status of such information. Following the FCC's and the NTIA's joint rejection of a USIA request for increased frequency allocations for Voice of America services, USIA officials responded by recruiting Carter's national security advisor, Zbigniew Brzezinski, to convince the President that VoA activities constituted yet another radio-spectrum priority. Despite the added opposition of the State Department (whose officials anticipated that the WARC ultimately would reject the request and, as such, the VoA 'priority' would be both a diplomatic miscalculation and a waste of time), Robinson was ordered by the President to override his three vice-chairs. The US delegation thus was committed to the inclusion of the VoA request as part of its many other demands at the WARC.[27]

In the end, the United States sent a sixty-seven-person brigade to the 1,600-delegate, 142-country WARC. State Department, FCC and Commerce Department officials constituted nearly one-half of the American contingent. The US private sector also participated in the American detachment, and these were dominated by telesatellite service providers and manufacturers. Comsat, for instance, sent three representatives to Geneva and Hughes Aircraft was represented by one.[28] This US delegation was both the largest and the most resourceful at the conference. Not only was it assisted in Geneva by a forty-person support staff, but the delegation also maintained a computer-satellite link to Washington where a database provided pre-planned back-up proposals for instantaneous use in situations in which compromise arrangements needed to be made. This kind of expertise and preparation provided the United States with the essential resources needed to negotiate what it considered to be acceptable agreements with relatively under-resourced LDC delegates.[29]

Those private sector interests that participated in preparations for WARC-79 or took part in the conference itself were relatively large corporations, all of whom possessed the resources to maintain full-time offices and established contacts in Washington with one or more of the three dominant state agencies. Most importantly, Comsat, AT&T and others provided extensively researched reports involving both economic and engineering analyses to substantiate their particular frequency allocation requests.[30]

In the absence of an established agency wholly responsible for US foreign communication policy, and in the presence of vague but inflexible calls for a free flow of information, the conflicts characterizing American preparations for WARC-79 and the seemingly arbitrary manner in which priorities were established again signalled the need for a reappraisal of the structural underpinnings of the US foreign communication policy process. Nevertheless, WARC-79 generally was seen to have been a good conference for the United States, given the success of its delegation in convincing many West European and communist states that a comprehensive pre-planned GSO and frequency regime was *not* in the interests of any country aspiring to become internationally competitive in satellite technologies and applications. Detailed planning for DBS developments had been agreed to among Region 1 and Region 3 countries in 1977, largely as a result of a widespread recognition that both a potentially uncontrolled in-flow of signals was undesirable and that US interests most probably would dominate such developments. At WARC-79, the ITU's approval of a similar arrangement for less threatening satellite technologies – particularly at this formative stage of the West European aerospace industry, and the aspirations of the Soviet Union in relation to its Intersputnik telesatellite system – was delayed at least until the first meeting of a two-part WARC on space communications took place in 1985.[31]

But as Washington-based consultant Morris H. Crawford wrote after WARC-79, 'a new and precarious course for international communications' was 'charted.' As Crawford saw it, 'the 1979 conference deviated from the past. It ended an era when allocations were decided on technical grounds.'[32] In part because the State Department, the FCC and Commerce were jointly charged with the responsibility of preparing for the 1985 and 1988 Space WARC meetings, new conflicts emerged as early as 1982.[33] However, by the time WARC-85 was convened a significant shift in US policy had been initiated – away from free flow and toward free trade. This change did not occur as a result of US policy agents somehow putting their policy-house in order. Instead, reforms emerged in an *ad hoc* manner in response to the ascendancy of a trade-based conception of international communication issues by American private sector interests increasingly concerned with future capacities to exploit their competitive strengths in a range of information-based activities.

## 5.3  SHIFTING DEMANDS AND STRUCTURAL REFORMS

Although the need for a more coordinated communication policy was first comprehensively addressed in the mid-1960s during the Rostow Commission proceedings, after the OTP upheaval little incentive existed among either elected or non-elected government officials to reform the ways in which the United States made and implemented foreign communication policy. By the early 1980s, however, the importance of international telecommunications for a growing number of private sector interests, and the apparent intransigence of UN agencies and the ITU, generated an organized push by some of America's largest corporations to reform US foreign communication policy agencies and their structural environment.

In the early 1970s, various state agencies struck committees and commissioned studies with the participation of US-based corporations to examine government policies in relation to the emerging American service sector. In formulating the 1974 Trade Act, for example, private sector input resulted in the recognition of service issues *as* trade issues. Driving this forward – particularly in the minds of TNC executives – was the development of communication capabilities involving the convergence of computer and telecommunication technologies. Through these advancements, the information and expertise held by US-based businesses became increasingly sellable to spatially dislocated markets. In the words of William Drake and Kalypso Nicolaidis, 'As transmission capacity increased and costs fell, buyers could in principle purchase on-line services from abroad almost as easily as from across the street.'[34]

In 1979, the combined market for computer and communications hardware and services in the United States totalled approximately $150 billion. By 1982, many analysts predicted that this market would more than double within six years. US defense-based research and development funding enabled American corporations to hold a dominant position in these fields.[35] One of the most diligent companies aspiring to raise public and private sector awareness of the emerging economic importance of international information-based services, and the reforms required to capitalize on the relative strengths of US companies in this area, was American Express.[36] In 1982, its executives were primarily concerned with the general issue of transborder data flows. Amidst the emerging recognition that different kinds of information were or could become valuable commodities, foreign nation-state officials became increasingly concerned with developing the ability to control domestic electronic information movements. These were usually related to their goal of protecting domestic industries and/or the desire to tax these new commodity flows. Because of these emerging overseas efforts to treat information-based services like material commodities,[37] American Express senior vice president Joan Edelman Spero recommended that 'Washington must work to develop an international regime to preserve the free flow of information *through* agreed international *trade* rules.'[38]

As a result of the emerging discrepancy between international communications and domestic service sector capacities, US-based TNCs orchestrated a global 'consciousness-raising' campaign.[39] American Express and others recognized that the United States was unlikely to reform foreign attitudes toward information-based services through a unilateral attempt to reform existing international institutions. Spero, for instance, wrote that to be successful, Americans had to convince foreign governments that a free flow of information was in *their* long-term economic interest also. This would be possible only through a concerted effort to promote the righteousness of neo-liberal trade ideals concerning this particular sector. According to Spero:

> countries should recognize that liberalization of trade in communications and information products and services will provide the same benefits as liberalization of trade in goods. Furthermore, lifting [data flow] restrictions will contribute to the expansion of trade in goods and services. Finally, liberalization will be in the interest of countries seeking to export information goods and services to the US market, where signs of protectionism are also beginning to emerge.[40]

Due to the fragmented character of intra-state policy making agencies, the United States lacked the structural framework needed to work in conjunction with private sector interests on this project. Spero believed that because of the strong economic growth of computer and communication activities, and the long-established dominance of AT&T and Comsat in leading US relations with foreign telecommunications officials, US government personnel generally had neglected this policy area.[41] Due to the rapid internationalization of corporate information and communication activities, and the accompanying growth of a coordinated foreign resistance to it, 'the organizational fragmentation, the scarcity of resources, and the absence of high-level attention' resulted in a crisis for American interests seeking to arrest overseas opposition. The US government's fundamental problem, according to Spero, was that 'no one is in charge.'[42]

European, Japanese and Canadian-based TNC executives became the primary targets of American corporate efforts to modify the perspectives of foreign governments. As service providers, some of these overseas corporations would presumably be opposed to US competitors in their domestic markets. To counter this, US-based TNCs promoted the recognition of foreign corporations *as service consumers* and emphasized the potential benefits available to foreign TNCs once their access to US advertising, consultancy, financial and other relatively advanced American-based services were established.[43] US-based interests subsequently pushed ahead of American state officials in efforts to modify the ways in which foreigners perceived both free flow and free trade. In this project, in the words of Karl Sauvant, US-based TNCs forged 'a sophisticated organizational infrastructure through which...[their] interests...[could] be identified, formulated and promoted.'[44]

In response to these developments, US foreign communication policy officials themselves began to reconceptualize free flow of information issues to involve concerns involving trade also. In 1983, the Department of Commerce issued a report on 'Long Range Goals in International Telecommunications and Information.' It recommended that the United States 'place a high priority on the reduction of non-tariff trade barriers affecting the telecommunications and information industries through vigorous multilateral and bilateral negotiations in the GATT and elsewhere, but without insisting on rigid reciprocity.'[45] Foreshadowing revisions to Section-301 of the US Trade and Tariff Act, the report recommended that possible amendments to US trade law would protect domestic interests from 'unfair industry-targeting practices and other anti-competitive policies of other countries.'[46] Finally, the report recommended that an enforceable international regime of intellectual property rights should be pursued – one that could adequately protect 'new forms of intellectual property' involving a ban on 'unauthorised commercial reception and use of copyrighted material transmitted by satellite.'[47]

Also in 1983, the US Senate commissioned Jane Bortnick to prepare a report on 'International Telecommunications and Information Policy.' One conclusion was that there existed a 'need' for the United States 'to respond to [protective] foreign actions and [to] influence the proceedings of international organizations.' However, the Senate report admitted that 'the best mechanism to accomplish this, given existing political realities and institutional inertia, is less clear.'[48] During Senate hearings, the underdevelopment of American state capacities to formulate and implement a coherent and relevant foreign communication policy was repeatedly addressed. Even FCC Chairman Marc Fowler – just one year after he told another Congressional committee that the current policy structures, headed by the SIG, constituted a satisfactory coordinating mechanism – testified that efforts to centralize US policy making in the hands of the executive branch should proceed. In response to questioning by Senator Barry Goldwater, Fowler explained that 'what has changed over the past year which leads me now to support a very high-level approach to coordination in the executive branch has been that, more than ever, telecommunications has become important to our country.... [I]ncreasingly, it has an important trade implication.'[49]

Dating from 1982, Department of State officials unilaterally sought the formation of a new office in charge of all foreign communication policy activities.[50] In 1983, Secretary of State George Shultz asserted his department's leadership in this policy field by establishing the Office of the Coordinator for International Communication and Information Policy, and President Reagan appointed Diana Dougan to be its Coordinator. In September, Shultz submitted to the Senate a letter outlining the three general objectives of the United States in this policy field. The first objective Shultz listed was the principle of the free flow of information. The second committed the United States to 'support the advancement of international commerce through the efficient and innovative use of communications resources.' Finally, Shultz wrote that it was the objective of the US government to 'expand information access and communications capabilities of developing countries.'[51] To achieve these somewhat mixed objectives, Shultz noted that trade policy would play a role in more general attempts to promote 'competitive' and 'deregulatory' policies in foreign countries. Perhaps in the hope of minimizing intra-state conflict over this State Department assertion of policy leadership, the Secretary stressed that 'No single agency possesses the resources or expertise necessary to advance... the interests of the United States in this area.' As such, Diana Dougan was to become the *Coordinator* for International Communication and Information Policy.[52]

The formation of Dougan's office, however, did not necessarily signal the sudden realization of the importance of government efforts to shape and implement a coherent foreign communication policy on behalf of the President – the constitutional head of foreign policy. More accurately, the Reagan administration had little interest in facilitating any kind of definitive public sector leadership in this area. This was made apparent in its heavy reliance on private sector participation at the 1982 ITU Plenipotentiary Conference held in Nairobi. Moreover, the long-standing practice of appointing senior policy personnel on the basis of party patronage rather than the development of a knowledgeable and capable cast of policy officials continued. The most extreme example of this came to light when former Reagan bodyguard, Dennis LeBlanc, was given an executive position at the NTIA (see Chapter 1). Diana Dougan's qualifications to lead the State Department office that was supposed to coordinate all US foreign communication policy were not much better. While Dougan had been a local television producer in Salt Lake City, then a Promotions Director for Time, Inc., and then a Reagan-appointed Board Member of the Corporation for Public Broadcasting, more importantly, she was a life-long Republican Party activist.[53]

In the first year of her appointment, Dougan vaguely recognized that while foreign communication policy 'plays a prominent role in international trade,' the communications–trade relationship was, at this stage, imprecisely understood.[54] However, echoing the views of American Express and others, Dougan explained that,

> as we deal with the trade issue, we must be careful how it is packaged, because this commodity approach has particular appeal to governments inclined to view information services as a source of tax revenue. This approach could, in fact, sanction Government controls of the free flow of information, which is of deep concern to our country.[55]

Despite her generally uncontroversial viewpoints, Dougan and her new office of seven officials faced resistance both from other agencies and even from within the State Department itself. Throughout 1984, for example, the NTIA consistently asserted its jurisdictional role (as prescribed under President Carter's Executive Order 12046) 'in developing and supporting US telecommunications industry in both domestic and international markets.'[56] In response to the efforts of Secretary Shultz to increase Dougan's staff by at least thirty officials and to upgrade the status of her Office to that of a Bureau, State and Commerce Department communication policy consultations were held less and less frequently.[57] The focus of this chilling of inter-agency relations was the State Department's attempt to amalgamate existing NTIA and more general Commerce Department responsibilities, including its proposed dominance in emerging trade issues involving telecommunications.[58] By the end of 1984, this conflict was temporarily resolved when Shultz and Secretary of Commerce Malcolm Baldridge exchanged memoranda clarifying the lines of responsibility held by their agencies: State Department responsibilities were to include the coordination of foreign policy and foreign relations for all government-to-government relations, and the coordination of US delegations for all inter-governmental meetings; the Commerce Department was to be responsible for ongoing consultations with its foreign government counterparts and the substantive preparations of US delegates for all inter-governmental meetings. Not only did the State–Commerce respite also reaffirm the NTIA's continuing role as the President's representative on issues concerning domestic telecommunications, more significantly it marked the end of conscious efforts by any one public sector agency to lead US foreign communication policy.[59]

By the mid-1980s, a complex overlapping of US trade policy with communication policy had emerged. US corporations recognized that international telecommunications had become not only the essential lifeblood of their operations, but TNCs in general, regardless of their activities, came to recognize through the concept of free trade that their *ongoing* ability to conduct business and sell commodities was dependent on *expanding communication capabilities*. In 1983, the US Chamber of Commerce was followed by the International Chamber of Commerce in endorsing the formulation of multilateral agreements that would recognize and promote the international flow of information. While the former explicitly recognized the General Agreement on Tariffs and Trade to be the ideal institutional forum in which this free flow ideal could be entrenched,[60] the latter – representing business interests in approximately fifty countries – was not yet convinced to take this step.

## 5.4  CONCLUSIONS

A detailed analysis of the structural conditions characterizing US foreign communication policy and the historical context of their development for the most part has been absent in the writings of Schiller and other proponents of the cultural imperialism paradigm. As such, the dynamics and implications of the structural conditions addressed in this chapter have been underplayed. The bias of US policy making that was perpetuated by these conditions can be described as the tendency to focus on short-term issues – such as corporate plans in relation to an upcoming ITU conference – rather than relatively long-term concerns – such as a coordinated intra-state effort to institutionalise the free flow of information in international law. Following the failed effort by State Department officials to take on a leadership position in US foreign communication policy, the Senior Interagency Group for International Communication Policy provided the National Security Council with its first comprehensive overview of the policy problems in this field.[61] But despite these and lesser responses to the free flow crisis, the US public sector ultimately was incapable of meeting the long-term needs of its private sector. A core component of this public sector inability readily to reform itself was reflected at and prior to WARC-79. The extraordinary size and complex make-up of the American delegation was the result of more than just the political and economic importance of the conference. It also reflected the nature of US foreign communication policy structures. The wealthiest, best organized and most 'connected' American corporations, rather than just being heard in the domestic negotiations that preceded the meeting, also were directly represented in Geneva. The assumed necessity of sending sixty-seven officials and a forty-person support staff underscored more than the significance of international communications to the United States; it underlined (as early as 1979) the presence of a structural disparity between the significance of free flow and the ability of American state officials to act competently on behalf of free flow interests.

These structures and related policy-making biases directly influenced the domestic policy developments discussed in the next chapter. To some extent, the liberalization of US communication activities, vigorously pursued in the early 1980s, generated an unforeseen escalation of the foreign communication policy crisis. The haste and ideological fervor in which US communications were re-regulated ironically hastened the efforts of established corporate interests to resist both foreign and domestic competition. One of the more unsavory examples of this resistance during the 1980s was the role played by US cable television companies in monopolizing local markets, dominating national programing activities, and subsequently conspiring to block competitive DBS developments.

Modifications to state structures usually follow a complex of external political-economic pressures and domestic realignments. How this process has taken place in US foreign communication policy constitutes the undercurrent issue flowing through the next two chapters. As indicated thus far, as a result of mostly economic and technological developments, US foreign communication policy was brought to the political-economic fore in the 1980s. Established distinctions between domestic and international information-based commodity activities became increasingly blurred as the activities of a broad range of American corporations were being globalized and/or becoming more and more dependent on international communications. Intra-state jurisdictions became obscured while new state agencies directly participated in communication policy making. To sort out these shifting state mechanisms, Chapter 6 focuses on mostly domestic developments, while Chapter 7 will tend more to analyze the international forces at work. Again, DBS constitutes a focal point for much of what follows.

## NOTES

1   Dante R. Fascell, 'Modern Communications and Foreign Policy,' p. 3R.
2   Hearings on 'Satellite Broadcasting: Implications for Foreign Policy,' p. 3R.
3   See, for instance, Hearings on 'The Role and Control of International Communications and Information.'
4   Joel H. Woldman, 'The View Ahead: Direct Satellite Broadcasting and International Communications.' Report to the United States Senate. Committee on Foreign Relations. Reprinted in United States Congress. Senate. Committee on Foreign Relations. Subcommittee on International Operations. Hearings on 'The Role and Control of International communications and Information,' 95th Cong., 1st sess., June 1977, p. 46.
5   *Ibid.*, p. 48.
6   Gardner quoted in Hearings on 'Satellite Broadcasting: Implications for Foreign Policy,' pp. 64–5.
7   Michael J. Stoil, 'The Executive Branch and International Telecommunications Policy: The Case of WARC "79",' in John J. Havick (ed.), *Communications Policy and the Political Process* (Westport, Conn.: Greenwood Press, 1983) p. 90.

8    On general executive branch powers in foreign communication policy, see Alan Pearce, 'Telecom Policy and the White House,' *Telecommunications* (November 1980) 16.

9    See Mark Freiman, 'Consumer Sovereignty and National Sovereignty in Domestic and International Broadcasting' in Canadian–US Conference on Communications Policy, *Cultures in Collision* (New York: Praeger, 1984) pp. 111–13; and Robert Horwitz, 'The First Amendment Meets Some New Technologies,' *Theory and Society*, 20 (1) (February 1991) 21–72.

10   Jeremy Tunstall, *Communications Deregulation* (Oxford: Basil Blackwell, 1986) pp. 198–9.

11   On the efforts of Ted Turner's Cable Network News to overcome these obstacles, see United States Congress. House. Committee on Energy and Commerce. Subcommittee on Telecommunications, Consumer Protection, and Finance. Hearings on 'International Satellite Issues'. 98th Cong., 2nd sess., 13 June; 25 and 26 July 1984, pp. 372–5.

12   The FCC also is responsible for regulating the common carrier activities of Comsat.

13   Personal interview with John McKee, President DirecTV Canada, 21 June 1993, Toronto.

14   Current FCC regulations prohibit foreign nationals from controlling domestic DBS services. Moreover, DBS applicants must satisfy an annual 'due diligence' requirement involving the contracting/construction of the satellite within one year of receiving an FCC license. Only then does the FCC make GSO and frequency assignments.

15   Federal Communications Commission, 'Policies for Regulation of Direct Broadcast Satellites.' Staff Report (unpublished: FCC Office of Plans and Policy, 1980). Also, personal interview with Mark Bykowsky, Senior Economist, National Telecommunications and Information Administration, US Department of Commerce, 1 September 1992, Washington, DC. The FCC has not yet determined how to classify a DBS system in regulatory terms: is DBS a 'common carrier' or a 'broadcasting entity'? In practice, the FCC employs elements of both classifications. The DBS uplink generally is considered to be the activity of a 'common carrier.' The downlink, however, generally is understood as the action taken by a 'broadcaster.' Rather than selecting one of the two, or re-writing its regulatory classifications altogether, the Commission maintains that DBS constitutes a unique hybrid form of telecommunication.

16   Put another way, DBS constitutes an inconvenient anomaly to traditional classifications and as such the FCC has opted not to classify it using established definitions.

17   Office of the Federal Register, National Archives and Records Administration, *The United States Government Manual 1991/92* (London, MD: Bernan Press, 1991), p. 737.

18   *Ibid.* Also see Allen C. Hansen, *USIA, Diplomacy in the Computer Age* (New York: Praeger Publishers, 1984).

19   Robert E. Elder, *The Information Machine, the United States Information Agency and American Foreign Policy* (Syracuse, NY: Syracuse University Press, 1968) p. 42.

20    Executive Order No.12046 (1978), 'Transfer of Telecommunications
      Functions', Sections 2–401, 2–404, and 2–410 respectively.
21    *Ibid.*, Section 2–404.
22    The State Department's Bureau of International Communications and
      Information Policy (ICIP) coordinates and leads US delegations at
      international conferences following consultations with other agencies
      and relevant private sector interests. When other departments or agen-
      cies represent the United States at international meetings, it must be
      done with the consent of the State Department. See Department of
      Commerce, 'Long-Range Goals in International Telecommunications
      and Information,' p. 73. According to the head of the ICIP in the
      mid-1980s, Diana Dougan,

> The process by which the US government develops the positions it
> takes at international conferences is long, complex, and arduous
> because of the primacy we place on the private sector as well as the
> diverse expertise and perspectives of the numerous US Government
> agencies which contribute to our policy process – *Diana Lady Dougan*,
> 'The US and the Caribbean: Partners in Communication'. Address to
> the Caribbean Seminar on Space WARC and the Transborder Use of
> US Domestic Satellites. Montego Bay, 2 October 1984 (Washington
> DC: US State Department, 1984), p. 2.

      The ICIP is responsible for identifying 'key international communica-
      tions and information policy issues'; incorporating 'foreign policy con-
      siderations into United States positions'; bringing 'these issues to
      decision by coordinating a United States position'; and promoting
      'these positions internationally'. US Department of State, 'Bureau of
      International Communications and Information Policy' (Department of
      State Publication 9860: March 1991).
23    Among other things, Executive Order 12188, issued in 1979, assigns to
      the USTR the task of being the President's 'principal advisor . . . on
      international trade policy.'
24    See 'US Development Communications Assistance Programs' and
      'Summary Excerpts SIG Report to NSC,' *Chronicle of International
      Communication*, V (9) (November 1984).
25    Stoil, 'The Executive Branch and International Telecommunications
      Policy,' p. 92.
26    *Ibid.*, pp. 92–4.
27    *Ibid.*, pp. 94–5.
28    Also, AT&T sent one delegate, as did Motorola, Rockwell Interna-
      tional, Satellite Business Systems, and Western Union.
29    Larry Martinez, *Communication Satellites: Power Politics in Space*
      (Dedham, Mass.: Artech House, 1985) pp. 126–7.
30    In his study of the WARC-79 preparations, Stoil contrasts these rela-
      tively sophisticated efforts with an unnamed 'educational association'
      which advocated the need for a quasi-DBS system to service the needs of
      educators in both developed and less developed countries. This kind of
      relatively vague request for more spectrum – rather than a detailed

'action plan' – was doomed to fail, especially in the absence of support from a powerful proponent in the White House. Stoil, 'The Executive Branch and International Telecommunications Policy,' p. 99.

31  Martinez, *Communication Satellites*, pp. 126–30.

32  Morris H. Crawford, 'The US Mobilizes for WARC – but Bickers over Political Aims,' *Transnational Data Report*, V (6) (September 1982) 313.

33  *Ibid.*, pp. 313–16.

34  William J. Drake and Kalypso Nicolaidis, 'Ideas, Interests, and Institutionalization: 'Trade in Services' and the Uruguay Round,' in *International Organization*, 46 (1) (Winter 1992) 48.

35  The data-processing sales of the world's twenty largest computer companies totalled over $31 billion in 1979, and US companies held a 77.6% share of this total. Also in 1979, 80% of the data base information used in the world originated in the United States. Joan Edelman Spero, 'Information: The Policy Void,' *Foreign Policy*, 48 (Fall 1982) 145–6. From 1986 to 1992, total exports of database services increased from $124 billion to $592 billion, while imports rose from $23 billion to $85 billion over these same years. From US Government, *Survey of Current Business* (September 1993) Table 2, p. 122.

36  On the role played by American Express executives during the formative stages of the Canada–United States Free Trade Agreement, see Linda McQuaig, *The Quick and the Dead, Brian Mulroney, Big Business and the Seduction of Canada* (Toronto: Viking, 1991).

37  Methods applied by nation states to control or monitor transborder information flows included the imposition of legal restrictions to closed information systems; requirements that data processing be conducted in host countries; restricted licensing of the operation of or access to particular transmission media; tariffs and taxes placed on telecommunication network use; and many others. The United States applied a number of its own restrictions to information flows – such as the items on a list generated by the Department of Defense of banned technology exports – despite its ongoing promotion of free flow principles. See Colleen Roach, 'The US Position on the New World Information and Communication Order,' *Journal of Communication*, 37 (4) (Fall 1987).

38  Spero, 'Information: The Policy Void,' p. 140 (emphases added).

39  TNC organizations involved in this effort included the International Chamber of Commerce which, in 1981, endorsed the inclusion of services in the GATT negotiations; the US Council for International Business whose Committee on Transborder Data Flow was established in 1979, and whose Committee on International Telecommunications was established one year later; and the International Trade and Investment Task Force of the Business Roundtable, founded in 1972. Other significant TNC organizations are listed in Karl P. Sauvant, *International Transactions in Services: The Politics of Transborder Data Flows* (Boulder, Col.: Westview Press, 1986) pp. 194–9.

40  Spero, 'Information: The Policy Void,' p. 155.

41  Also see testimony of William J. Hilsman, Director of the Department of Defense Communications Agency, in United States Congress. Senate. Committee on Commerce, Science, and Transportation. Subcommittee

on Communications. Hearings on 'The International Telecommunications Act of 1983'. 98th Cong., 1st sess., 10 and 11 May 1983, p. 122.

42 Spero, 'Information: The Policy Void,' pp. 150–1. At a 1983 Congressional hearing, Phillip C. Onstead, a representative of Control Data Corporation agreed with Spero, adding that 'there is . . . very little understanding [among American state officials] of the critical but increasing importance of the availability of unrestricted state-of-the-art telecommunications to the future of our nation and to achieving such national goals as improving foreign trade and also national security.' Onstead in Hearings on 'The International Telecommunications Act of 1983,' p. 179.

43 Drake and Nicolaidis, 'Ideas, Interests, and Institutionalization,' *International Organization*, p. 49.

44 Sauvant, *International Transactions in Services*, p. 199. For an example of how some US corporations sought to convince foreign companies and governments that free flow constituted a universal economic good, see article by American Express Senior Vice President Harry L. Freeman, 'Impeding the Flow of Information Damages National Interests,' *Transnational Data Report*, VI (1) (January–February 1983) 19. Geza Feketekuty, while Counsellor to the USTR in 1985, wrote that

All segments of the American business community have identified international data flows as one of the top priorities for a new round of trade negotiations. In fact, it is one of the few issues, along with the importance of intellectual property, on which there was common agreement.–*Feketekuty*, quoted from his 'The Telecommunications and Services Market Worldwide: A US View' (unpublished mimeo: USTR, 1985) p. 10.

Feketekuty is generally considered to have been 'the most visible, prolific, and influential analyst at the time. His activism in Congressional hearings, efforts in organizing interagency and business coalitions, and writing and speaking activities have led some to regard him as the "father of trade in services." ' Moreover, due to the general absence of knowledge regarding service trade issues, Feketekuty's analyses, despite his affiliation with the USTR, were well respected by many foreign officials. See Drake and Nicolaidis, 'Ideas, Interests, and Institutionalization,' p. 50 and fn.21.

45 Department of Commerce, 'Long Range Goals in International Telecommunications and Information,' pp. 20–1.

46 The report also recommended 'the integration of telecommunications and information services into the overall US trade effort, by identifying the barriers encountered by US suppliers and users of such services abroad and vigorously seeking their reduction.' *Ibid.*, p. 21.

47 *Ibid.*, p. 22.

48 Jane Bortnick, 'International Telecommunications and Information Policy: Selected Issues for the 1980s.' Report prepared for the US Senate, Committee on Foreign Affairs (unpublished: 1983) p. 16.

49   Fowler in Hearings on 'The International Telecommunications Act of 1983', pp. 43–4.
50   See *ibid.*, pp. 180–1.
51   George Shultz, letter to Chairman of the Senate Committee on Foreign Relations, 21 September, 1983. Reprinted in Senate Hearings on 'International Communication and Information Policy,' p. 4.
52   *Ibid.*, p. 5.
53   Interview with Diana Dougan; Tunstall, *Communications Deregulation*, p. 211; 'The Right Stuff, Ambassador Diana Lady Dougan,' *Broadcasting* (18 March 1985) np.
54   Dougan testimony in Hearings on 'International Communication and Information Policy,' p. 11.
55   *Ibid.*, p. 14. Dougan added that 'we also see the developing countries pursuing policies that are often quite restrictive in order to develop their own fledgling industries in this sector. Further, the less developed countries are afraid that they are going to be left behind ... and they are concerned with concepts like technological ... [and] cultural imperialism.' – p. 15.
56   'Summer Theatre on the Hill,' *Chronicle of International Communication*, V (4) (May 1984) 4–5.
57   'Making Room at the Table of Organization,' *Chronicle of International Communication*, V (5) (June 1984) 1–2. Congressional leaders concerned about foreign communication policy also were at odds over the more general question of how to coordinate policy. Resistance to State Department efforts to expand Dougan's role and responsibilities, for example, were led by the Chair of the Senate Foreign Relations Committee, Richard Lugar, who generally rejected the notion of solving problems by creating new bureaucracies. House Foreign Relations Chair Dante Fascell, however, supported State's efforts to take on this leadership position. See 'Change and Chance at the Organizational Wheel,' *Chronicle of International Communication*, VI (1) (January–February 1985) 5–6.
58   'Freedom of Business Communication Vital,' *Transnational Data Report*, VI (6) (September 1983) 302–5.
59   'For the Record and Subject to Change,' *Chronicle of International Communication*, V (10) (December 1984) 7.
60   'Information Flow Vital to World Economy,' *Transnational Data Report*, VI (5) (July–August 1983) 239–42.
61   United States National Security Council, 'National Security Decision Directive Number 130' (unpublished mimeo: 6 March 1984).

# 6 Exporting Liberalization and the Ascendancy of Trade

The term commonly used to characterize US communication policy in the 1980s – 'deregulation' – is a misnomer. In any regulatory regime, the practices or behavior of most private sector entities are, to varying degrees, monitored by state officials. Corporate activities also can be regulated through the structural constraints present in the market-place itself. The former more hands-on type of regulation has been called 'behavioral regulation' and the latter, less direct form, 'structural regulation.'[1] With this distinction in mind, deregulation essentially involves a shift away from behavioral regulation and toward the assumed constraints of inter-corporate and supply-and-demand relations. Deregulation thus constitutes a shift in regulatory emphasis rather than some kind of absolute 'freeing-up.'

One of the most significant steps toward structural regulation and away from behavioral regulation emerged as a result of a US Department of Justice (DoJ) antitrust suit filed against AT&T and implemented through federal courts. Although this action was initiated in 1974, it was not until 1982 that a negotiated settlement was reached. AT&T officials agreed to divest its twenty-two Bell operating companies.[2] In return, AT&T was allowed to retain its long-distance services, its manufacturing subsidiary (Western Electric) and its research wing (Bell Labs). More importantly, AT&T was allowed to expand into new business ventures.[3] Judge Harold H. Greene, who presided over the divestiture, approved the settlement, which included a plan by AT&T executives to reorganize the Bell operating companies under the umbrellas of seven regional holding companies (RBOCs).[4] In effect, the AT&T divestiture constituted both the release of the world's largest telecommunications company into international markets and a promotion of domestic long-distance competition. The related surge in domestic telecommunications activity compounded state policy problems in that more public and private sector participants and increased foreign participation in the US market perpetuated the inability of existing state structures to redress unforeseen problems emerging as a result of re-regulation.

A catalyst for this and other regulatory and more general conceptual changes in US policy were technological advancements involving telesatellites. When Intelsat was first established, the capacity of satellites to focus transmissions onto particular regions through spot beams was limited. With advancements in transponder technologies and power capabilities, not only could pre-specified areas be serviced but spot-beam locations could be modified in accordance with shifting market strategies or demands. As of 1985, the French Telecom 1 telesatellite possessed the capacity to redirect its transmissions to markets outside of Western Europe. Moreover, similarly capable systems were about to be launched in Europe and elsewhere. Apart from US companies seeking to provide international telecommunication services, some West European and Japanese PTTs also favored some degree of international regulatory liberalization in order to take advantage of their existing or planned telesatellite capabilities. But the main proponents of liberalization were large business users seeking lower rates and more specialized services.[5] As David Markey told a Congressional hearing in 1985 (when Markey was the Assistant Secretary for Communications and Information at the Department of Commerce and, as such, a spokesman for the Reagan administration), 'We just want competition, which we think will be to the benefit of the American *user*.'[6]

The general shift from behavioral to structural regulation produced some important unanticipated results. One result of the adoption of a structural regulation/liberalization model involved the dramatic decline in the US share of the world telecommunication hardware market following the AT&T divestiture. While in 1987 the US equipment and services market accounted for 40 per cent of the world market, since 1984 domestic employment in this sector had fallen by 30 per cent.[7] More importantly, in 1986, for the first time, the United States posted a trade deficit of $2.6 billion in high technology goods – a remarkable decline from its $27 billion surplus six years earlier.[8]

As this chapter chronicles, this mounting crisis generated a rare consensus among US-based corporations in this policy field. Competition in the American market was workable only if domestic liberalization reforms could be exported to foreign markets. Rather than a reassertion of behavioral regulation at home, foreign communication policy officials were compelled to reform *international* communication regimes. In other words, the State Department, the FCC, the NTIA and others came under increasing pressure to do something they were, for the most part, structurally incapable of doing. Out of crisis, 'free' trade became the centerpiece of US foreign communication policy. As argued below, its ascent was the direct but complex outcome of the vacuum left by the collapse of the free flow of information policy.

## 6.1   THE FAILURE OF FREE FLOW

In the early 1980s, Reagan administration officials, despite intra-state opposition, set out to nullify (if not to destroy) those international agencies where proponents of a New World Information and Communication Order had organized in opposition to the free flow of information. UNESCO became the primary target. This initiative did not necessarily imply that the White House was pursuing a well-conceived reform strategy. While ignoring the advice of officials from the State Department, the FCC, and even recommendations from its own appointees to UNESCO, the 1984 withdrawal was not charted on a larger strategic road map pointing toward a universal free flow regime through the auspices of free trade. What the Reagan assault did produce, however, was a policy leadership vacuum, eradicating what had been a generalized and uncoordinated but nevertheless an occasionally cooperative inter-agency approach to foreign communication policy. It was in this historical and structural context that the services trade issue took on its prominent position among US foreign communication policy officials.

Before the Reagan administration could withdraw the US from UNESCO and threaten to do the same with the ITU, the conditions for a *domestic* rejection of the free flow policy approach first would emerge. Indeed, in the early 1980s, the strategic weaknesses and intra-state conflicts associated with the free flow of information approach became increasingly apparent. Given the growing awareness of the importance of information-based activities in the international economy, and the dominant position of US companies in such activities, foreign nation-state officials understood free flow policy to be almost entirely based on America's competitive advantages. Because the free flow 'principle' was widely seen as a ruse calculated to pry open foreign markets, the arguments made by American officials that free flow was *more* fundamentally a human rights issue held little sway in efforts to generate free flow converts.

By the early 1980s, it had become clear that the free flow policy was an inadequate means through which substantive international reforms could be generated. This was due to the absence of the leverage needed to compel other countries to accept free flow as a legal principle which, under most conditions, would be prescient in relation to prior consent. But even if they were to become universally recognized, the failure of free flow also stemmed from the unenforceable nature of such principles. In light of a mounting corporate reliance on international communications and information services, and the enormous costs involved in constructing 'seamless' world-wide telecommunications infrastructures, finding answers to questions concerning the legality and enforceability of free flow became matters of great urgency.

In the past, US telecommunications interests had been almost wholly identified with the interests of AT&T and Comsat. A common acceptance of these monopolies and their complementary relations with Intelsat and PTTs persisted until the 1970s. But by the early 1980s, the growing number of US-based companies that had become dependent on international communications, and *their* demands for specialized services and lower costs, generated a wide-scale reassessment of both free flow policy and the persistence of largely uncompetitive telecommunications markets[9]. Washington-based communications consultant Roland Homet told Congress in 1983 that 'until we in the US exert ourselves to redirect the swirl of 'sovereignty' forces along more constructive paths, we face a potentially calamitous disintegration of information resources and relationships that will benefit neither United States interests nor the international community.'[10]

From an intra-state perspective, dissatisfaction with free flow emerged in step with the application of new technologies. For example, as a result of the use of conventional telecommunication facilities to transfer computer software across national borders, the Department of Defense established the means to monitor such transmissions. When this practice became public knowledge in 1983, the State Department was deluged with complaints from foreign governments that this and other forms of US spying contravened the spirit of America's own free flow of information.[11] The resulting State Department–DoD conflict sharpened State–White House frictions over the issue of executive branch restrictions to so-called 'strategic exports' involving limitations in the availability of US technologies and scientific research to 'ideologically friendly' countries. In the minds of foreign officials, these ally-to-ally restrictions undermined the credibility of official US statements that such free flow exceptions were based solely on national security interests.[12]

State Department relations with the White House were further soured during and after the UNESCO withdrawal. Statements by Gregory Newell – Reagan's appointee for the position of State Department Assistant Secretary for International Organizations – that a core motivation for leaving UNESCO was to enable the United States to free up US $50 million for development projects without UN 'obstruction' or 'administrative waste' produced only more tensions in US–LDC relations. The limited investments subsequently made as a result of these 'savings,' and their almost exclusive support for telecommunication infrastructure projects designed to enhance TNC communication and market-building capabilities, placed State Department officials in an increasingly untenable position when arguing that free flow was primarily a human rights/free speech issue.[13]

More significant to officials in the State Department, but also to some in the FCC, Commerce and other agencies (not to mention AT&T and other telecommunications interests), were White House-led discussions on the future of the ITU. The option of withdrawing from the Union was first publicly debated in 1982 following the ITU's Plenipotentiary Conference in Nairobi. At this conference, delegate concerns went well beyond subjects such as spectrum allocation and conflicts concerning international standards. For the first time in its history, an ITU member country – Algeria – officially raised a 'political' issue not primarily concerning telecommunications: Israel's invasion of Lebanon. Much conference time was spent on the question of whether or not Israel should be expelled from the Union.[14] According to Michael R. Gardner, the head of the American delegation in Nairobi, 'Had Israel been thrown out of the ITU... [w]e would have been forced... to find an alternative' to the Union.[15]

Also of concern to US interests was the failure to get America's preferred candidate elected as the new Secretary General of the Union – apparently another indication of the ITU's 'politicization.' Instead, Australian Richard Butler won the position largely on the basis of his extensive lobbying of LDC delegates.[16] As Richard B. Nichols, an AT&T Vice President and a US delegate to Nairobi, explained to a Congressional hearing, Butler's 'leftist' leanings apparently meant that 'he can be bought [by anti-free-flow interests and]... you might even be able to buy some of his staff.' Nichols continued to explain that 'they [Butler's ITU executive] could set standards that would specifically benefit the developing countries at the expense of the developed.'[17] Michael Gardner reported to Congress that this 'negative trend' in the ITU warranted a reconsideration of US efforts to 'maintain the staus quo' and to investigate pursuing a more proactive position: 'So while the US must try to assert more effective leadership within the ITU ... we should not fail to seriously consider compatible alternatives to the ITU.'[18]

The dominant position held by the US public and private sectors in international communications meant that the ITU could not exist without America's direct support. The Nairobi conference produced not only the belief that the Union's reform was necessary but also that US threats should be used in the process. But instead of confronting the ITU with specific demands and a formal withdrawal deadline, as had been done with UNESCO, US officials opted to reform the Union using indirect methods. Gardner, for example, suggested that through expanded US private and public sector aid in the education of foreign telecommunication officials, 'we [can] build bridges to these people so they do not vote against us in ... important forums'.[19] As a consequence, unlike UNESCO, the ITU played a substantive role in the ongoing maintenance of an orderly international communications environment, and AT&T, IBM, American Express and other large US corporations made innumerable representations to Reagan administration officials explaining their ongoing dependency on an orderly international telecommunications regime.[20] Less direct methods of reform thus constituted the only feasible option given this state of essential interdependence. In addition to educational and other development programs, US officials soon discovered that by placing issues directly affecting established ITU activities on the international trade agenda, some degree of cooperation between the Union and the GATT process could be attained.

The effectiveness of this GATT-based ITU reform strategy became apparent at the Union's 1988 World Administrative Telegraph and Telephone Conference (WATTC-88). At this conference, a conflict involving the technical conditions facilitating market access for service providers and nation-state controls over domestic communications emerged. On the one hand, delegates from the US, Britain and a small number of other countries argued that regulations affecting the growth of financial and other telecommunication-dependent services should be minimal. On the other hand, delegates from mostly less developed countries argued that the application of reforms and regulations facilitating a level *competitive* playing field for all service providers, carriers and users was more essential. In sum, the US and other countries recognized that because transnational telecommunications are becoming inextricably linked with the international growth of a broad range of economic (service sector and non-service sector) commercial activities, regulations hindering their development constituted a fundamental barrier to world-wide economic growth.

Already in 1987, an ITU Legal Symposium had examined international telecommunication issues as *trade* issues in order to coordinate these concerns with those emerging in the GATT. In part, this GATT-ization of the ITU was a response to suggestions that the technical regulations set by the Union should be evaluated as trade facilitators or impediments. Again, suggestions from some US officials emerged that if the ITU failed to promote a free trade agenda, an international telecommunications regime based on private sector proprietary standards should be considered as an alternative to the Union itself. Given the existence of an ITU *status quo* whose policies and decisions took into account the development needs of LDCs and the protection of state-controlled PTT monopolies,[21] some telecommunication and information-based service sector corporations began to consider that even 'an effective state of anarchy' would offer better opportunities for economic growth than would existing ITU regulatory priorities.[22]

With this US-led challenge in place, WATTC-88 produced a compromise agreement in which privately owned telecommunication networks were, to some extent, exempted from future ITU regulations. Moreover, those regulations that were established at the Conference – mostly affecting state-controlled telecommunications entities – were *not* legally binding. Most remarkably, WATTC-88 formally recognized that future telecommunication services regimes should be negotiated as 'trade' regimes. Despite these concessions, American interests criticized the conference for not formally condemning PTTs as unacceptable institutional barriers to the development of the international service economy.[23]

## 6.2   THE EMERGENCE OF FREE TRADE

The emerging awareness of service sector activities as significant components of the world economy has been associated with the shifting competitive capabilities of relatively advanced capitalist economies.[24] In 1972, the Organization for Economic Cooperation and

Development (OECD) initiated a general rethinking of services through its coordination of an international conference on long-term changes in the global economy. In the US, this ground-breaking conference and its subsequent report were much-welcomed developments.[25] In directly associating service transactions with international trade, a new coalition of diverse corporate interests could be mobilized and greater weight could be provided to their otherwise isolated appeals for the liberalization of various activities. Moreover, from a strategic perspective, these corporations were empowered with a new discursive weapon through which they could relate isolated market access and reciprocity problems with a more general crusade against 'protectionism.'

Among American state officials, the services issue-as-trade-issue equation provided the USTR with greater responsibilities. Related to the enthusiasm of USTR officials for adopting the services trade issue was the emergence of academic and popular publications espousing an emerging so-called 'post-industrial society.'[26] Elected members of the US Congress and executive branch officials acknowledged both the economic growth prospects of the relatively advanced US service sector and its potential role in providing the US with a leadership position in the emerging international information economy. As such, American state officials began to promote the idea that the economic revitalization of the US was attainable through the internationalization of US-based service sector activities.[27]

From the early 1970s, various government agencies struck committees and commissioned studies with the participation of US-based TNCs. In formulating the 1974 Trade Act, for example, private sector input resulted in the recognition of service issues as potential trade issues and the option of taking unilateral action against countries impeding service sector trade. In 1984, a USTR study on the growing role of services in the international economy (which included a 56-page appendix containing previously undocumented statistics on GATT member service activities) was submitted to the GATT.[28] Not only did this constitute the first comprehensive American state study on services submitted to the multilateral trade organization, in general terms it established national policy objectives for the services trade issue.[29] Other advanced industrialized countries subsequently undertook detailed studies of their domestic service activities while LDCs generally did not. Neither the 1984 USTR study, nor any major private or public sector study preceding it, had addressed the issue of the relationship of services to LDC development concerns. In the absence of theoretical or empirical arguments, LDCs, led by Brazil and India, refused to consider even the possibility of service transactions as trade issues. As a Brazilian delegate to the GATT argued in 1987, liberalization in the trade of services 'could contribute to a new international division of labor where we [LDCs] are granted some advantages in certain manufactures but will be permanently excluded from passing on to a post-industrial or more services-oriented economy as is happening in the developed world.'[30]

US foreign communication policy officials began to re-conceptualize free flow of information issues in terms of free trade in the early 1980s. In 1983, the Commerce Department report on 'Long-Range Goals in International Telecommunications and Information' recommended that the US government 'place a high priority on the reduction of non-tariff trade barriers affecting the telecommunications and information industries through vigorous multilateral and bilateral negotiations in the GATT and elsewhere, but without insisting on rigid reciprocity.'[31] Foreshadowing revisions to Section-301 of the US Trade and Tariff Act, the report recommends possible amendments to US trade law to protect domestic interests from 'unfair industry-targeting practices and other anti-competitive policies of other countries.'[32]

In the minds of many US state and corporate officials, this modified approach was not difficult to accept given the general failure of free flow.[33] In a 1985 survey prepared by the USTR on the views of US corporate representatives on the upcoming GATT Uruguay Round, free flow of information issues were directly linked to US trade policy. Among other private sector groups, the National Foreign Trade Council told the USTR that 'emphasis should be placed upon those service sectors, such as communications, which form the infrastructure of services trade.' Likewise, the Services Policy Advisory Committee submitted that

> Telecommunications plays a central role in the international trade of all information based services because it is the primary distribution channel for these services.... For this reason, policies or practices that create barriers to the flow of information or to the use of telecommunications services should be accorded a special priority in any trade in services negotiations.[34]

In another paper prepared in 1985 by a US government Interagency Working Group on Transborder Data Flow, both the free flow of information and a commitment to a competitive capitalist market system were recognized to be the 'two broad principles' driving 'US telecommunications and information policy.'[35] More specifically, the paper specifies eight policy goals:

1 enhance the free flow of information and ideas among nations subject only to the most compelling national security and privacy limitations;
2 promote harmonious international relations and contribute to world peace and understanding through communications;
3 promote, in cooperation with other nations, the development of efficient, innovative and cost-effective international communications services responsive to the needs of users and supportive of the expanding requirements of commerce and trade by broadening opportunities for competition and investment;
4 ensure efficient utilization of geostationary orbit and electromagnetic frequency spectrum;
5 expand information access and communications capabilities of developing countries to facilitate their economic developments;
6 ensure the flexibility and continuity of communications and information required to maintain national defense and international peace and security;
7 promote competition and reliance on market mechanisms to ensure efficient prices, quality of services, and efficient resource utilization; and
8 promote the continuing evolution of an international system of communication services that can meet the needs of all nations of the world, with attention directed toward providing such services to economically less-developed countries.[36]

These goals have direct and indirect implications for the international development of DBS and the prospective internationalization of US information-based products and services. For example, the third goal is fundamental to the efficient maintenance and development of markets for international advertisers – the initial source of DBS revenues. More generally, in defining free flow of information principles as trade issues involving a debate between free traders and protectionists (rather than free flow versus prior consent), information-based producers and service providers positioned themselves on what became the free trade common-sense high ground. However, this revised way of thinking about economic development required the recruitment and political engagement of foreign proponents.

Recognizing that other countries would need to be pulled toward this reconceptualization of communication issues as trade issues (rather than being more crudely pushed into it), the Reagan administration, with Congressional support, instructed the USTR to pursue bilateral service and intellectual property rights agreements. Through the establishment of trade precedents with Israel and Canada, and industry-specific deals with Japan and the European Community (EC), precedents and standards were set for future GATT negotiations. More importantly, these agreements would compel GATT members to take part in multilateral negotiations or face potential exclusion from the US market.

This strategy was supplemented in the Trade and Tariff Act of 1984. Under Title III of the Act, services were provided with the same legal status as material goods. While the Act recommends the pursuit of bilaterally and multilaterally negotiated solutions to foreign barriers, it also empowers the executive branch to take unilateral retaliatory action against 'unfair' and restrictive trade practices involving services and other sectors, including restrictions to foreign direct investment.[37] While the 1974 Trade Act recognized services for the first time, its Section 301 was amended in the 1984 legislation to provide the President with remarkable retaliatory authority.

In 1985, the European Community agreed to include services in the upcoming GATT round negotiations.[38] LDCs, on the other hand, opted to utilize the United Nations Conference on Trade and Development (UNCTAD) to undertake studies and promote their concerns regarding the impact of such an agreement on economic development. The services-as-trade concept thus became a North versus South rather than a US versus 'the world' issue. However, despite the mobilization of UNCTAD, LDCs were unable to develop a substantive counter-proposal to free trade. Outside the UN, relatively few studies were conducted by LDC or Northern analysts.[39] Unlike lawyers involved in free flow versus prior consent debates, even economists who were directly engaged in trade in services issues had little theoretical or even empirical understanding of services issues. As such, little intellectual grounding existed for a relatively informed debate of the services trade question to take place.[40] Moreover, LDCs and sympathetic trade analysts were unable to present a feasible alternative to a free trade in services agreement that would even begin to satisfy the overarching demands of TNCs as represented both in US policy and TNC-based lobbying efforts.

In the mid-1980s, the US and its GATT allies publicly admonished a small number of 'radical,' 'hardline' and 'selfish' LDCs for their opposition to an emerging GATT agreement that apparently would provide 'moderate' LDCs with new opportunities to access First World markets. This group of hold-outs – Brazil, India, Argentina, Cuba, Egypt, Nicaragua, Nigeria, Peru, Tanzania and Yugoslavia – was commonly referred to as the Group of Ten, while the moderate LDCs were called the Group of Twenty (led by Jamaica and Colombia). However, from this divisive environment, fears among the Group of Twenty of prospective and exclusionary bilateral agreements, and the gradual recognition by First World officials that development issues should be addressed, the emergence of a 'common working platform' between Brazil, India and the EC was achieved on the eve of the Punta del Este Uruguay Round meeting in 1986.[41]

During the Uruguay Round negotiations, US officials rarely applied either a 'carrot' or a 'stick' in efforts to bring about a services agreement: they used both. In 1988, the US Congress passed the Omnibus Trade and Competitiveness Act. As an extension of Section 301 of the US Trade Act of 1974 (revised in 1984), which originally enabled the US government to challenge and retaliate against 'unfair trade practices' under GATT procedures, the new so-called Super-301 enabled Congress to act against foreign countries for practices *not* covered by the GATT. Another significant modification was the so-called Special-301 provision. Unlike Super-301, Special-301 specifically addresses intellectual property rights. Rather than the GATT method of negotiating agreements based on mutual trade concessions, Super-301 and Special-301 were designed to compel foreign governments to make specified trade concessions or accept the unilateral suspension of their existing access to US markets. Moreover, retaliatory measures could be imposed on an entire country, rather than just an offending industry as prescribed in the original 1974 Act. Super/Special-301 assigns the USTR the task of identifying countries and trade blocs whose laws and/or practices will *probably* hamper potential American exports. Either a domestic party *or* the USTR could launch a complaint under these new provisions.

In both empowering the USTR to present an annual report to Congress on 'priority' countries and enabling its officials to initiate complaints independently, Congress provided the private sector with a comprehensive research service while shielding those US-based corporations reluctant to launch complaints against host countries. After these priority countries and their offensive practices are identified,

USTR officials are mandated to grant them from one year to eighteen months to negotiate a settlement or face retaliatory action.[42] If, following negotiations, the executive branch (in practice, the USTR and the President) determined that the policies or practices of the priority country were 'inconsistent with the provisions of, or otherwise denies benefits to the US under, any trade agreement, or . . . is unjustifiable, unreasonable, or discriminatory and burdens or restricts US commerce,'[43] the President is compelled to take action against the offending country.[44] As Sauvant interprets Section 301:

> [its working] definitions are very broad. In fact, the definition of 'unreasonable' applies even to acts that are 'not necessarily in violation of or inconsistent with the international legal rights of the United States.' In other words, the perceived interests of the US are placed above the strict letter of international agreements . . . [Because] no internationally recognized standards to govern [services and intellectual property exist,] . . . until such standards are established, the US will be able to determine and apply its own concept of 'unreasonable.'[45]

It is difficult to imagine any other country carrying out this kind of trade policy. The assertion of unilateral trade sanctions against priority countries (initiated by the US Congress largely due to mounting corporate constituency pressures and an ongoing national balance-of-payments crisis) in part was meant to stimulate the successful conclusion of the Uruguay GATT process. Yet Super/Special-301 is explicitly illegal under existing GATT rules. In the US and elsewhere, international treaties, such as the GATT, have the legal force of domestic law. Nevertheless, retaliatory measures continued to be taken especially in the services sector due to its status as a 'priority area.'[46]

As previously mentioned, the Uruguay Round also involved negotiations on trade-related intellectual property rights (TRIPS).[47] This inclusion was accepted by relatively advanced industrialized GATT members largely in response to the general ineffectiveness of existing international agreements as remedies against the unauthorized use (or 'piracy') of information-based commodities. The Berne Convention, the Universal Copyright Convention (administered by the UN), and the Paris Convention for the Protection of Industrial Property (protecting patents and trademarks), all lacked effective enforcement mechanisms and dispute settlement procedures.

Many LDCs, relative to most advanced industrialized countries, considered the effects of an enforceable intellectual property rights regime to be exclusionary. In the absence of enforceable agreements, LDC-based businesses could maintain their access to relatively inexpensive supplies of pirated information-based products, including valuable software programs and new technologies. Moreover, by copying only the most successful products, research and development costs can be significantly reduced and marketing risks minimized. LDC state officials generally recognized that industries producing counterfeit goods can employ thousands of people. All in all, despite TNC threats to withdraw investments, LDCs and the entrepreneurs operating in them generally have been more interested in maintaining their access to a relatively inexpensive supply of information-based resources than in remunerating foreign owners.[48]

A central role in the development of a GATT-based intellectual property rights regime subsequently was played by elements of the US private sector. Broad-based organizations such as the Intellectual Property Committee, the US Chamber of Commerce, the Council for International Business, and others, developed 'minimal standards acceptable to industry' that were communicated through various official and unofficial channels to both US and foreign government personnel.[49] This GATT-based intellectual property agreement also was pursued by two interrelated organizations – the Motion Picture Association of America (MPAA) and the International Intellectual Property Alliance (IIPA).[50]

## 6.3  FREE TRADE AND INTERNATIONAL INSTITUTIONS

In November 1990, in response to pressures by AT&T and several other US-based TNCs, USTR GATT negotiators announced that countries not granting US firms the same kind of access that their corporations enjoy in the American services market would be excluded from any prospective agreement. One of 'the most active and arguably the most crucial'[51] of service trade negotiating groups that emerged with these reciprocity ideals in mind was the Working Group on Telecommunications Services. Established in May of that year, the group first debated the 'proper place' of telecommunications within the GATT as a whole. At this time the key question for trade negotiators was whether a telecommunications agreement should be handled within the framework of a general agreement on the delivery of services or whether it should be drafted as a narrower sectoral annotation. On this issue, US negotiators pressed for the negotiations to be part of the GATT's overall definition of trade in services. Through this inclusion, a broad range of telecommunications and intellectual property issues could be 'de-politicized' in that they would be treated as issues requiring more or less the same open-market trade approach already applied to toasters and video cameras. On the other hand, if telecommunication issues were instead to be considered the subjects of a separate sub-agreement, questions concerning market access, for example, would require an independent negotiating process, potentially leading to an agreement accommodating 'protectionist' interests. Debate also centered on whether or not all telecommunication services should be covered or whether some services should be exempted. This issue involved the possibility of subdividing telecommunications into 'basic' (transmission only) and 'enhanced' or 'value-added' services. USTR negotiators insisted that this sub-division not only would shield PTTs from direct competition, it would also prejudicially advantage non-American corporations in their ability to take part in *both* basic *and* value-added activities in the American market while US corporations would not be able to engage in similar activities in other countries.

In July 1990, a preliminary working draft emerged from the General Agreement on Trade in Services (GATS) negotiations concerning telecommunications. One provision obligated the parties to insure that domestic entities exercising monopoly or exclusive rights outside the scope of their domestic mandates would not engage in anticompetitive practices in relation to entities from other countries.[52] Importantly, at this early stage, a significant concession was made to LDCs through a provision that would provide countries with the right to apply for temporary restrictions on the services trade agreement in the event of balance-of-payments difficulties. This provision also suggested the development of an assistance program through the International Monetary Fund (IMF) to help remedy such 'difficulties.'[53]

By the end of 1992, a relatively developed draft agreement was produced, providing the prospective services agreement with an over-arching Most Favored Nation (MFN) rule. This committed all GATT members to set tariff rates that would not grant any firm or country preferential treatment. Important exceptions, however, were made. Existing regional trading blocs, for example, such as the EC or the NAFTA would be allowed to continue to provide their members with extended benefits. The draft agreement also involved a national treatment rule for value-added telecommunications and computer services. This means that in these important sub-sectors, the legal and regulatory conditions for domestic firms must be applied to foreigners also. However, the services draft agreement gave countries the option to include or exclude particular sub-sectors from these national treatment provisions. Canada, for example, refused to include its 'cultural sector' in the agreement draft.[54] In the draft agreement's 'Annex on Telecommunications,' however, the US gained the right of GATT members to have full access to one another's public and private telecommunication networks.[55]

The Uruguay Round negotiations were completed at the end of 1993. Last moment resistance by France resulted in the formal but temporary exclusion of an open market agreement being reached on television and film products. While the Clinton administration was berated by the MPAA and other US interests for this omission, the more general provisions in the agreement on services, telecommunications and intellectual property, in conjunction with ongoing developments involving digital technologies and transnational communications, will no doubt facilitate the rapid transnationalization of *all* information-based commodity activities. Specifically, unlike the apparent exclusion of so-called culture industries in the Canada–US Free Trade Agreement (where, in the words of one commentator, Canada gained 'the freedom of the mouse facing the snake, not daring to move any more'),[56] and in light of the ever-present US threat to apply Section 301 retaliatory measures, the EC agreed only to apply general GATS provisions to its audio-visual sector. Under the MFN provision, for example, the EC listed some audio-visual sector activities under its allowed exemptions – exemptions valid for a maximum of ten years. However, because a progressive liberalization of these activities must begin before this decade-long exemption ends, the Europeans have relatively little time to develop the capabilities of the regional production and distribution needed to compete in a digitalized, international, free-trade environment.[57]

Through digitalized transmissions, the ability of officials of nation states to make distinctions between the cross-border flow of a Hollywood film and a financial transaction is virtually erased. Whereas information-based commodities produced outside of the European Union and carried over European DBS systems, for instance, can still face legal restrictions because of the temporary video services exemption, it is the digitalized character of the signals which ultimately will make such services indistinguishable relative to the free flow of other GATT-sanctioned enhanced or value-added services. As such, the effectiveness of current regulatory definitions based on past technological distinctions will continue to diminish largely as a result of ongoing developments in digital transmission.[58] While the new GATT Telecommunications Annex covers enhanced and value-added services, a group of twenty, mostly OECD countries, including the US, have committed themselves to negotiate a complementary basic services agreement.[59]

In light of the developments outlined above, by the end of 1980s the ITU had become, in the words of R. Brian Woodrow, decidedly 'schizophrenic':

> On the one hand, there was a desire to project a positive image in support of the Uruguay Round negotiations and their objectives and to assist-telecommunications liberalization. On the other hand, there was also irritation and concern that these negotiations could lead to a services trade regime which might disrupt established patterns of international telecommunications regulation and challenge the authority of the Union in certain areas.[60]

In 1989, Secretary General Butler came to believe that the survival of the Union required it to cooperate with the GATT process. As a result, ITU procedures – traditionally dominated by nation-state officials and interested hardware manufacturers – were increasingly opened up to business, industrial and scientific organizations as a means of directly incorporating the interests of telecommunication distributors and users into the regulatory process. In 1989, a High-Level Committee was established to review the ITU's mandate and activities and to recommend structural reforms. Its report, completed in 1991, included the recommendation that a new Bureau for Tele-communications Development be established in order to include, for the first time, officials from transnational corporations to act as advisors on LDC development and investment strategies.[61]

Butler's successor, Pekka Tarjanne (elected in 1989), has expressed support for institutional cooperation between the Union and the GATT. His speeches convey a belief that TNC-based pressures will compel the ITU to reform itself so as not to be a barrier to the changes taking place in an increasingly liberalized international economy. In two speeches made in January and February 1990, Tarjanne suggested that international telecommunications should now be considered by ITU officials as 'tools for trade.'[62]

The internal reorganization of the ITU and its direct participation in GATT services negotiations led Union officials to endorse a prospective GATT agreement. At the Union's Nice Plenipotentiary in April 1991, its High-Level Committee reported that,

> Although the purposes and approach of the GATS and the ITU are different, ... they are complementary. While there is likely to be some overlapping or 'grey' areas between the two, we do not foresee any major or fundamental conflict or incompatibility. The ITU is evolving to provide for an increasing range and variety of networks, services and participants, and to work with new organizations concerned with the provision and use of telecommunications. It is working in an increasingly liberal environment, and seeking to promote innovation and efficiency .... *The philosophy and spirit of the ITU's evolution are, therefore, not fundamentally different from those emerging in GATS.* It is understood that the latest draft Annex on Trade in Telecommunication Services recognizes the role of the ITU and the needs of developing countries. *There is no reason, therefore, why the ITU and GATT should not continue to proceed along similar paths.*[63]

In 1993, the ITU announced that it was to undertake structural changes in keeping with its commitment to become more 'market orientated.' Rather than making frequency allocations at ITU conferences, business and nation-state officials are now directly involved in the allocation process. Union expenditures have been reduced and personnel eliminated in part through the creation of industry advisory panels. According to Thomas Irmer, the Director of the ITU's Coordinating Committee on International Telephone & Telecommunications (to be consolidated under the plan with the International Radio Consultative Committee), these and other reforms aim to make the Union more 'businesslike' and 'market oriented.'[64]

As for UN-based efforts to establish a New World Information and Communication Order, 'the NWICO, as a major international policy debate, is dead.'[65] UNESCO, for instance, under Director General Fredico Mayor of Spain, has even sanctioned American free flow of information principles despite the fact that the US remains a non-member.[66] As with relatively developed countries, many LDCs now are pursuing communication policies aimed at attracting loans and investments targeted at building their telecommunication infrastructures. It should be noted here that the institutional, technological and political-economic developments presented in this study, all facilitating open-market international communications, are finding their apogee in DBS applications. Through new GATT-negotiated and WTO-applied corporate rights and freedoms, and the use of DBS systems both to establish almost instantaneous transnational information networks and to promote more general consumer demands, direct broadcasting will be an increasingly significant vehicle advancing the general aspirations of many TNCs. As Earl L. Jones, Jr, Chairman and Chief Executive Officer of International Broadcast Systems Ltd, explained to a Congressional subcommittee:

> the privatization of European broadcasting [for example] opens up new opportunities for American companies that advertise heavily on television. These companies are looking for global markets, and they need a global means through which to reach new customers on a cost effective basis.... [T]he more that American companies advertise abroad, the more of their products they will sell abroad, thereby contributing in a very positive way to the US balance of trade.[67]

## 6.4  CONCLUSIONS

The disparate character of the American state has played a significant role in the ascendancy of trade. It was not a coincidence that this policy shift took place during a period of national economic crisis and in a failed policy environment in which US free flow aspirations had become both urgent and seemingly unobtainable.

The GATT services and intellectual property rights agreements have neutralized or modified those international institutions capable of accommodating an organized resistance to US free flow aspirations. Without well-defined and 'realistic' counter-proposals to a services and intellectual property trade agreement, opposition to the GATT (especially by the Group of Ten) appeared to many moderate LDCs to be reactionary and self-serving, particularly given the collapse of the NIEO and the NWICO, and the pressing need to penetrate Northern markets.

As a result of the apparent need to do battle with the anti-free flow and anti-liberalization assumptions of overseas officials, the mid-1980s constituted the *beginning* of the kind of widespread awareness of cultural power among American officials that Schiller and others assumed had already been well established. Recognizing that transnational information activities constitute 'key policy instrument[s]' in larger efforts to shape overseas perspectives and outlooks, a National Security Council Decision Directive (NSCDD-130) of March 1984 acknowledged the need both to reform US foreign communication policy structures and to give USIA and CIA broadcasting exports 'the highest priority.' According to NSCDD-130, the use of DBS should be pursued by the USIA in response to assumed Soviet preparations to utilize them.[68] In response to Japanese and West European public and private sector plans to pursue DBS and other communication and information applications, US corporations with mass-media interests began to participate directly in preliminary GATT-based services, trade and intellectual property negotiations.[69]

*Officials involved in US foreign communication policy today generally recognize the cultural-power implications of information-based commodity exports.* According to the Department of Commerce, 'it appears that the global dissemination of electronic media and technology is playing an increasingly significant role in promoting US foreign policy by fostering demand for democratic reforms internationally.'[70] The reception of West European television and radio signals in Eastern Europe, the distribution of mostly pirated US-productions on videotape, and the long-standing propaganda activities of the VoA, RL and RFE are now commonly cited as important components facilitating the end of the Cold War.[71] DBS and other forces facilitating the expansion of information-based commodity activities almost regardless of domestic regulations will, it is believed, continue to promote democracy and consumerism overseas.[72] Moreover, the recent regeneration, at least in Washington, of terms like 'radical perestroika,' reflects the emerging common-sense belief among policy makers that the international distribution of corporate-produced information serves to undermine popular support in foreign countries for apparently anti-corporate (and, to some extent, anti-American) policies.[73] In the words of USTR official Emory Simon, 'we have gotten a lot further away from counting beans and pairs of shoes... *[to focusing on instead] the overall environment that creates our competitiveness.*'[74]

The failure of free flow policy and the related importance and success of the free-trade strategy has involved an overall rise in the status of foreign communication policy within the American state. Ironically, in implementing what were essentially free flow reforms through USTR-based agreements, the emerging importance of communication and information commodity interests has not necessarily produced a concurrent growth in the authority of established foreign communication policy agencies. The complex intra-state character of this policy field remains largely unchanged since facing its crisis period in the 1980s. What has changed is that the USTR has taken foreign communication concerns to a higher level – reflecting the centrality of these concerns among a diversity of corporate interests – while the State Department, FCC, NTIA and others constitute resource centers utilized by trade and other officials. While inter-state battles over the meanings and applications of new trade agreements will continue through the WTO and other forums, *the USTR will almost certainly remain the core conceptual and instrumental mediator of US foreign communication policy. The status and responsibilities now shouldered by USTR and related public officials reflect the now unquestioned centrality of information-based commodity producers and distributors in the US political economy.*[75] The very public and potentially very damaging 1995 trade dispute between the US and the People's Republic of China (not a member of the WTO) over PRC-based software piracy activities underlined, for instance, the elevated status of International Intellectual Property Alliance corporations in the 1990s.

As outlined in this and the preceding chapter, domestic reforms fueled the foreign communication policy crisis and the direct intervention of private sector interests in restructuring both the American state and international institutions. Of course these domestic reforms, involving the ascendancy of trade agreements and the USTR, were crafted to enable the American state to mediate the needs of what arguably was becoming the most important economic sector in the US. Through US threats involving market access, threats to the ITU, and even – in the case of UNESCO – the near-eradication of relatively weak and unaccommodating international organizations, *free flow of information principles have been institutionalized through free trade.*

Rather than interpreting these recent and dramatic changes in international communications to be the result of the ascendancy of transnational capital over nation states, the US clearly has acted as the essential mediator of these reforms. Moreover, the continuing centrality of the USTR indicates that even though the WTO and other international reform goals have been achieved, US and foreign-based TNCs remain dependent on nation states to act or react on their behalf. Perhaps most fundamental and least understood is the role played by the state in the negotiation of common-sense perceptions of 'reality' in the international political economy. Since the late 1980s, the only state capable of mediating such conceptual transformations has been the American state. The end of the twentieth century has been a moment of historic transition involving, among other things, a struggle to reform the structural *and* conceptual bases through which capitalist activities will continue.

The domestic structures through which US foreign communication policy is articulated were reformed in response to the crisis involving the disjuncture between free flow policy and the needs of the American information economy. In response to a diversity of mostly US-based service sector corporations, existing communication policy agencies began to adopt free trade as a complementary policy approach. Meanwhile, the USTR emerged to pursue unprecedented international trade in services and intellectual property rights agreements. The ascendancy of the USTR and its adoption of telecommunications and other free flow-related issues previously handled by the State Department, Commerce and others compelled a more comprehensive but not altogether unproblematic restructuring of these agencies under the new free-trade effort. This period in which the American state was reformed in order *then* to reform international institutions and foreign government policies successfully involved not only changes in the mechanics of communication policy, it also involved changes in the ways in which officials think about policy.

## NOTES

1   Jill Hills, *The Democracy Gap* (New York: Greenwood Press, 1991) p. 51. It should be noted that Hills' use of the term 'structural regulation' is not related to references to state structures found in this book.
2   These companies collectively constituted about three-quarters of AT&T's 1981 assets of $145 billion. On the divestiture, see Jeremy Tunstall, *Communications Deregulation* (Oxford: Basil Blackwell, 1986) pp. 89–114. Also see US Department of Commerce, 'NTIA Telecom 2000: Charting the Course for a New Century' (Washington, DC: NTIA, October 1988) pp. 430–3.
3   While communications 'deregulation' most notably began with a Supreme Court ruling in 1968 permitting users of the telephone system to connect non-AT&T equipment onto the system, the AT&T divestiture constituted a radical leap toward structural regulation due to its mammoth scale. Just before its divestiture in 1984, AT&T was the largest

corporation in the world. Called the Bell System, it employed almost 1 million people and its annual revenues were nearly $70 billion, constituting approximately 2% of US GNP.

4    These RBOCs are Nynex, Bell Atlantic, Bell South, Ameritech, Pacific Telesis, US West and Southwestern Bell. Judge Greene barred them from taking part in three areas of business: long-distance services; telecommunication hardware manufacturing; and the provision of information services. The RBOCs always have considered these conditions to have been unreasonable, and have waged protracted campaigns to win the legal right to offer 'content-related' services, including the delivery of television signals direct into homes through telephone lines. The federal courts defined 'information services' as a broad range of activities, from cable television to electronic publishing. In 1970, the FCC adopted rules that prevented potential telephone companies competing with cable television operators in order to provide the latter with an opportunity to establish themselves. These commonly called 'telco-cable cross-ownership rules' were incorporated into the Cable Communications Policy Act of 1984 and involved an amendment to the Communications Act of 1934. These provisions were radically rolled back, however, through the Telecommunications Act of 1996. This extraordinary piece of regulatory liberalization legislation will be addressed in chapter 7.

5    Robert R. Bruce, 'Intelsat in Transition,' *Chronicle of International Communication*, VI (3) (April 1985) 5–7.

6    Markey testimony in US Congress. House. Committee on Foreign Affairs. Subcommittees on International Operations and on International Economic Policy and Trade. Hearings on 'Foreign Policy Implications of Competition in International Telecommunications.' 99th Congr., 1st sess., 19 February; 6, 28 March 1985, p. 46 (emphasis added).

7    Jochen K.H. Schlegel, 'Competition in International Communications,' *Transnational Data and Communications Report*, X (5) (May 1987) 19; and Hills, *The Democracy Gap*, p. 57.

8    Meheroo Jussawalla, 'Economics and Global Impact of Telecom Deregulation,' *Transnational Data and Communications Report*, XI (3) (March 1988) 15. Other factors for declining US equipment exports included the relocation of US manufacturing activities to relatively low-wage countries and the (temporary) lack of experience of American companies in the equipment export market relative to Japanese and European competitors. Schlegel, 'Competition in International Communications,' p. 20. As Jill Hills points out, however, the liberalization of equipment had begun prior to the divestiture. As such, this balance-of-trade decline had begun prior to 1982. Hills, 'Dynamics of US International Telecom Policy,' *Transnational Data Report*, XII (2) (February 1989) 15.

9    Joan E. Spero, 'Information: the Policy Void,' *Foreign Policy*, 48 (Fall 1982) 150.

10    Homet in Hearings on 'International Communication and Information Policy,' p. 178.

11    Tunstall, *Communications Deregulation*, pp. 202–3.

12      *Ibid.*, p. 203. Also see Colleen Roach, 'The US Position on the New World Information and Communication Order,' *Journal of Communication*, 37(4) (Autumn 1987) 44; and 'Blocking Scientific-Technical Data Exports,' *Chronicle of International Communication*, VI (5) (June 1985) 1–2.

13      'Crimping the Commitment,' *Chronicle of International Communication*, VI (5) (June 1985) 6–7. Also see 'The Gang that Wouldn't Shoot Straight,' in *Chronicle of International Communication*, V (10) (December 1984) 1–3. For speeches, articles and statements by Gregory Newell during this period, see Bibliography.

14      Israel was not expelled thanks largely to an orchestrated effort by British delegates which resulted in the Plenipotentiary merely condemning the invasion.

15      Gardner quoted in Hearings on 'The International Telecommunications Act of 1983,' pp. 59–60.

16      Tunstall, *Communications Deregulation*, p. 214.

17      Nichols' testimony in Hearings on 'The International Telecommunications Act of 1983,' p. 173.

18      Gardner's testimony in *ibid.*, p. 60.

19      *Ibid.*, p. 65.

20      Interview with Jean Pruitt.

21      R. Brian Woodrow, 'Tilting Towards a Trade Regime, the ITU and the Uruguay Round Services Negotiations,' *Telecommunications Policy*, 15(4) (August 1991) 329 and 334.

22      Jean-Luc Renaud, 'The Role of the International Telecommunications Union,' in Kenneth Dyson and Peter Humphreys (eds), *The Political Economy of Communications* (London: Routledge, 1990) p. 47. This option would involve the construction of an international telecommunication regime based on the ongoing development of mostly *ad hoc* corporate-negotiated agreements and an accompanying comprehensive trade agreement in services and intellectual property rights through the GATT. Opponents of such a development among mostly LDCs generally recognized that the rapid growth of telecommunications and their consequent effects would restrict opportunities for relatively small domestic corporations which, given the absence of the time and support needed to develop the economic clout required to compete internationally, would be placed in an extremely tenuous position. For a summary of this perspective among Indian telecommunication interests, see Stephen D. McDowell, 'International Services Liberalization and Indian Telecommunications Policy,' in Edward A. Comor (ed.), *The Global Political Economy of Communication* (London and New York: Macmillan and St Martia's) pp. 103–24.

23      It should be noted that while ITU conferences usually come to agreements on a consensus basis, US resistance to the WATTC-88 compromise compelled a majority vote system to be adopted. The US was the only delegation that voted against the final Conference agreement. See R. Brian Woodrow, 'Tilting Towards a Trade Regime,' *Telecommunications Policy*, p. 331.

24   See William J. Drake and Kalypso Nicolaidis, 'Ideas, Interests, and Institutionalization', *International Organization*, 46(1) 43. A number of conceptual and analytical difficulties emerge when dealing with services as tradeable commodities. These include, (1) how should/can information be identified and/or measured?. (2) What is the relationship of time to the value of an information commodity?. (3) When is the flow of information across borders trade and when is it not?. And (4) how should/can information labor be classified/assessed? See Sandra Braman, 'Trade and Information Policy,' *Media, Culture and Society*, 12(3) (July 1990) 367–8.

25   Organization for Economic Cooperation and Development, *Report by the High Level Group on Trade and Related Problems* (Paris: OECD, 1973).

26   A formative work in this literature is Daniel Bell, *The Coming of Post-Industrial Society: A Venture in Social Forecasting* (New York: Basic Books, 1973).

27   Drake and Nicolaidis, 'Ideas, Interests, and Institutionalization,' pp. 45–6.

28   US Government, *US National Study on Trade in Services: A Submission by the US Government to the General Agreement on Tariffs and Trade* (Washington DC: Government Printing Office, 1984). This study was prepared in 1983.

29   Stated objectives included the establishment of a 'common framework applicable to all [service sub-]sectors with specific rules set out for [each],' *ibid.*, p. 8.

30   Unnamed delegate quoted in Drake and Nicolaidis, 'Ideas, Interests, and Institutionalization,' p. 57.

31   US Department of Commerce, 'Long-Range Goals in International Telecommunications and Information,' (unpublished, NTIA, 1983) pp. 20–1.

32   The Report also recommends 'the integration of telecommunications and information services into the overall US trade effort, by identifying the barriers encountered by US suppliers and users of such services abroad and vigorously seeking their reduction,' *ibid.*, p. 21.

33   Personal interview with Emory Simon, Deputy Assistant US Trade Representative, Office of the US Trade Representative, 9 September 1992, Washington, DC.

34   Both submissions quoted in Karl P. Sauvant, *International Transactions in Services* (Boulder, Col.: Westview Press, 1986) p. 204.

35   United States Government, Interagency Working Group on Transborder Data Flow, 'Communications and Transborder Data Flows in the US: A Background Paper' (unpublished mimeo: Interagency Working Group on TDF, 1985) p. 120.

36   *ibid.*, pp. 121–2.

37   Foreign direct investment traditionally has been the *sine qua non* of transnational service activities in that most services are produced and consumed simultaneously, often in one place. The pre-eminent role of telecommunications in extending service activities beyond this spatial limitation has been cited as a key direct stimulant to the general growth of service activities. Karl Sauvant outlines several reasons for the

preeminance of US efforts to secure free trade through the GATT and other means rather than an international foreign direct investment regime. One reason is that

> trade is a less sensitive matter than FDI [foreign direct investment] and, therefore, lends itself to faster action and results. FDI involves the [direct and visible] control of economic activities by foreigners and some key issues surrounding FDI... belong to the most intractable international public-policy issues, particularly between developed and developing countries.–*International Transactions in Services*, p. 311.

38    The inclusion of services was largely the result of three factors. First, most West European countries came to recognize that they held a potentially competitive position in services and telecommunications, but still preferred their *gradual* liberalization due to the recognition that some catching-up through a protected and cooperative EC industrial strategy was required. Second, the prospective development of a Canada-US FTA, and a North American FTA, led Europeans and other GATT members to consider a US GATT retreat and the emergence of a relatively closed regional policy to be a feasible US option. And third, foreign public and private sector officials took seriously the growing rhetoric emerging from the US Congress involving the application of new US protectionist strategies. See *Ibid*, pp. 464–65. A *New York Times* article published at the end of 1990 discussed the potential collapse of the GATT negotiations:

> 'Let's face it,' said an American negotiator who spoke on the condition that he not be identified,'there are other avenues that we can take – bilateral arrangements.... It's chiefly developing countries that will be hurt by a collapse here.'... Commerce Secretary Robert A. Mosbacher put it more succinctly in a conversation with several American reporters...: 'We could be okay either way. The US always could make regional or other agreements. In all truth, we're doing this now.' From Clyde H. Farnsworth, 'If One Conference Fails, the US Has Alternatives,' *New York Times* (4 December 1990) p. C5.

39    One reason for this was that analysts interested in LDC development tended to focus on present-day implications of direct TNC investment and related activities. Among established Northern analysts, little would be gained (either professionally or financially) from efforts radically to reconceptualize the terms on which the trade in services debate had recently developed. Drake and Nicolaidis, 'Ideas, Interests, and Institutionalization,' p. 64.

40    For a critique on the neoclassical economic assumptions informing most free trade in services proponents, see Robert E. Babe, 'Information Industries and Economic Analysis,' in Michael Gurevitch and Mark R. Levy (eds), *Mass Communication Review Yearbook*, vol. 5 (Beverly Hills: Sage, 1985) pp. 535–46. On conceptual and analytical problems concerning information commodities and the communicative

implications of all commodities, see Ian Parker, 'Commodities as Sign Systems' in Robert E. Babe (ed.) *Information and Communication in Economics* (Boston: Kluwer, 1994) chap. 3.

41    Drake and Nicolaidis, 'Ideas, Interests, and Institutionalization,' pp. 66–8. The opening of the Uruguay Round was delayed by two years in part due to the disagreement over the inclusion of services. Sandra Braman reports that EC industrial planning concerns also contributed to this delay. See Sandra Braman, 'Trade and Information Policy,' p. 365.

42    Jagdish N. Bhagwati, 'US Trade Policy at the Crossroads,' *The World Economy*, 12(4) (December 1989) 440–1.

43    US Trade and Tariff Act of 1984, Section 304(a).

44    Under Section 301 of the Trade Act of 1974, the President may 'suspend, withdraw, or prevent the application of, or may refrain from proclaiming, benefits of trade agreement to carry out a trade agreement' with the foreign entity involved, and may 'impose duties or other import restrictions on the products of such foreign country or instrumentality, and may impose fees or restrictions on the services of such foreign country or instrumentality, for such time as he deems appropriate.'

45    Sauvant, *International Transactions in Services*, p. 188.

46    See *ibid.*, p. 190. One of the first service industry complaints filed for review under the unrevised provisions of Section 301 involved a number of US television broadcasters who, in 1978, alleged that the Canadian Income Tax Act unreasonably denied tax deductions to Canadian advertisers running commercials directed at a Canadian audience over US border stations when such deductions were available on Canadian channels. By 1984, legislation was enacted in the US that mirrored the Canadian law. Another example took place in 1985 when the MPAA launched a complaint against South Korea because that country's review and rating system for foreign films was not applied to domestic productions. A significant aspect of the MPAA complaint involved the delays in releasing films caused by the process. Prior to filing the Section 301 complaint, the MPAA had lobbied the South Korean government and complained directly to the GATT, but to no effect. Eventually, South Korea agreed to cancel its review and rating system and the Section-301 proceedings were halted. See Brian L. Ross, ' "I Love Lucy," But the European Community Doesn't: Apparent Protectionism in the European Community's Broadcast Market,' *Brooklyn Journal of International Law*, XVI (3) (1990) 556 and fn.130.

47    The TRIPS mandate is as follows:

> In order to reduce the distortions and impediments to international trade, and taking into account the need to promote effective and adequate protection of intellectual property rights, and to ensure that measures and procedures to enforce intellectual property rights do not themselves become barriers to legitimate trade, the negotiations shall aim to clarify GATT provisions and elaborate as appropriate new rules and disciplines. Negotiations shall aim to develop a multilateral framework of principles, rules and disciplines dealing with international trade in counterfeit goods, taking into account work already

undertaken in GATT.' Reprinted in Marshall A. Leaffer, 'Protecting US Intellectual Property Abroad: Toward a New Multilateralism,' *Iowa Law Review*, 76(2) (January 1991) 277, fn.24.

48    It should be noted, however, that some LDC entrepreneurs are themselves victimized by pirating activities and many Third World officials take seriously threats concerning the withdrawal of capital investment. Some LDC-based consumer groups also have expressed concerns regarding the safety of some unauthorized products. Moreover, many LDC state officials were intimidated by America's Super/Special-301 provisions. See *ibid.*, pp. 281–3; and Thomas Cottier, 'The Prospects for Intellectual Property in GATT,' *Common Market Law Review*, 28(2) (Summer 1991) 389.

49    R. Michael Gadbaw and Rosemary E. Gwynn, 'Intellectual Property Rights in the New GATT Round,' in R. Michael Gadbaw and Timothy J. Richards (eds), *Intellectual Property Rights, Global Consensus, Global Conflict?* (Boulder, Col.: Westview Press, 1988) p. 66.

50    Personal interview with Fritz Attaway, Vice President, Motion Picture Association of America, 1 September 1992, Washington DC.

51    Woodrow, 'Tilting Towards a Trade Regime,' p. 338.

52    As Drake and Nicolaidis put it, 'telecommunications administrations [for example] should not use their control of underlying national networks to manipulate the conditions of interconnection for specialized service providers, nor should they use profits from reserved operations to cross-subsidize competitive ones.' – 'Ideas, Interests, and Institutionalization,' p. 74.

53    Klaus-Jurgen Kraatz, 'GATT and Telecommunications,' *International Business Lawyer*, 18(11) (December 1990) 517.

54    Robert Tritt, 'GATS, Son of GATT: A New Rule Book for Cross-Border Competition,' *InterMedia*, 20(6) (November–December 1992) 15–16.

55    Developing countries, moreover, received special conditions in particular circumstances.

56    K.F. Falkenberg, 'The Audio Visual Sector in the Uruguay Round' (unpublished: 18/19 November 1994) p. 243.

57    *Ibid.*, pp. 244–5. The MPAA estimates that this ten-year exemption will deny US film and television producers up to US$6.4 billion in foreign revenues. Figure in letter from Bonnie Richardson, Director of Federal Affairs, Motion Picture Export Association of America, to Donna R. Koehneke, Secretary of the International Trade Commission, 2 May 1994, p. 2 (unpublished).

58    The GATS, among other things, generally requires its signatories to pursue further bilateral negotiations to eliminate the restrictive business practices of public or private sector entities wherever they restrain services competition (Articles IX and XV). More specifically, it requires that national treatment be afforded to all GATS participants (Article XVII). The Uruguay Round TRIPS agreement also constitutes a precedent in that it provides not only comprehensive rules for the enforcement of ownership rights (in TRIPS Part III), but it also validates the

application of judicial procedures within nation states and provides for the use of GATT dispute settlement procedures (TRIPS Part V). For more detail, including GATS exceptions, see Ernst-Ulrich Petersmann, 'International Competition Rules for the GATT-MTO World Trade and Legal System,' *Journal of World Trade*, 27(6) (December 1993) 54–9. The Washington-based International Intellectual Property Alliance continues to argue in favor of applying Super-301 and Special-301 legislation as a means 'to smooth away [outstanding] trade barriers.' – Jay Berman, President of the Recording Industry Association of America, quoted in International Intellectual Property Alliance, 'People's Republic of China Tops IIPA's Special 301 Target List with Almost $830 Million in Estimated Losses Due to Piracy' (Washington: IIPA Press Release, 18 February 1994), p. 3.

59    Keith E. Bernard, 'New Global Network Arrangements, Regulatory and Trade Considerations,' *Telecommunications Policy*, 18(5) (July 1994) 390.

60    Woodrow, 'Tilting Towards a Trade Regime,' pp. 329–30.

61    One of the new ITU 'think-tanks' touted in the report was a Business Advisor Group. Jonathan Solomon, the Director of Corporate Business Development at the British-based TNC Cable & Wireless, called these recommendations and the ITU's institutional 'corporate restructuring' the beginning of its new role as 'the world telecommunication systems integrator.' Jonathan Solomon, 'The ITU in a Time of Change,' *Telecommunications Policy*, 15(4) (August 1991) 375.

62    Woodrow, 'Tilting Towards a Trade Regime,' p. 333.

63    Final Report of the High-Level Committee, *Tomorrow's ITU: The Challenge of Change* (Document 145–E, 26 April 1991); emphases added.

64    Irmer quoted in 'ITU Restructuring Is Intended to Make it More "Market-Oriented",' *Satellite Week*, 15(7) (15 February 1993) 5–6.

65    Thomas L. McPhail, 'Inquiry in International Communication' in Molefi Kete Asante and William B. Gudykunst (eds), *Handbook of International and Intercultural Communication* (Newbury Park, Ca.: Sage, 1989) p. 48.

66    Jill Hills, 'Communication, Information, and Transnational Enterprise,' in Babe (ed.), *Information and Communication in Economics*, p. 310.

67    Jones's testimony in Hearings on 'Television Broadcasting and the European Community,' p. 99.

68    See 'Tune Up for Term Two,' *Chronicle of International Communication*, V (6) (July–August 1984) and 7–8; and 'Tracking Red Television Beams; *Chronicle of International Communication*, VI (4) (May 1985) 5–6.

69    'Formidable Barriers Seen to Media Trade,' *Transnational Data Report*, VIII (1) (January–February 1985) 11.

70    US Department of Commerce, 'Comprehensive Study of the Globalization of Mass Media Firms.' Notice of Inquiry issued by National Telecommunications and Information Administration (February 1990), p. 7.

71    *Ibid.*, pp. 57–9.

72    *Ibid.*, pp. 51 and 53–6. Also, personal interviews with Mark Bykowsky, Senior Economist, NTIA, and Sharon Bywater, Office of International Affairs, NTIA, both on 1 September 1992, Washington, DC.

73    In the words of journalist Tony Snow of *USA Today: 'Blockades are not going to work. I'm one of the radical right-wingers who believes in radical perestroika for Cuba. Let's end the blockade. Let's flood them with goods and ideals. That's what's going to win the war.'* – From 2 September 1994 television broadcast of *'The McLaughlin Group'* on *PBS Television.*

74    Interview with Emory Simon (emphases added).

75    For example, see Mike Mills, 'The New Kings of Capitol Hill, Regional Bells Use Lobbying Clout to Push for New Markets,' *Washington Post* (23 April 1995) pp. H1 and H5.

# 7 Capital, Technology and the United States in an 'Open Market' Regime

United States domestic reforms have had anticipated and unanticipated implications for the international political economy. For example, the AT&T settlement was largely driven by the desire to create a more competitive US telecommunications market that, in turn, theoretically would reduce equipment and services costs for domestic (primarily business) customers. With the formation of the RBOCs and the ongoing liberalization of the American equipment market, the standardisation of hardware and software that had been imposed by AT&T's market dominance was replaced by a state of technological fragmentation. This, and the relative low cost and high quality of equipment produced overseas, generated a sharp rise in foreign imports. Moreover, the opening up of this market compelled the increased involvement of government agencies into communication policy, including more participation by officials from the Department of Justice, federal courts and by state government regulators.

The growing number and diversity of agents participating in the behavioral and structural regulation of domestic developments, in conjunction with the growing convergence of foreign and domestic communication activities, exacerbated concerns regarding the policy-leadership vacuum in Washington. This was a pressing issue due not only to the inroads that overseas manufacturers were making into the American market but, more generally, its seriousness involved the belief that a historic opportunity to exploit the most significant prospective growth sector in the US economy could well remain unrealized.[1] As Jane Bortnick reported to Congress in 1983,

other nations have been able to capitalize on American innovations to develop commercial products with comparable or higher quality and value without a heavy investment in basic research and development. At the same time ... actions by foreign governments to increase regulatory controls on telecommunications and information activities, erect protectionist

161

barriers to this trade, provide government support for indigenous telecommunications and data processing industries, and develop national strategies for increasing their share of the world market are significantly affecting the ability of US firms to maintain their predominance.[2]

Bortnick continued to explain that while foreign governments support local companies in their efforts to participate directly in the US market, these countries have also maintained tariff and non-tariff barriers to the free flow of information. As a result of the liberalization of the domestic market, US firms thus faced increased competition at home while encountering constraints in relation to equipment sales, data flows and electronic-based service exports in overseas markets. The ultimate result of this situation, if it persists, would be the obstruction of America's 'general economic growth.'[3]

Beyond such US market access opportunities, with few exceptions, foreign governments initially resisted US pressures to take up the structural regulation model. There were several reasons for this. Many used their PTTs both as alternative (non-taxation) revenue-generating vehicles and as levers through which the profits made from long-distance services could subsidize the development of local infrastructures. Resistance to the reciprocal market access demands raised by American interests thus involved more 'material' interests than cultural sovereignty concerns alone.[4]

By the mid-1980s, in part as an outcome of divestiture, AT&T had become perhaps the best positioned of all US corporations to participate in the prospective international enhanced services market. Reagan administration officials argued that the rapid internationalization of AT&T (and IBM) was necessary in order to compete with the growth of mostly Japanese-based companies in world markets. To some extent, divestiture had implications exceeding these and other such growth expectations. Domestic liberalization measures begat demands for reciprocity in foreign markets as well as new pressures to further domestic liberalization measures. The RBOCs, for instance, aggressively pursued FCC approval to participate in the distribution of television and other information-based services through their established telephone lines by arguing that their participation in the video services market constituted *the* essential revenue-generating vehicle needed to pay for their deployment of a national fiber-optic cable infrastructure. Using similar arguments, the US cable television industry, in 1984, convinced Congress to eliminate FCC oversight of the rates it charged in local monopolies.[5] In sum, new open-market opportunities granted to one sub-sector generated demands for similar opportunities by others.

More than twenty years after the Department of Justice antitrust suit against AT&T, Congress passed what arguably is the most sweeping piece of market liberalization legislation in US history – the Telecommunications Act of 1996. Similar to the divestiture, the Telecommunications Act is designed to further the interests of mostly large companies, some seeking opportunities to seize market share from rival communications and information interests, others also aspiring to consolidate existing market positions. Long-distance telephone interests – AT&T, MCI and Sprint – sought and obtained more opportunities to become full service communications and information corporations. This was achieved, for instance, through their direct access into local markets involving the Act's legalization of competitive cable television and other services. Similarly, the regional telephone companies (the RBOCs) were granted the right to provide customers with long-distance and other services, including television (or 'video'). Cable television companies also have been given permission to offer telephone and other services. From a legal perspective, the Telecommunications Act thus signals the start of a period of intensified corporate jockeying, deal-making and, in some instances, direct competition.

This is not to say that the Act is a precursor to the development of some sort of seamless *and* competitive national and perhaps international communications and information infrastructure. Long-distance telephone companies now appear well positioned to forge seamless *but largely non-competing* full-service infrastructures.[6] RBOCs, on the other hand, while free to provide long-distance services, now face direct competition locally and more legal restrictions relative to long-distance companies in servicing regional markets.[7] As for the cable television companies, their well-known debt-loads, when viewed in relation to the costs of upgrading infrastructures, will probably compel them to consolidate their positions through mergers, acquisitions and creative partnerships.[8]

Out of the complexity of the 1996 Telecommunications Act, and the political-economic ramifications of its implementation, come new opportunities and insecurities. *For most of the large-scale corporations directly involved in communications and information commodity activities, more competition is not an end in itself, but it is the means through which new markets potentially can be dominated.* In addition to these corporations, the Act was promoted by companies such as Citicorp, the world's largest financial services corporation. Like much of the US and international service sector, Citicorp continues to benefit from post-Fordist developments such as regulatory liberalization, international free-trade agreements and ongoing digital technology applications. The Telecommunications Act – because it facilitates the long-term development of relatively seamless (and oligopolistic) communications and information infrastructures – probably will generate more efficient and malleable service sector offerings. In keeping with the post-Fordist emphasis on production process flexibility, Citicorp and others thus will be better able to decentralize operations, penetrate markets *and* centralize control over their diverse activities.

In this chapter, the Telecommunications Act is treated as the latest and one of the most significant steps yet taken in the use of the American state as the mediator of corporate interests in international markets. Following the establishment of an international free trade in services and intellectual property rights regime through the GATT/ WTO, the White House – led by Vice President Al Gore – has promoted the need for a universal commitment by foreign state officials to facilitate corporate efforts in the construction a so-called Global Information Infrastructure (GII). It is in this context that *Business Week* magazine reported, one month after President Clinton signed the Telecommunications Act, that 'more important than better prices . . . the players know where they stand, they can finally build the long-awaited high speed (so-called broadband) links of the Information Superhighway.'[9] Beyond a model for 'freeing up' the private sector in efforts to construct a GII, the Telecommunications Act will fuel its development not despite its probable oligopolistic outcomes but more probably as a partial result of them. Using DBS as a focal point, the following pages relate these developments to domestic and international corporate activities directly involving the information economy. The implications of introducing digital technologies, particularly those involving high-definition television, to mass consumers and their implications also are addressed.

## 7.1  DBS IN AN 'OPEN MARKET'

Following the failure of the first domestic license holders in the early 1980s, American state officials – despite their growing awareness of the potential technological and economic significance of direct broadcasting – left the development of DBS to the vagaries of corporate competition. But such structural regulatory practices, in effect, provided the cable television industry with the opportunity in fact to *avoid* competition. The liberalization of the cable television industry had previously facilitated its tremendous growth and eventual marketplace dominance as both television distributors and producers. From 1976 to 1991, US cable revenues grew by more than 2,100 per cent and the number of households subscribing to cable rose from 10.8 to 55.8 million. By this latter date, three of the largest cable operators – Tele-Communications Inc. (TCI), Time Warner and Continental Cablevision – together serviced almost 40 per cent of this market.[10] From 1980 to 1990, the monthly 'basic service' subscription rate charged to households by cable operators increased 223 per cent.[11] Practically all of the cable programing services developed since the late 1980s are owned or have involved significant equity participation by at least one of the country's largest cable distributors. Most US cable channels also became participants in emerging overseas cable developments. These investments have been financed, in large part, by revenues generated by their domestic local monopolies.[12]

Despite this success, since the end of the 1980s cable companies have had good reason to fear DBS. While DBS has always had cost advantages over terrestrial distribution systems in three markets – areas with low population densities; areas where cable lines are limited in the scope of their coverage; and areas where cable systems are, in relative terms, technologically obsolete – digital technology developments have provided DBS distributors with immediate advantages due to their signal compression capabilities. In effect, because compression enables more information to be transmitted over existing bandwidths (in the mid-1990s providing distributors with an eight-fold increase in television signal transmission capacity), and because a DBS system can accommodate this compression at virtually no cost in relation to the complex and expensive infrastructure upgrades facing cable operators, economic efficiencies and relative per-household distribution costs provide direct broadcasting operators with obvious competitive advantages.[13]

In North America, especially in areas where cable has not already been laid, DBS is particularly cost effective. In order to reach its subscribers, cable companies must install lines and equipment past every household *en route*. DBS, in contrast, enjoys much greater flexibility in that the overhead cost of installing one reception unit will not require the enormous investment found in a cabled neighborhood. Moreover, if the DBS subscriber decides to stop receiving signals, the reception unit can be removed and, at minimal cost, can be installed again at another location. Moreover, given its continent-size coverage area, DBS systems, unlike most cable services, are not dependent on their successful deployment in pre-specified territories. If a DBS service fails to 'catch on' in Canada or Florida, for example, the same DBS operator can shift his or her marketing efforts toward any number of alternate locations – perhaps Mexico and California. Cable, on the other hand, *must* succeed in pre-established markets. This extraordinary flexibility also enables DBS operators to 'poach' from cable company subscribers, whereas cable's capability to do the same to DBS is limited.

All of these relative advantages are largely the result of cable's . physical limitations, the fragmented and localized character of most cable markets, and the fact that in North America DBS, in the 1990s, has a relatively small clientele from which cable can lure away subscribers.[14] One study estimates that the cost per channel of reaching all US television households through cable is $378 million, whereas for DBS the cost is just $3.7 million.[15] Given the size of the North American market, the price for a DBS system essentially to 'wire' the continent works out to US $1.67 per household.[16]

After just one year in business, the most successful North American DBS enterprise, DirecTV, had 1.3 million household subscribers.[17] While this penetration into homes probably will not continue far beyond 15 million by the year 2000 – due largely to the efforts of terrestrial-based systems to provide digital video technologies to their existing subscribers – it constitutes an unprecedented growth rate for any post-1945 in-home technology. In Britain, as of 1996, after seven years in service, 5.5 million households receive DBS signals.[18] In Europe, the Astra system (the telesatellites carrying BSkyB services and many others) was received by more than 65 million homes at the end of 1995, up from just over 20 million in 1990.[19] *As the cutting-edge transnational and digital communications technology*, corporate investors of DBS developments now include practically every TNC directly involved in information and communication commodity activities, including AT&T.[20]

Until 1994, the only operating DBS system in the United States was Primestar – a company owned by a partnership of the country's largest cable television companies. Originally called K-Prime Partners, its participants have included Comcast, Continental, Cox, New Vision,[21] TCI, United Artists,[22] Viacom,[23] Warner Cable and the

General Electric (GE) satellite subsidiary GE American Communications (GE Americom). In 1992, following the initiation of a federal Department of Justice antitrust investigation, the New York State Attorney General charged these companies ('Primestar Partners LP') with a number of illegal activities. According to the Official Complaint, 'the nation's largest cable system operators... by their conduct, monopolized, attempted to monopolize, combined and conspired to monopolize and restrained trade in the delivery of multichannel subscription television programming to consumers.'[24]

The Complaint argues that due to the size of the companies that constitute Primestar and the large number of cable systems they control, their collective ability to purchase or control programing involved a conscious and successful effort to 'restrict actual or potential competitors access to programming services necessary to compete.'[25] The New York Attorney General claims that the country's most successful programers – including HBO, Showtime, Cinemax and MTV – were not made available to prospective US DBS operators in order to restrict their ability to compete with existing cable systems.[26] The Complaint explains that

> Commencing sometime in or before 1986,... and continuing to the present, the defendant MSOs [cable companies] and their co-conspirators have engaged in a continuing contract, combination or conspiracy in unreasonable restraint of trade in an effort to suppress and eliminate DBS competition in the delivery of multichannel subscription television programming to consumers.[27]

These cable companies also were accused of acquiring control of GE Americom's K-1 satellite in 1990 – then the only North American system readily capable of providing a DBS service – 'in order to reduce the potential for direct competition' with prospective DBS companies and among one another's cable operations.[28] In December 1990, when the K-Prime partnership was reformulated and re-named Primestar, an agreement was made with the FCC DBS applicant Tempo Satellite (owned by TCI) to transfer the medium-power Primestar service onto Tempo's prospective high power DBS. 'The efforts... to acquire Tempo and other high-power DBS applicants,' states the Complaint, were explicitly designed 'to eliminate potential competitors.'[29]

In or before 1985, when Hughes Communications began to formulate its DirecTV DBS service, its officials attempted to contract programers such as Turner Broadcasting, ESPN, HBO, Playboy Entertainment, the Disney Channel and others. Cable companies responded by threatening 'to drop any programmer who went direct to the home' rather than deliver their services through cable company 'middlemen.' Recognizing the desire of cable companies to control programing, Hughes then pursued 'a cable friendly approach' offering to provide 'programming services "complementary" to those offered by cable systems.' Hughes executives also offered cable companies a financial interest in DirecTV and guaranteed them a degree of exclusivity in the distribution of programs in their established franchise areas. Recognizing the Hughes DBS system to be a competitive threat, in November 1988 General Electric (a direct competitor to Hughes in satellite manufacturing and the owner of its own broadcasting interests) offered the cable companies its K-1 satellite as a cable-controlled alternative to a prospective Hughes agreement. GE executives argued that through its telesatellite, cable interests could tie up programing in order to make it difficult for the Hughes DBS system to attract viewers.

In the context of these activities, Congress passed the Satellite Home Viewer Act in October 1988. This legislation created a compulsory copyright license authorizing the retransmission of broadcast signals – including so-called superstations and network transmissions – to the owners of home satellite reception equipment.[30] For the first time in the United States, a DBS venture theoretically could provide programing *without* the consent of cable companies and other programers. However, the compulsory license provision also enabled cable companies to distribute the same programing, thereby extending the scope and attractiveness of their already established services. Nevertheless, in May 1989, a preliminary agreement was signed between cable companies and GE for the use of the K-1 satellite. K-Prime/Primestar officials agreed to provide a national DBS service that would be tailored to curtail the development of emerging DBS operators and, through this service, provide a non-competitive programing package relative to the cable interests represented in the partnership.

Related to these practices, in 1992 Congress countered the anticompetitive behavior of cable operators. Due in part to the activism of the National League of Cities and other 'citizen's groups,' vaguely justified cable rate increases since the 1984 liberalisation, and mounting complaints regarding poor or inadequate service, Congress was compelled to re-regulate 'free market' activities. As a result of the 1992 Cable Regulation Act, the FCC has imposed 'reasonable access' rules on cable operators requiring cable-controlled programing to be made available to DBS broadcasters. In April 1993, the Commission placed the burden of proof onto the shoulders of cable programers in legal conflicts in which access issues arise.

Like the US cable television industry, television and radio broadcasters have opposed DBS. In general, the National Association of Broadcasters has been anxious about more competition. One of the core arguments used by the NAB against DBS is its potential threat to the economic viability of local stations and network affiliates. Over-the-air broadcasters believe that because of the low costs involved in reaching *each* consumer through DBS, direct broadcasters pose a direct threat to their audience share.

The Motion Picture Association of America (MPAA), representing much of the US film and television production sector (namely, Hollywood), has mixed views on DBS. As Fritz Attaway of the MPAA explains:

> We are always looking for new outlets for our programming. However, we have to factor in the effect that new outlets have on existing markets. We would not want the DBS system in Hong Kong [Star TV], for instance, to result in a severe decrease in theatrical attendance because we [now] make more money per viewer in theaters than we do on television. Similarly, we would not want DBS to produce a major adverse affect on home videos because again we [now] make more money per viewer on video than television. Television is really the last in the sequence of exploitation.... So one has to be careful, when you're in the business of marketing ... [our] product that the new outlets don't cannabalise the old.[31]

At least until direct broadcasters garner enough spending power to make their delivery systems at least as profitable as theaters and videotape rentals, the MPAA remains reluctant to embrace DBS. In the United States, existing subscription movie channels, such as HBO, usually do not broadcast films until most theater and video rental revenues have been tapped. With DBS and the development of cable pay-per-view services, Attaway explains that 'one of the big marketing questions' facing MPAA members is 'what's going to happen to the existing home video market if films are released on pay-per-view simultaneously with home videotape release?'[32]

As described above, the development of an 'open market' communications regime in the United States – featuring the relative retreat of behavioral regulation – has enabled established companies to consolidate their holdings and, when possible, undermine prospective competitors. As represented in the cable television industry's attempt to block DBS, the recent history of the domestic communications and information market again and again has featured such anticompetitive activities. The relative efficiencies of DBS systems impelled established cable operators to conspire against their introduction in the domestic market. In light of the transnational broadcasting capabilities of DBS, this conspiracy produced quite the opposite of what the cultural imperialism paradigm might anticipate: the cable companies actively worked to prevent the development of expanding North American markets for *their* programing and, in effect, more general corporate promotions. While the long-term establishment of such transnational markets mostly benefiting US-based TNCs may well come about, the case of DBS again raises the need for more precise theorizations and detailed research. American state structures took many years to redress these anti-competitive activities, and FCC efforts to encourage DBS developments using a policy approach almost totally absent of behavioral regulation proved to be an illusory remedy.


## 7.2   DBS, DIGITALIZATION AND HDTV

The two corporations most active in DBS developments – General Motors (GM) (through its subsidiary Hughes Communications) and News Corporation International – also control a range of related information-based commodity interests. In 1984, General Motors, in pursuing a policy of restructuring and corporate 'rationalization' involving wage-restraint packages, worker lay-offs and plant relocations, purchased the world's largest data-processing company, Electronic Data Systems, for $2.5 billion. One year later it bought Hughes Aircraft for $5 billion. GM's long-term rationale for this entry into communications and information-based activities involved the formation of a fully integrated intra-corporate computerized information system with the capability of instantaneously linking internationally segmented factory floors with head office. Beyond its attempts at setting a world standard for such technologies, GM, like many other TNCs, applied these resources in efforts to reduce day-to-day production costs (including labor costs through the use of computers and factory robotics), to increase the efficiency and flexibility of its diverse international operations, and to channel its resources into producing and distributing a range of new information-based services.[33]

Through subsidiary Hughes Communications, with its established telesatellite capabilities, and its historic leadership in promoting direct broadcast technologies in the United States, GM has established DirecTV, North America's first high-power DBS system. As noted above, its 150–channel capability has an advantage over many established cable distributors in that it can already provide digitalized services to its customers (whereas terrestrial systems will have this capability no sooner than the end of the 1990s).[34] This provides GM with a platform from which to provide the North American market with a broad range of information-based services – including those from its database and financial services subsidiaries – as well as a continental medium through which its manufacturing interests can be promoted.[35]

Recognizing the potential transformative influence that a DBS system can have on consumer demand and cultural practices in relatively less developed regions, in 1993 News Corp. paid US $525 million for a controlling interest in a Hong Kong-based, low-power DBS system called Star TV. This investment was remarkable in that Star TV itself projected that its losses would reach US $200 million by 1995 and that the first year of profit would not come until at least 2001. Following an expensive upgrading of Star TV equipment – including the launch of more powerful satellites and the application of signal compression technologies – News Corp. officials believe that the potential of Star TV to reach fifty-five Asian and Middle Eastern countries justifies these expenditures. The most important of these are India and the People's Republic of China (PRC).[36]

In the PRC, while state officials have banned the direct reception of Star TV signals, variations in the local application of the ban and the impracticality of tracking down privately held reception dishes have contributed to the decision to develop and promote multipurpose cable systems throughout the country.[37] As of 1993, an estimated 4.8 million Chinese households already received Star TV broadcasts, while reception units are being sold to PRC citizens at a rate of over 10,000 each month. Having recognized the general impracticality of controlling the direct reception of DBS transmissions, state officials have negotiated with News Corp. executives to use selected Star TV programing on these cable systems in order to exercise some degree of censorship. As Star TV transmission upgrades increase the number of channels available using smaller and more discrete household reception units, the emerging PRC 'middle class' may well turn away from these state-controlled systems and, in effect, will become increasingly discriminating consumers. In the words of Dennis Brownlee, an executive with United States Satellite Broadcasting (USSB) – another North American DBS broadcaster – DBS investors are banking on the belief that 'people want ... and will pay for programming that is more personally meaningful.'[38]

Simon Murray, a former Managing Director of Star TV, has asked 'What can governments do anyway? If people want to put up dishes, what can the government do to stop them?'[39] Senior US Commerce Department official Jean Pruitt also recognizes this. According to Pruitt, the significance of DBS directly involves its impact on recasting the regulatory capacities of even the most totalitarian of nation states:

> As a distributor of a good or service, the thing you most want is local support. As soon as you've got some people using your product or making money off your product you are almost free [*sic*] .... The thing about DBS [receivers]...is they are ubiquitous .... No one really knows you're doing it [receiving transmissions] until after the fact.[40]

The Star TV acquisition can best be understood in terms of the European and North American activities of News Corp. in relation to more general digital technology developments. News Corp. subsidiary News Datacom owns the VideoCrypt signal encryption (or 'scrambling') technology. Through its adoption by the dominant direct broadcasting system in Europe – Astra – and the first high-power North American system – DirecTV – VideoCrypt is on the verge of becoming the *de facto* global DBS encryption standard. More significantly, News Corp. continues to upgrade both Star TV and its European DBS interests (most notably BSkyB) to accommodate compressed digitalized signals utilizing the upgraded version of Video-Crypt already used by DirecTV. These investments will substantially increase the quantity and quality of Asian and European transmissions and will enable News Corp. to service transnational markets with its international publishing, television and film holdings, downloaded from its satellites to consumers using smaller and smaller reception dishes. In the PRC alone, following its equipment upgrade, News Corp. anticipates that Star TV video services will be watched by 185 million Chinese households by 2003. In sum, through DBS, News

Corp. has positioned itself as a core agent in digital information highway constructions involving the development of mass and specialized consumer markets on a global scale.[41]

Through compression, digital technologies will continue to reduce the bandwidth required for the transmission of video and other signals. Digitalization also will lower production costs through the use of computer-based production equipment. Over the next twenty years or so, digital technology will give television the potential to become the centerpiece of middle-class, day-to-day household communication *and* economic activities. With this in mind, there is little doubt that in the late 1990s DBS constitutes the ideal medium for the *introduction* of digital high-definition television receivers. While most DBS systems already have the capacity to transmit digitalized high definition television (HDTV) signals, most terrestrial over-the-air and cable-based services still require costly upgrades in order to participate.[42]

In sum, digitally compressed transmissions constitute catalysts in larger efforts to transform the very status of the television receiver. From its established role as an entertainment and information medium into *the* household communication centerpiece, HDTV may constitute, in the words of Vincent Porter, 'the locomotive for an entire industrial system, which not only keeps the programme makers in business and gives politicians a platform for their views, but . . . also keeps afloat the consumer electronics industry.'[43] A new generation of digital receivers employing HDTV technical standards not only will require the reconstruction of the technological infrastructures of the film and television industries, but its qualitative superiority to analogue-based receivers will potentially stimulate significant growth in the electronic services and equipment markets.

In the 1970s, DBS became a medium of great interest to a number of governments and corporations primarily due to its potential as a vehicle for introducing HDTV to mass consumers. It was in this context, and as a result of Japanese DBS-delivered HDTV experiments, that the US Academy of Engineering recommended that NASA re-establish its direct funding for research involving telesatellite technologies.[44] The digitalization of communications and its far-reaching economic and general cultural-power potentials were cited by the Bortnick Congressional study as a core reason for the US government to promote advances in DBS.[45] Also, as the Department of Commerce recognized five years later, European states and private sector interests understood DBS to constitute the ideal vehicle through which digital services (including HDTV) could be introduced on a mass scale.[46] All in all, the most lucrative long-term pay-off involving DBS may involve its application in efforts to establish international HDTV markets as a means of generating a vast range of spin-off hardware and software opportunities.

Television sets produced by Dutch-based company Philips and French-based Thomson (and their subsidiaries) together account for over one-third of the world TV monitor market and about two-thirds of the West European market.[47] In order, at the very least, to preserve this European market share relative to prospective Japanese and US HDTV equipment manufacturers, Philips and Thomson pressed EC officials to impose on member states an *independent* European HDTV standard. In 1991 the European Commission responded and directed DBS operators, manufacturers of relatively large-screen television sets, DBS dish makers and cable television systems to institute a single transmission standard called D2–MAC.

Remarkably, this decision was adopted without consultations with relevant consumer associations nor any consideration as to how broadcasters and viewers were to pay for the adaptation. It soon became apparent that the MAC Directive was impractical. A number of modifications were made.[48] Commercial telesatellite systems, such as Astra, were allowed to continue their transmissions using the PAL standard. The D2–MAC standard would be introduced over a five-year period through simulcasts with the financial assistance of an EC subsidy of more than $500 million. However, some of the largest terrestrial broadcasters in Europe began developing advanced PAL-compatible systems that would accommodate standard and wide-screen ('quasi-HDTV') transmissions without exceeding current terrestrial bandwidth allocations. The French government, in the meantime, maintained that its broadcasters and telesatellite operators should use the domestic SECAM system.

In the face of these developments, the European Union has shown itself largely incapable of redressing the concerns of competitive European corporate and national interests. It now appears that any successful HDTV system must be capable of receiving D2–MAC, PAL-Plus *and* SECAM transmissions. Moreover, these various transmission standards will have to be encrypted and decoded involving the continent-wide coordination of billing facilities. These developments will require extraordinary private sector investments and levels of cooperation. The EU, given its limited financial resources, is unlikely to provide for more than a fraction of these costs. Corporations and, indirectly, home consumers, therefore will almost certainly be European HDTV's primary financiers. A study conducted by financial consultants Coopers and Lybrand, however, estimates that the cost of upgrading the equipment now already used by European consumers to enable them to receive a universal European D2–MAC signal would be in excess of $20 billion from 1993 to 2001.[49] Moreover, to view a high-definition signal, the initial price for a receiver will be approximately $4,000.[50]

At the end of 1992, a $1 billion EC 'action plan' to promote MAC-based HDTV was blocked by the British and Dutch governments. Philips, Europe's largest prospective manufacturer of HDTV receivers, subsequently announced that it would not proceed with its MAC-compatible production plans,[51] The subsequent European action from requiring both medium-and high-power DBS systems to adopt the D2–MAC standard now is complete and, in part, it illustrates the market dominance of the Astra system. The European private sector thus has been left to establish a *de facto* continental DBS transmission standard, rendering the MAC Directive industrial policy stillborn.

Unlike the European Union, formative commercial US HDTV developments have been decentralized to such an extent that the FCC refused even to consider an HDTV standards policy until 1988. After twenty-five years of research and development and approximately $500 million in investment, Japanese interests already have initiated analogue HDTV services over NHK's DBS system. In the United States, on the other hand, private sector expenditures, up until 1991, totaled no more than $20 million and, until 1997, HDTV technical standards remained unresolved.[52]

American public sector officials have taken a wait-and-see approach to HDTV standards. Of special concern to the FCC were questions regarding the compatibility of different HDTV systems to existing NTSC television broadcasting standards and the financial costs associated with their industry-wide implementation. US delays have been most directly influenced by the NAB and its members who see HDTV as a threat to the ongoing viability of their holdings. This is the result of HDTV's need for large amounts of bandwidth – capacities now available over most DBS systems and soon to become plentiful through fiber-optic cabling. As a result of the insistence of NAB officials that any prospective HDTV standard must be NTSC-compatible, this fundamental NTSC-compatibility requirement dominated all US HDTV proposals.

US-based telephone companies – already most advanced in fiber-cabling efforts and in a strong financial position relative to cable television operators – have been one of HDTV's most active proponents. They generally consider HDTV to be an important component of their future participation in developments of the mass market information highway and have pressed the FCC to adopt a digital standard (as opposed to established Japanese analogue HDTV technologies) in order to maximize the prospective compatibility of the US system with a range of anticipated digital services. Other key agents promoting a digital standard are US consumer electronics manufacturers hoping to reclaim a significant share of the domestic and world industry.[53]

In contrast to the Europeans, in 1987 the FCC created an Advisory Committee on Advanced Television Service (better known publicly as the 'HDTV Blue Ribbon Committee'), involving representatives from .all large-scale private sector HDTV and related interests. Its mandate was to develop a general consensus on HDTV standards that the FCC could use as the basis for its standards decision. Because of the likelihood that such deliberations would take a good amount of time, it was commonly feared that the lead already established by Japanese-based TNCs (and their acquisition of US film, video and audio production facilities and 'libraries') would result in a *de facto* foreign-based world HDTV standard. Staggering estimates were placed on potential economic losses if this were to be allowed to take place. From 1990–2010, for example, cumulative direct and indirect job losses of 1.5 million and a trade deficit over US $2 trillion were forecast. On the other hand, the economic impact resulting from the successful development of a US-based HDTV system was seen to be extremely positive.[54]

In 1993, after twenty-three different HDTV system proposals were submitted to the FCC, proponents of an all-digital system agreed to form what has been called a 'grand alliance.' AT&T executives consented to work with other corporate interests to create a single prototype that US officials believe could become the *de facto* world HDTV standard. As a result of this collaboration, grand alliance participants hope to avoid the costs and delays stemming from uncoordinated research and development efforts, lengthy FCC hearings and subsequent court challenges to Commission decisions. The first digital US HDTV sets now are scheduled for production in 1997 or 1998 at a retail price no more than US $1,000 above comparable large-screen NTSC sets. In order to facilitate the compatibility of

HDTV with existing computer monitors, the alliance is committed to a standard that uses a process called 'progressive scanning.' In addition, the US HDTV receivers will be 'smart sets,' in the sense that they will automatically interpret an incoming signal to be either NTSC or the new standard and thus able to display either transmission.[55]

Although this example of the HDTV policy process illustrates the overarching influence of *status quo* corporate interests in US decision-making, and the time delays involved in developing any kind of private sector consensus before undertaking such major initiatives, it is important to note that the positive outlook now held by US interests in relation to developments in digital technology has directly involved the structural conditions through which US communication policy activities take place. Whereas they were publicly promoted as the positive outcome of 'letting the free market decide,' alternatively it can be argued that the historical anti-competitive activities of cable television operators through their control over US programing constituted an essential pre-condition preventing Japanese corporate interests (such as Sony) from dominating American HDTV developments. Arguably, had early DBS systems been allowed to compete, US HDTV would be undergoing a much different history. Given the underdevelopment of compression technologies in the 1980s, US DBS operators could well have provided HDTV-type services (as many had planned) and might have developed a far larger market for special events than now exist in order to stimulate sales. Japanese-based corporations might well have subsidized a fledgling HDTV (NTSC-compatible) US monitor market in order to establish a *de facto* standard. Given these developments, the FCC's wait-and-see policy, largely a result of the structural inability of the American state to lead such a development (itself publicly justified by a general faith in 'market forces'), could have produced disastrous consequences for many US-based TNCs now hoping to use a digital HDTV standard to reclaim a large portion of the home electronics market. Instead, through the launch of DirecTV, the United States has taken advantage of its late start and is now home to the first fully digitalized high-power DBS system.[56]

Through digitalization, the new HDTV standard, free trade, DBS and the Telecommunications Act, a number of corporations are positioning themselves to implement virtually seamless national and potentially international communications and information service infrastructures. Large-scale corporations (like Citicorp, as discussed earlier), seeking the one-stop services offered by prospective winners of this race to lead information highway developments, may well use their economic clout to compel similarly seamless offerings to be extended to their international operations. Related to this pressure, AT&T, for instance, will probably intensify its push for further overseas liberalization reforms, using not just the WTO but also the lobbying efforts of executives and neo-classical economists in the pay of foreign businesses who also desire these services. Those US corporations that are slow or unsuccessful will be compelled to look overseas for significant growth opportunities. For example, if or when RBOCs reach ceilings in their efforts to establish comprehensive service networks, it is likely that vehicles such as the new WTO services provisions will be used to further pry open foreign markets. Cable television companies, facing new competitors in the United States and in need of financial support, may well look to foreign partnerships and pursue increasingly international agendas.

· As with most significant legislative reforms, the market opportunities released by the Telecommunications Act will generate corporate winners and losers. Short-term winners will include business interests located in large urban centers where markets are big and dense enough to justify the construction of truly competitive infrastructures. Communications and information corporations able to provide a seamless menu of services will probably dominate the domestic sector. The losers in this domestic struggle and those companies stymied by the winners' entrenched control in 'open' markets, may seek overseas partnerships and market opportunities. Likewise, the domestic winners – in order to service their largest and most valued clients – probably will pursue regulatory reforms in other countries in the image of the US Telecommunications Act. It is important to point out, however, that the international forces released by this domestic legislation at this historical juncture only serve to intensify what corporate interests already have been anticipating. In the next section, dynamics in the capitalist marketplace directly involving DBS are highlighted to illustrate this point.

## 7.3   DBS AND GLOBAL MARKETS

In addition to the re-regulation of cable television and the technological and economic advantages represented by DBS systems, both in themselves and in relation to more general digital applications, another development that stimulated investments in direct broadcasting has been the general economic slow-down of relatively developed economies that began in the late 1980s. This economic downturn, coinciding with the introduction of new television services, produced a general slowing in the annual growth of advertising expenditures.[57] As with other information-based corporations, the world's largest advertising and market research firms also were involved in new partnerships, mergers and takeovers.[58] The ongoing internationalization of a range of consumer goods and services has encouraged an increasing number of TNCs to use a single advertising-marketing firm in order to minimize expenses. Moreover, the increasing availability of mass-market transnational media, such as DBS, itself has encouraged TNCs to create and disseminate more and more advertising for a global audience. As Les Margulis of international advertising firm BBDO Worldwide explains, 'more and more clients in the USA and Europe are looking to develop products and advertising products over a broader geographic area.' Margulis explains that companies in the past, when marketing in Europe and Asia, 'may have had one product that they would advertise in thirteen different countries.' However, 'because of the various signals in Europe that are trans-geographic,' thanks in large part to DBS systems, there now exists greater flexibility in the option of funneling resources into a far smaller number of distribution outlets. 'Clients,' explains Margulis, 'are looking to save money, to reach the audience with less work.'[59] Comparing this emerging perspective 'with the old days,' he explains the activities of one of his clients – Gillette:

> Gillette used to have marketing groups in each of the countries [in which it sold its products] .... They would do their own manufacturing, do their own distribution.... You had to produce different ads. Do you know how much it costs to produce an ad of that quality, times twelve? So now, they do it times one. All they do is put the voice track on a separate audio channel, they strip the voice track and drop down the local language. It doesn't cost a whole lot of money to do voice tracks, but it costs a whole lot of money to get a camera crew of twenty people to shoot [twelve different ads].[60]

To reduce costs further, a range of additional strategies are being pursued. One involves efforts to sell advertising and distribute promotional material across a coordinated range of mass-media outlets. In return for relatively large-scale commitments, advertisers pay lower rates than they would for multiple (and relatively fragmented) promotions. Corporate clients also receive opportunities to coordinate the timing and spatial organization of promotions better. International advertising and marketing firms, because they are able to accommodate globalized multi-media strategies, are increasingly able to exclude smaller, less capable competitors from gaining a share of the transnational promotional environment. Strategic partnerships also have emerged between small and large companies in order to share in these promotions and to complement segments of the market not controlled by larger advertising-marketing TNCs.[61]

Another advantage of using a coordinated large-scale advertising-marketing firm involves the application of new communication technologies. Marketing efficiency – reaching *only* those consumers who are potential buyers of the product or service – is being refined through the use of interactive technologies and electronic databases. Marketing efficiency now involves the ability to anticipate the day-to-day movements and activities of consumers, 'following them through the course of their day as they turn to different sources for news and entertainment.'[62] According to Keith L. Reinhard, the Chairman and Chief Executive Officer of DDB Needham Worldwide, the result is that

> We are no longer thinking media form or media vehicles until we have tracked the target consumer. We no longer think of print versus TV versus radio but, rather, in terms of how can we *combine* vehicles to which the consumer is extremely loyal in some sensible consumer pattern.[63]

An example of this approach is Time Warner's practice of linking its database information on consumer interests and preferences with high-speed printing and binding technologies. Individualized advertisements are incorporated into subscribers' magazines such as *Time, Sports Illustrated, People, Fortune, Life* and others. Companies such as Kraft Foods and General Motors now favor advertising-marketing firms that can effectively target consumers over a broad range of media outlets including DBS.[64] New technologies and a limited pool of advertising revenue also have led to a resurgence of direct marketing techniques and event promotions. Databases detailing customer preferences and activities have provided new options in efforts to market products and services more efficiently. Demographic and 'lifestyle' information can be applied to a range of synergistic strategies.

For example, the use of brand-name products in films can have a subtle but impressionistic effect on potential consumers. Companies utilize well-known products and personalities to create positive associations with apparently unrelated services or products. While so-called creative rights have long been for sale, recent developments constitute a marked expansion of these practices. The Domino's Pizza chain, for example, leased the right to use Teenage Mutant Ninja Turtles on their pizza boxes – a direct reference to the Turtles' favorite food.[65]

Also driving these developments is the highly competitive character of international advertising and marketing. According to Margulis:

> Most advertisers are quite conservative because it's their money, i.e. their jobs are on the line. They have to sell products. Clients are only interested [in]... what they can do over the next eighteen months.... You're either up or you're out.... Honest to God, they've got to move boxes of razors, or Pepsi, or something. They've got to move it now. That's why they have promotions and tie-ins.[66]

The general shift away from mass advertising toward direct program and event sponsorship is, according to Margulis, all about companies seeking to 'control the environment.' For TNCs in general, and globalized advertising-marketing firms in particular, DBS constitutes an opportunity to make 'more efficient buys' in the business of promoting consumption.[67]

These emerging practices have been significant for recently established transnational DBS systems because advertising and sponsorships constitute – at least initially – their most important sources of revenue. The reason for this is that the primary market for most new direct broadcasting services are not only the already 'developed' regions of the world but also urban centers in the 'less developed.' In the latter, for instance, where a 'middle class' is emerging, TNCs have supported and will probably continue to support DBS systems facilitating the dissemination of their mass consumer products. News Corp's Star TV is an example of this. By providing TNCs with significant discounts, Star TV's original owner, Hong Kong-based Hutchison Whampoa, secured approximately $300 million in advance funds. Explaining these commitments, one advertising executive asked, 'Can I walk away from this, because it might be massive?... If the price is right, the advertising buy is right.'[68]

The other kind of DBS system that is likely to succeed can be termed 'global narrowcasting.' A core reason for the slowdown in the growth of television advertising revenues has involved TV's tarnished image in relation to its past status as the ideal medium for reaching potential consumers. Television programers have responded by seeking better ways in which to satisfy corporate demands for more efficient buys. Unprecedented pressures have surfaced, compelling programers to guarantee the delivery of a specified group of targeted consumers to the advertiser-client. With the development of digital compression and increasingly secure encryption technologies, both DBS and cable-based systems constitute ideal vehicles for gathering large groups of consumers who share both common interests and consumer lifestyles. Especially in regions where cable infrastructures are relatively underdeveloped, DBS will enable broadcasters to charge high advertising fees in return for the delivery of an international audience that is both interested in luxury or specialized products and is financially able to purchase these types of goods and services.

A corporation that controls software but not the accompanying means of distribution is vulnerable in relation to competitors who control distribution. In the film, television and video sector, for instance, distribution has become *the* essential component of business activities. As New York investment analyst, Michael Garin, puts it, 'you produce to feed a distribution machine.'[69] Survival in emerging information-based production and distribution activities depends on the integration of all aspects of the production process, involving production, distribution *and* consumption. Increasingly, this involves the capacity to control the *entire* process through, for example, News Corp's control over the encryption technology used by Astra and its use on Star TV. In this case, News Corp has positioned itself to coordinate much of the world's DBS-based production, distribution and viewing activities. In 1996, News Corp entered into partnerships with the second largest telecommunications company in the world, British Telecom (second largest, next to AT&T, as a result of its 1996 acquisition of MCI). Also that year, News Corp signed agreements with European-based mass-media TNCs Canal Plus and Bertelsmann. These and other agreements aim to make Rupert Murdoch's News Corp *the* core agent through which others must deal when seeking access onto the digital information highway.[70] According to Vinton Bower, Vice President of HBO Satellite Services, through its tele-satellite, software and encryption holdings, News Corp has 'built a system that basically gives ... [it] a captive audience.'[71]

As with other technological applications, some DBS developments are being directly influenced by the labor-intensive character of some information-based activities. This, according to international media consultant and former BBC executive David Webster, involves 'squeezing more out of existing product.' In the broadcasting industry, for example, because labor costs tend to increase and equipment and per-viewer transmission costs, over time, tend to go down, 'what ever you're doing you've got to take down [or minimize] employing people.' For example, in order to produce an international around-the-clock television news service most efficiently, Webster explains that a corporation should *not*

> employ journalists to regurgitate the news – they cost a lot of money. Instead, the ideal method involves the real-time transmission of news programming from various sources over a satellite system and their retransmission to various regional DBS operators. These regional operators would then replace the commercials that come with the signal with advertising targeted at their particular markets. The real-time signal is then transmitted to homes and hotels through DBS. And while this would mean that the *MacNeil-Lehrer Report* [for example] would be broadcast in Paris at midnight instead of seven o'clock in the United States, the dedicated English-speaking viewer of *MacNeil-Lehrer* would have the option of videotaping the programming while he or she sleeps.[72]

Also, because of the multi-language track capability of digital DBS systems, French, German, Spanish and other sub-titles or voice-dubbing can be provided. Studio and equipment costs can be minimized through this method, and labor costs, for the most part, can be limited to translators (if necessary) and 'guys sitting in a control room snapping their fingers.'[73]

Initial DBS developments have promoted and will continue to promote the redistribution of established broadcasting services. Music Television (MTV) in North America, for instance, is now transmitted by satellite to Hong Kong where modifications are made involving little more than the replacement of US with Asian-based advertising. On the impact of DBS on the international production sector, joint production arrangements between US and European-based companies appears to be more a reflection of attempts to minimize risk than of the need to redress the prospective unused transmission capacities generated by new distribution platforms. The European Television Directive, for example, has stimulated a trend among some US and European production interests to invest in one another's markets. For many European companies, such as Canal Plus, the best way to access major Hollywood 'hits' is to invest in their production. For US-based producers, insuring access to European-based markets by becoming legally 'European,' and the recognition that local companies often are better able to produce programing that is attractive to local markets, have become important considerations. The desire to lower production costs and the high risks inherent in the film and television production sector more generally have led some US producers to enter into relatively complex production and distribution deals with foreign-based companies in order to share costs and guarantee access into preferred markets.[74]

As for the development of transnational television advertising through DBS, European television has experienced some accidental indications of the effectiveness of cross-border promotions. Advertisers who had not intended to sell products in a particular national market have experienced instances of unanticipated consumer demand as a result of incidental signal spillovers.[75] According to Eric Scheck, of BBDO Worldwide, transnational advertising has grown dramatically in recent years. As of 1992, it constituted 2 per cent of all advertising expenditures in Latin America and 10 per cent of expenditures in Europe (the latter totaling US $8 billion).[76] David Webster believes that there will be an ongoing movement toward globalized advertising

> because ... the homogenization of markets [is already taking place and] will [continue to] ... take place. Also, certain economies can be applied by the advertising business, [i.e.] using some of the same ingredients used in other markets, modifying some version rather than starting from square one. There is also the whole business of satellite signals ... [which is already] changing the geography of existing markets.[77]

Les Margulis surmises that the ongoing development of transnational communication and advertising outlets will compel 'broadcasters to pick programming that is attractive to a larger audience, so that Star[TV] has movies [and] has MTV ... [Transnational broadcasters must] appeal to audiences that are ... [culturally] different.'[78] Eric Scheck adds that what this will result in is the ongoing *but globalized* search for the cultural 'lowest common denominator.'[79] However, in the long-term, because compression technologies also compel narrowcasting developments, increased transnational competition will provide advertisers with significantly lower rates *and* will stimulate, on an international scale, the funneling of advertising dollars toward much more targeted marketing.[80]

Direct broadcasting activities increasingly will involve the coordination of a broad range of information-based interests, especially telephone, cable television, financial services and computer companies. As discussed, this is because digital DBS now constitutes the best means through which transnational customers can be reached and offered a range of integrated information services. DBS provides information commodity capitalists with an immediate and largely unmediated transnational reach. In light of the competitive pressures released by new technologies, free trade, and the Telecommunications Act, DBS, with complementary terrestrial infrastructures, now provides a select number of corporations with the capacity to establish full-service global information infrastructures. News Corporation International, Hughes Communications, British Telecom, AT&T and others, appear well positioned to take advantage of re-regulation. Their quest is to construct and dominate the media used by virtually all participants in the emerging information economy.

## 7.4  CONCLUSIONS

More so than even the AT&T divestiture, the US Telecommunications Act both reflects and modifies larger post-Fordist historical forces. The development of what Al Gore now calls a Global Information Infrastructure is the primary goal shaping these and related information economy developments. Beyond a model for 'freeing up' the private sector in efforts to construct the GII, the Telecommunications Act and other US initiatives will fuel its construction not despite its probable oligopolistic outcomes but more probably because of them. In the words of TCI's Senior Vice President of Communications Policy and Planning, Robert Thomson, 'the race to market ... began on February 8 when the telecommunications bill was passed.'[81]

In relation to the concerns of this book, among other things these developments underline how the cultural imperialism paradigm remains ill-equipped to articulate the complex character of inter-corporate activities and their relationship to the American state. As in the 1960s and 1970s – decades in which behavioral regulation was dominant – the 1980s and 1990s – (a period in which structural regulation reached its apogee) large-scale communications and information commodity corporations have sought growth and dominance with 'competition' as only the means to an end. The more essential forces compelling market liberalization in this sector have involved capitalists seeking better services at lower prices in order to accommodate more expansive and diversified global production, distribution and consumption activities. Together, this bloc of interests has emerged with the not unproblematic (but essential) assistance of the American state. The cultural imperialism paradigm, because it lacks a developed theory of such inter-corporate dynamics and their relationship to the more general structures involved in historical change, lacks the capacity to 'make sense' of the complexities of contemporary developments and the role of the United States.

At this juncture in history – one involving dynamic, technology-based developments and their disruptive implications – the disparate character of the American state has provided US-based capital with unanticipated advantages. The inability of a single communication policy agent to take on a leadership position enabled the USTR to emerge as the *de facto* coordinator of US free flow efforts under the auspices of free trade. HDTV developments, because of the recent confluence of digitalization, DBS, and an enforceable free trade in services regime, constitute one concrete illustration of the distinct advantage held by US-based interests in the emerging information economy. Unlike European and Japanese efforts to challenge American interests, US-based companies resisted making significant HDTV commitments until industry leaders – especially AT&T and IBM – began to commit themselves to an integrated digital technology future. Quite unlike American state agencies, both the EC and Japan attempted to orchestrate a HDTV head-start without the compliance of key US interests. Beyond the obvious point about the economic dominance of US corporations in information-based commodity activities *in toto* (probably *the* key consideration from a perspective of cultural imperialism), what is significant is the fact that attempts by some foreign states and corporations to avoid an emulation of US HDTV developments for the most part have failed. Core international policy developments and key technological practices are being *generated in or mediated through* the United States. Information economy developments thus are not 'globally driven.' Nor are they reducible to the somehow coordinated orchestrations of US interests.

For the most part, while European HDTV policies, for instance, have been directly linked to the economic interests of 'national champions,' private sector developments in the United States will continue to define the contextual parameters in which European, Japanese and other national and regional interests are pursued. If consent constitutes an essential component of hegemonic order, the ascendancy of global information-based commodity activities, accommodated through free trade, raises at least the potential for a revived but different form of *Pax Americana.*

## NOTES

1    Jill Hills, *The Democracy Gap* (Greenwood Press, 1991) pp. 57–60.
2    Bortnick, 'International Telecommunications and Information Policy,' US Senate, Committee on Foreign Affairs, 1983, p. 13.
3    *Ibid.*, p. 24.
4    US Department of Commerce, 'NTIA Telecom 2000,' p. 122.
5    Hills, *The Democracy Gap*, pp. 95–6.
6    For example, the standards for an RBOC to offer in-region, long-distance services include a number of pro-competitive requirements. The Act requires local telephone companies to sell telephone services to long-distance companies at wholesale prices (defined as the retail rate minus marketing, billing, collection and other costs). AT&T, for instance, now can buy local services from NYNEX, repackage them and then resell them to customers. Because this kind of 'competition' is based on different companies offering services based on virtually identical infrastructures, price and service quality improvements are unlikely to change significantly as a result of the Act.
7    Despite these restrictions, such long-distance opportunities represent a significant revenue base for the RBOCs. If Bell Atlantic, for instance, captured just 10% of the long-distance traffic originating in its region, it would generate approximately $10 billion in annual revenues. Pablo Galarza, 'Happy Independence Day,' *Financial World*, 165 (7), 41
8    TCI, the world's largest cable company, owed more than $10 billion as of September 1995. In 1994, TCI revenues totaled $4.9 billion. Cable, company debts generally are the results of the high costs of expansion activities in the 1980s (including mergers and acquisitions) and the rising costs of programing. Given the competitive necessity to install fiber-optic cables and related equipment, such debt burdens are likely to continue. Martin Peers, 'Regulatory Climate Improving for Cable Giant,' *Atlanta Constitution* (31 August 1995) p. F4.
9    Catherine Arnst, 'The Coming Telescramble,' *Business Week*, 3470 (8 April 1996) 65.

188     Communication, Commerce and Power

10   National Cable Television Association, 'Cable Television Develop-
     ments' (Washington, DC: NCTA Research & Policy Department, May
     1992), pp. 2–A, 8–A and 14–A.
11   Ibid., pp. 2A, 6A and 8A.
12   See, Kevin Pearce, 'The World Is My Franchise,' Channels (3 December,
     1990) 30 and National Cable Television Association, 'Facts at a Glance:
     International Cable' (Washington, DC: NCTA Research & Policy
     Department, March 1991), p. 4.
13   One estimate of the relative costs of a DBS system's delivery of the same
     number of channels as a cable system calculates that the overhead costs
     for each subscriber reached will fall far more rapidly for DBS than for
     cable as total numbers increase. While the physical differences between
     DBS and cable will mean higher costs in one area relative to another
     (for example, the maintenance costs of cable lines are much greater than
     those associated with satellite monitoring), it can be assumed that DBS
     and cable systems involve similar administrative and management costs.
     Leland L. Johnson and Deborah R. Castleman, Direct Broadcast Satel-
     lites: A Competitive Alternative to Cable Television? (Santa Monica,
     CA.: Rand Corporation, 1991), p. 25.
14   Further discussion on the relative positions of DBS and cable can be
     found in ibid, pp. 31–3.
15   Calculation based on figures in ibid., p. 17.
16   'Is DBS Finally Here? Stanley Hubbard Thinks So,' DBS Report, 26 (20
     July 1992) 5. In sum, according to Johnson and Castleman,

     the DBS operator has greater flexibility than does a wire-line operator.
     With the whole nation as a market, the DBS operator can draw from
     millions of potential subscribers. Unlike the case of wireline, the DBS
     operator does not need a large minimum penetration level in any given
     community to break even. Rather, the challenge is to aggregate enough
     subscribers across the nation to cover total cost.' Johnson and Castle-
     man, Direct Broadcast Satellites, p. 33.

17   'Special Report: Open Architecture DBS,' Video Technology News, 9 (7)
     (25 March 1996) n.p.
18   'Sky Money Machine' Cable and Satellite Europe, 154 (October 1996) 12
     and 14; and 'Marketplace News,' Cable and Satellite Europe, 146 (Feb-
     ruary 1996) 52.
19   Paul Barker, 'Double Illumination,' Cable and Satellite Europe, 151
     (July 1996) 25–6; and 'Quarterly Connections,' Cable and Satellite Eur-
     ope, 153 (September 1996) 50.
20   Jim McConville, 'DBS at Top of Murdoch Wish List,' Broadcasting &
     Cable, 126 (15) (8 April 1996) 16; Harry A. Jessell, 'Going for It in
     DBS,' Broadcasting & Cable, 126 (19) (29 April 1996) 6; 'DBS Providers
     to Eclipse Cable in Multichannel Future,' Video Technology News, 9 (9)
     (22 April 1996) n.p.; 'PanAmSat Likely Will Attract a Host of Aero-
     space, Telco Suitors,' Satellite News, 19 (15) (8 April 1996) n.p.
21   The parent company of New Vision is Newhouse Broadcasting Cor-
     poration.

22    United Artists K-1 Investments, Inc. is a wholly owned subsidiary of TCI.
23    In November 1991, Viacom initiated its withdrawal from the Primestar Partnership.
24    *State of New York v. Primestar Partners LP* Complaint 93 Civ. No.3868, p. 2.
25    *Ibid.*, p. 17.
26    *Ibid.* As of 1991, the defendants held equity interests in fourteen of the twenty largest programing services, including the country's most and third-most subscribed pay networks HBO and Cinemax (owned by Time Warner), and the second and fifth most subscribed pay services, Showtime and The Movie Channel (owned by Viacom).
27    *Ibid.*, p. 19.
28    *Ibid.*, p. 21
29    *Ibid*, p. 22. In 1990, the defendants, through Tempo, also sought to acquire two other DBS applicants – Direct Broadcast Satellite Corporation and DirectSat Corporation.
30    This legislation was promoted by copyright owners demanding compensation for the retransmission by satellite companies of programing sent to cable companies for the latter's exclusive redistribution. The resulting Act legalized these unsolicited retransmissions but compelled the satellite companies to pay fees to copyright owners.
31    Interview with Fritz Attaway.
32    These concerns, says Attaway, have slowed the growth of pay-per-view services. *Ibid.*
33    Karl P. Sauvant, *International Transactions in Services* (Boulder, Col.: Westview Press, 1986) pp. 88–9. Also, interview with John McKee.
34    Cynthia Ritchie, 'Prime Focus: DirecTV,' *Cable and Satellite Europe* 116 (August 1993) 30.
35    Interview with John McKee.
36    See Simon Twiston Davies, 'Mandarin Will Be Plum,' *Cable and Satellite Europe*, 117 (September 1993) 20–1 In India, as of 1993, Star TV programs and ads primarily are targeted at upper-middle class consumers who receive signals directly or through one of approximately 14,000 private local cable operators. Star TV signals are entering Indian homes at a growth rate of 10,000 *each day.* As of 1996, approximately 11 million households subscribed to Star TV services throughout its footprint area. Goldman Sachs estimates that by the year 2000, this number will increase to 60 million. Asoka Raina, 'Star-struck,' *Cable and Satellite Europe*, 112 (April 1993) 42 and 44; and 'Hanging on a Brighter Star,' *Cable and Satellite Europe*, 150 (June 1996) 80.
37    Joseph Man Chan, 'Media Internationalization in China: Processes and Tensions,' *Journal of Communication*, 44 (3) (Summer 1994) 82.
38    Brownlee quoted in Scott Chase, 'Horses for Courses,' *Cable and Satellite Europe*, 109 (January 1993) 30.
39    Murray quoted in Margaret Scott, 'Dishing the Rules,' *Far Eastern Economic Review*, 148 (24) (14 June 1990) 35.
40    Interview with Jean Pruitt.

41    Barry Flynn, 'The Scramble for Europe,' *Cable and Satellite Europe*, 118 (October 1993) 48. Joseph Man Chan, 'National Responses and Accessibility to Star TV in Asia,' *Journal of Communication*, 44 (3) (Summer 1994) 120.

42    A study by the Columbia Broadcasting System (CBS) predicts a conversion time of at least five years, costing local broadcast stations at least $5 million each. Johnson and Castleman, *Direct Broadcast Satellites*, p. 36, fn.36. As at least one study recognizes, 'cable systems and broadcasting stations will provide only patchwork coverage for HDTV during its early years. Depending on the sales growth of HDTV receivers, the emergence of HDTV could provide an additional impetus to market penetration by DBS systems, and *vice versa*' (*ibid*, p. 36). Because HDTV television sets generally will have the built-in capacity to receive digital signals without the need for conversion equipment, the widespread adoption of DBS could itself become a core stimulant to its rapid deployment.

43    Vincent Porter, 'Film and Television in the Single European Market' in *Journal of Media Law & Practice*, 13 (1) (1992) 149.

44    Hills, *The Democracy Gap*, p. 99.

45    See Bortnick, 'International Telecommunications and Information Policy,' esp. p. 23.

46    US Department of Commerce, 'NTIA Telecom 2000,' pp. 278–80.

47    Vincent Porter, 'Film and Television in the Single European Market,' p. 149.

48    See 'Yes It Was a Fudge,' *Cable and Satellite Europe*, 92 (August 1991) 42. Also, Simon Baker, 'An Audible Sigh of Relief,' *Cable and Satellite Europe*, 98 (February 1992) 42.

49    Study cited in Porter, 'Film and Television in the Single European Market,' p. 150.

50    *Ibid.*

51    Philip Carse and Mark Shurmer, 'Why the US Standard Will Have the Clearest "Market Focus",' *InterMedia*, 21 (2) (March–April 1993) 31.

52    David J. Schaefer and David Atkin, 'An Analysis of Policy Options for High-Definition Television,' *Telecommunications Policy*, 15 (5) (October 1991) 412. It should be noted, however, that basic research underlying HDTV has been supported by the US state indirectly through Cold War military research allocations to private sector interests. President Bush's budget in 1990 allocated $30 million directly to HDTV research through the National Science Foundation. Additional funds have been allocated through the Defense Advanced Research Project Agency (DARPA) which is administered by the DoD. See Jarice Hanson, Thomas J. Conroy and David Donnelly, 'Initiatives and Ownership, HDTV and the Influence of Corporatism in the United States,' *Communication Research*, 19 (6) (December 1992) 810–11.

53    Schaefer and Atkin, 'An Analysis of Policy Options for High-Definition Television,' p. 411.

54    Various figures based on a range of assumptions are provided in Robert B. Cohen and Kenneth Donow, *Telecommunications Policy, High Definition Television, and US Competitiveness* (Washington, DC: Economic

Policy Institute, 1989). Cohen and Donow argue that the losses noted above are based on the prospective impact of the convergence of tele-communication and computer technologies utilizing HDTV-type systems over future fiber-based integrated broadband networks. See esp. pp. 30–42.

55 The alliance also is committed to using square pixels on screens which, like the progressive scanning process, is designed to accommodate existing computer standards. John Abel, the Vice President of Operations for the NAB, commented that 'The computer industry appears to have gotten more out of this than the broadcasting industry did.' Abel quoted in Sean Scully, 'The "Grand Alliance" Becomes Reality,' *Broadcasting & Cable*, 123 (22) (31 May 1993) 59–60.

56 According to Washington-based communications consultant and former Comsat executive, Michael Alpert, this 'will lead to HDTV.' Given these structural *and* incidental developments, a 'specific policy on HDTV is [not] needed [in the United States] since industry is doing it.' Interview with Alpert.

57 Advertiser-financed media, such as television broadcasting, had until this time enjoyed annual advertising price increases of up to 15%. Interview with Jonathan Levy.

58 See Armand Mattelart, *Advertising International, The Privatisation of Public Space* (London: Routledge, 1991).

59 Personal interview with Les Margulis, International Media Director, BBDO Worldwide, 21 April 1993, New York City.

60 *Ibid.*

61 Joseph Turow, 'The Organizational Underpinnings of Contemporary Media Conglomerates,' *Communication Research*, 19 (6) (December 1992) 692.

62 *Ibid.*

63 Reinhard quoted in *ibid.*, pp. 692–3 (emphasis added).

64 Turow, 'The Organizational Underpinnings of Contemporary Media Conglomerates,' pp. 692–3.

65 Domino's Pizza also was visually referenced once in the film *Teenage Mutant Ninja Turtles*. This motion picture also had references to 17 other brand names including the 'Burger King Whopper,' 'Diet Pepsi,' 'Mountain Dew' soda, 'Kodak' film; 'Turtle Wax', and another Disney film called *Critters*. Other US productions of 1990 employing brand-name references include *Ghost* (sixteen references including 'Reebok,' 'Ivory Soap,' 'Pall Mall' cigarettes, 'VO' liquor, 'Tide' detergent); *Pretty Woman* (eighteen references including the 'Lotus Esprit' automobile, 'Coca-Cola,' 'Miller' beer, 'Evian' water); *Home Alone* (thirty-one references including 'American Airlines', 'Crunch Tators' snack foods, 'Dodge' van, 'Right Guard' deodorant, 'Brut' cologne, 'Aqua Fresh' toothpaste, 'Pampers' diapers); and *Total Recall* (twenty-eight references including 'Hilton' hotels, 'Pepsi,' 'Coca-Cola,' 'Bicardi' rum, 'Kodak,' 'Sony,' 'Coors' beer, 'Jack in the Box' restaurants). Janet Wasko, Mark Phillips and Chris Purdie, 'Hollywood Meets Madison Avenue: the Commercialization of US Films' in *Media, Culture and Society*, 15 (2) (April 1993) pp. 290–1, Appendix.

66    Interview with Les Margulis.
67    *Ibid.*
68    See Michael Westlake, 'Reach for the Stars,' *Far Eastern Economic Review*, 151 (22) (30 May 1991) 61.
69    Garin quoted in Geoffry Foisie, 'Banking on Syndication,' *Broadcasting* (21 January 1992) 51.
70    Eleonora Zamparutti and Piero Muscara, 'Code Red,' *Cable and Satellite Europe*, 149 (May 1996) 42, 44 and 45, and Paul Barker, 'A Meeting of Minds,' *Cable and Satellite Europe*, 150 (June 1996) 4.
71    Personal interview with Vinton Bower, Vice President HBO Satellite Services, 23 April 1993, New York City.
72    Personal interview with David Webster, International Communications Consultant and President of the Trans Atlantic Dialogue on European Broadcasting, 11 September 1992, Washington, DC.
73    *Ibid.*
74    Significantly, however, while US-based firms sold more than US $3.7 billion worth of film, television and video products to Europe in 1993, US-EC co-productions occupied only a small fraction of on-air television broadcasting time. In Germany, for example, while in 1993 35% of all television was made up of US productions, only another 1.2% were European-US co-productions. In Britain, these figures stood at 15% and 1.1%, and in France, 22% and 0.3%. Meredith Amdur, 'US Broadcasters Berate GATT,' *Broadcasting & Cable*, 123 (51) (20 December 1993) 14.
75    Interview with David Webster.
76    Personal interview with Eric Scheck, International Media Supervisor, BBDO Worldwide, 21 April 1993, New York City. Scheck was unable to provide an accurate time frame for this growth, but he estimated these figures have doubled over the past five years. The figures he cites are from confidential BBDO studies.
77    Interview with Webster.
78    Interview with Margulis.
79    Interview with Eric Scheck.
80    Geoffrey Foisie, 'Banking on Syndication,' p. 56.
81    Thomson quoted in Noel Meyer, 'In Units We Trust,' *Cable and Satellite Europe*, 148 (April 1996) 74–5.

# 8 Conclusion: Communication, Culture and American Hegemony

Until recently, despite its status as a relatively ideal transnational broadcasting technology, proponents of DBS in the United States for the most part have been marginally positioned in relation to dominant corporate interests and the priorities of foreign policy officials. Instances of *status quo* information commodity corporations promoting direct broadcasting developments – such as Comsat's failed efforts in the early 1980s – are rare, whereas instances of other powerful interests working to suppress DBS developments – such as the efforts of the US cable television industry – are not. More generally, US foreign communication policy, historically uncoordinated and leaderless, in the 1980s became the target of an evolving private sector campaign to recast free flow legal efforts into trade-based services and intellectual property rights negotiations. The subsequent ascendancy of the USTR and its largely unanticipated role as a powerful and centrally positioned foreign communication policy agency has helped elevate both the status of information-based commodity interests and has itself successfully produced a *de facto* free flow of information regime through free trade.

Out of hegemonic crisis, US dominance in information-based commodity activities has emerged despite a general ignorance among American state policy makers regarding the sector's cultural-power implications. Decades of military-related research and development funding, a domestic market that has been the wealthiest in the world, and the presence of entrenched state agents that are relatively disparate – dominated by private interests and thus generally responsive to the policy priorities of powerful corporations – all constitute factors that have facilitated America's renewal.

The domestic liberalization of communication activities unintentionally compelled American telecommunications interests to promote US re-regulation models world-wide. Out of a foreign communication policy crisis came a remarkable domestic consensus in which the American state, quite incapable of deflecting such seemingly universal

193

demands, proceeded with the task of *reforming itself in order to reform the world*. The subsequent capacity of US-based corporations to dominate international information-based commodity developments and their direct and indirect potential to promote liberal and consumerist ideals overseas remain, however, according to the Assistant Secretary for Communications and Information in the Department of Commerce under the Reagan and Bush administrations, Janice Obuchowski, a 'somewhat fragmented [concept] among government agencies.' Nevertheless, this awareness appears to be increasing among 'key officials, such as those in the USTR.'[1]

American-based transnational corporations directly involved in information-based products and services, since the early 1980s, have promoted a shared assumption that communication technologies will facilitate the development of new economic opportunities leading to greater national wealth. Especially since the 1970s, virtually every sector of the international economy has been influenced by technological change directly involving convergence. Through the application of digital and compression technologies, a broad range of integration opportunities continue to develop, including the integration of different transmission media into a single mega-network; the integration of different telecommunications services into this network; the switching of voice with data with video over a single communications circuit, facilitating direct linkages between telephones, computers and video transmissions; and the conversion of messages from one system (or 'protocol') to others, enabling, for example, the integration of a range of communications standards.[2] Not only has direct broadcasting become a core component in this emerging digital mega-network, but the very presence of DBS – as a result of its use in establishing unprecedented transnational communication capabilities – itself is stimulating these developments.

Because the ideals of individualism, competition and equality under the law are to some degree promulgated through everyday interactions in the capitalist marketplace, the workplace, and through the ownership and use of household and portable 'personal' technologies, the atomistic world view of liberalism constitutes both a reflection of predominant conceptions of reality and day-to-day practices. Liberalism therefore reflects not only a particular kind of common sense, for many people it also constitutes, quite literally, 'the way it is.' Both its ongoing practice and conceptualization thus accommodate social fragmentation over mass organization – the latter constituting the precondition for the development of a widespread, sustainable and 'realistic' counter-hegemonic movement. As for the role of direct broadcasting in maintaining or extending a neo-liberal world order among non-elites, the promotion of mostly mass market products and services will dominate DBS information and entertainment transmissions, at least for the foreseeable future. New York-based international advertising executive Eric Scheck believes that DBS has played a significant role in the recent internationalization of US-dominated television and advertising activities:

> In the last five to seven years . . . we've gone from the US being principally the sole commercial market in television, with a few very small exceptions, to basically a worldwide commercial television [market]. . . . Governments are letting go of their control over the broadcasting medium . . . [and] a lot of it has to do with governments . . . [saying] 'we've given up trying to block the signals.'[3]

The scope, scale and dynamism of US information-based commodity activities have not discouraged the maintenance of a generally unco-ordinated and disparate state, and this, in relation to the pervasiveness of contemporary communication and information technology applications, has been a factor making the United States the central arbiter of world information economy developments. The positive implications for the United States of the successful Uruguay Round GATT on services and intellectual property underlines the point that *the new free trade consensus not only has been a US-mediated development but also, in effect, may well constitute the essential foundation for the economic and even hegemonic renewal of the United States*. The contemporary free flow of information 'consensus' is being fueled by this universalization of neo-liberal principles, the collapse of the Soviet Union and thus its potential support for alternative forms of international organization, and the implementation of DBS and other transnational and relatively 'personal' technologies. Again, in the context of these and other developments, *DBS now constitutes the technological wedge through which the construction of a transnational information highway can take place*. The WTO, for example, provides information economy capitalists with the international legal stability needed to make the required investments to construct a virtually seamless, world-wide communications infrastructure. Knowledge that the United States will probably lead retaliatory efforts against potentially uncooperative countries constitutes a crucial step forward for these

TNCs. Through the medium of DBS, in conjunction with established telecommunications links, and the use of sports, rock videos, sex, violence and perhaps even on-line gambling to attract mass transnational audiences to participate in the information economy, Al Gore's dream of a Global Information Infrastructure appears set to come true.

## 8.1  ASSESSING CULTURAL IMPERIALISM

Cultural imperialism is being exercised but not in the form postulated by most cultural imperialism theorists. Rather than primarily a systematic expression of capitalism or an outcome of elite-based structures and orchestrations, its expression largely has been defined by complex structures and mediations. In not recognizing this, Schiller, for one, now has replaced the American state with transnational capital as the core agent of this sub-set of imperialism. The institutionalization of the free flow of information has, as Schiller believed it would, entrenched the dominant position of mostly US-based corporations in late-twentieth-century information economy developments. However, in not articulating the processes and structural dynamics of this history, and in not explicitly recognizing the distinction between the American state as 'mediator' versus its role as an imperialistic 'orchestrator' or 'functionary,' the precise nature of cultural imperialism and its problematic and potentially contradictory features cannot be directly addressed.

Based on the research presented in this book, the cultural imperialism paradigm fails adequately to explicate intra-state and intercorporate conflicts. It does not clearly recognize the barriers and the related historically based policy-making structural biases that shape the day-to-day perspectives of public sector officials. Lastly, and perhaps most importantly, it is limited in its ability to theorize change. For example, on the Carter administration's formation of the IPDC, Schiller assessed American motivations as follows:

> [T]he US business system would secure world markets for its high-tech products and services, bind more closely than ever into its world-wide commercial system the balky nations of Africa, Asia, and Latin America, and neatest of all, in an ideological sense, convince the poor world that it was embarking on a course of economic improvement and national autonomy. All these benefits

to the transnational corporate order might be derived from persuading the least advantaged states to install and hook into the new electronic networks.[4]

Although these motivations and interests, at some level, are probably accurate, it conveys an 'America-equals-imperialist' and 'LDCs/UN-equals-anti-imperialist' generalization that itself requires much elaboration. Fundamentally, this perspective tends only to locate the agents of change in existing or potentially collectivist anti-*status quo* organizations, such as UNESCO. Without the analytical capacity to pin-point tensions and potential contradictions stemming from the peculiarities of more particular historical conditions or structural forms, the imperialist process – short of revolution – becomes virtually unalterable.

Beyond its empirical and theoretical limitations, this concentration on core–periphery relations itself can generate strategic problems. To assume that the NWICO, for example, represented a truly counter-hegemonic movement and that the LDCs supporting it were bullied or co-opted into their subsequent acceptance of a neo-liberal world order is naïve and ahistorical. Also, to view Third World leaders as champions of their publics in the struggle for social justice, rather than their roles in servicing the interests of domestic capitalists and state officials, too often mistakes public pronouncements for actual material interests and motivations. Rather than assuming free trade, World Bank support for telecommunications investments and the privatization of broadcasting services and many other developments to be the outcomes of the triumph of US or Northern interests over the South (which, at one level, they certainly are), an account of the material and structural changes that have taken place *in* LDCs would provide a more complex and accurate account. Of course this is not to say that some peripheral elites (and certainly some peripheral masses) have not been bullied or swept along in the sea of information economy and neo-liberal hype. It is to say, however, that to understand counter-hegemonic strategic options at any given place and time, an explicit analysis of the 'victims' of cultural imperialism is an important but neglected task. Ultimately, the emphasis found in the cultural imperialism paradigm on the assumed interests of the United States and capital in relation to the assumed interests of LDCs and 'the exploited' is analytically thin and, in itself, strategically unhelpful.

In relation to assumptions raised by some analysts working within the boundaries of the cultural imperialism paradigm, this book has directly challenged assertions that the American state functions in ways that instrumentally serve US information-based corporations. The DBS example underlines the often anti-competitive tendencies of most mass-media and related industry activities. This history illustrates that far from being universally instrumental, the US state at times has been dominated by some information-based corporations or sub-sectors at the expense of others. Moreover, the state is not the structurally or systemically homogeneous entity implied by Schiller. Instead, *the preceding chapters portray an American state that is itself usually uncoordinated and often characterized by intra-state conflict. Moreover, because the state exists and functions in a larger social-economic context, state activities are directly affected but not necessarily directly determined by non-state forces.*

Technological convergence, its widespread application, and related information economy developments together constitute one general example of a historical and widespread context in which state officials now operate. This contextual shift facilitated DBS developments in the United States, first through challenges to the AT&T and Comsat monopolies and later through efforts to redress the cable television industry's anti-DBS behavior in a 'competitive' neo-liberal environment. In order to understand the role of the American state in the development of the contemporary information economy, state structures, and the capacities held by public and private sector agents to act in relation to established interests and emerging demands, must all be assessed using a historically dynamic analysis.

This book has examined the role of the American state and US-based corporations, purposely not focusing on the cultural-power *effects* of US-based developments largely because the former has been neglected by critical analysts. While this itself substantiates the attention paid to the state in the present study, the findings of this history directly inform evaluations of cultural-power capacities and their relevancy in efforts to re-tool American hegemony. In recognizing the US state to be the complex mediator of international reforms facilitating ongoing information economy developments, the concept of US cultural imperialism remains a salient perspective despite its many problems. But again, such an analysis requires a detailed assessment of historical moments in relation to structural capacities and the social-economic forces shaping the interests and actions of key agents. In recognizing both the ongoing centrality of the American state in the international political economy and the opportunities and limitations furnished by its structural capacities, Schiller and others need not turn toward a vague conception of transnational capital as the new 'center' of cultural imperialism. Rather than a choice between the nation state or TNCs as *the* imperialist, a more nuanced and accurate approach would situate the American state as the complex mediator of a cultural imperialism characterized by the explicit and/or implicit promotion of consumerism and liberal ideals.

## 8.2 THE INTERNATIONALIZING STATE AND US HEGEMONY

Aspects of the work of Robert Cox and Gramscian international political economists can be used to develop the paradigm of cultural imperialism. The concept of hegemony, for instance, represents a process that involves the capacity to engage in and dominate institutional developments and, when necessary, control the form of mediated compromises. Cox elaborates that hegemony constitutes

a structure of values and understandings about the nature of order that permeates a whole system of states and non-state entities. In a hegemonic order these values and understandings are relatively stable and unquestioned. They appear to most actors as the natural order. Such a structure of meanings is underpinned by a structure of power, in which most probably one state is dominant but that state's dominance is not sufficient to create hegemony. *Hegemony derives from the dominant social strata of the dominant states in so far as these ways of doing and thinking have acquired the acquiescence of the dominant social strata of other states.*[5]

It is through predominant and far-reaching social-economic nodal points – such as organizations, international institutions and complex political-economic regimes – that hegemony is structurally expressed and potentially challenged. As elaborated above, the United States continues to act as the core mediator among capitalists and other domestic and international agents. As such, Schiller's recent emphasis on organizing the American working class – although obtuse given his argument that transnational forces now have taken charge of the cultural imperialism project – is a remarkably relevant suggestion. Given the centrality of the United States in this period of 'globalization,' the American state will continue to be a central site in which to organize both domestic and international priorities. But again, ongoing changes in the form in which states act as domestic–global mediators – and the increasingly porous qualities of the capitalist–nation state dichotomy (that is, the capacity of capital to act as 'good corporate citizens' *and/or* as mobile and flexible transnational actors) – problematizes even the theoretical status of US workers as ideal agents of 'progressive' reform. This caveat underlines not just the dialectical nature in which national and global forces affect one another, also it reflects the temporal immediacy and political-economic volatility accompanying late-twentieth-century communication and information developments – developments that the American state has aggressively pushed forward and must continually learn to live with.

As outlined in Chapter 2, what Cox calls the internationalization of the state involves tensions between global forces and national structures. As shown in this study, the American state has been restructured in ways that have prioritized international free flow of information reforms through mostly trade-related agencies. The complex forces at work have reflected and involved a realignment of dominant class relationships. The general competitive needs of corporate producers and consumers of information-based commodities now, for the most part, are being accommodated in the United States, international organizations, institutions and even LDCs. While the American state may be structurally disparate, it also is a complex institution characterized by historically constructed rigidities and policy-making biases. State structures can be dangerously inflexible in response to shifting needs and the changing make-up of dominant interests. Importantly, however, because these conditions are historically constructed, they are by no means unalterable.

The ups and downs of the American hegemonic project have been traced in this book through the capacities held by state officials to maintain or modify relevant international mediators – that is, the regimes, institutions and organizations mediating international relations – on behalf of mostly US-based interests. Long-standing efforts to counter prior-consent international legal regimes with free flow principles, for example, have constituted one of the core struggles waged by the United States. The relative decline of the United States, dating from the early 1970s, presented LDCs and others with opportunities to reform the existing world order through, for instance, the movement of various international institutions and organizations away from an American world view. Facing this crisis, in conjunction with the recognition that information-based commodity activities constitute America's most promising growth sector, rebellious (but not revolutionary) international organizations were contained or disassembled. In conjunction with this, American officials radically modified the very ground on which the free flow struggle was to take place and elevated it into the quest for free trade. During these years, the ITU was restructured to reflect the new 'realities' of international business and the GATT became the core nodal point through which neo-liberal reforms could be institutionalized and ideologically promulgated. By the mid–1990s, even UNESCO (with the United States remaining a non-member!) officially recognized the practical (if not legal) supremacy of the free flow of information.

Although Cox understands the state to act as a mediator in the internationalization process (and the contemporary role of the state in legitimizing the neo-liberal reordering of domestic and international relations),[6] elaborations of inter-corporate and intra-state capacities, structural disparities and outright conflicts are lacking. This is a result of his tendency to focus on complex capital–labour relationships rather than the organizational and institutional nodal points that directly shape these relations. But unlike the work of Schiller, for Cox, this has been a sin of research neglect rather than theoretical omission. While production and class relations are central to Cox's methodology, 'other factors enter into the formation or nonformation of real historical classes.' These, Cox explains, include 'agencies of collective action that can evoke and channel class consciousness.'[7] Thus, while Cox stresses capital-labour relations, these are understood to be dynamic and directly conditioned by organizations and institutions that mediate these relations. These mediations directly influence the intellectual capacities of human agents. The spatial and temporal integration of such relations constitute historical structures, structures, that are both constructed *and* usually resistant to deconstruction efforts. In these processes, Cox understands the state to be a central agent, consecrating dominant forms of production both institutionally and ideologically. 'How the state does this,' writes Cox, 'has to be explained because it in turn explains the structuring of power within society.'[8]

However, in Cox's *Production, Power, and World Order*, and in his subsequent work, the focus has been on macro-processes. The lack of research by Cox and other Gramscians on micro-processes – particularly those shaping American state mediations – has contributed to a view that the future holds few opportunities for the United States to construct a new hegemonic order. In analyzing US micro processes in the context of relatively macro (national and international) conditions, the potential for this kind of renewal can, I think, be identified. Due perhaps to a lack of detailed research on the nature of domestic US structures, and as a result of a recent tendency to privilege global forces over domestic, Cox and others have found it difficult to conceptualize this. Given that the history presented in this book reveals that the American state has acted as the mediator among and on behalf of mostly US-based corporations in international agencies involving their structural reform, *such attention to domestic structures and struggles not only remains analytically relevant, it is strategically essential.*

In response to the crisis in foreign communication policy of the 1980s, components of the American state were reformed in order to facilitate its mediation of more comprehensive efforts in global restructuring. In sum, the American state – through the ascendancy of trade – underwent reforms enabling it to service the political and legal needs of mostly transnational corporations and international business consumers directly involved in information economy developments. These modifications, in turn, altered aspects of US relations with transnational capital. Rather than viewing this in terms of an 'either/or' nation-state or global-capital dichotomy, an analytical emphasis on structures and media direct us toward a more sophisticated conceptualization. This is not to say that the American state, by 'freeing up' mostly US-based and other private sector interests to become increasingly transnational actors has not set in motion problematic tendencies involving, for example, the capacity of US-based corporations to become geographically decentralized and mobile in relation to their 'home' nation state. Rather than contradictions stemming from reduced state capabilities to influence capital, a focus on structures and media suggests that core contradictions will involve *the form* in which the United States relates to capital.[9]

While the dominant position of the United States in service sector activities has been greatly enhanced through the Uruguay Round GATT agreement and related international reforms, the doors that these have opened for US-based corporations, however, could presage problems for the American and, indeed, the international political economy. The globalization of information-based commodity activities – facilitated through new technologies like DBS and complementary institutional reforms – are now, for example, directly affecting the form in which the United States deals with international financial crises. Due to the rapid growth in the volume, rapidity and subsequent volatility of financial market activities, US mediated reforms of the GATT and the ITU already are conditioning challenges to the structural capacities of the American state. The decision in 1995 by President Clinton to exercise executive branch authority in response to the collapse of the Mexican peso – forgoing the two or three weeks needed to attain Congressional approval for a federal loan plan – reflects the temporal problematic of democratic debate. In facilitating the free flow of information in general, and electronically based economic activities in particular, the old Hollywood adage 'Time is money' is taking on an extraordinary new meaning. This brings to the surface a contradiction involving the form in which US-capital relations take place: the sometimes inflexible characteristics of the American state will compel continuing tension, frequent crises and ongoing change. In other words, in this period of post-Fordist political, economic and cultural change, the state will not always possess the structural capacities needed to accommodate change. In Marxist terms, *the state is the core but ever-problematic mediator of the ongoing dialectic involving global forces and relations of production.*

The hegemonic implications of US and world capitalist dependencies on stable and expanding international communication infrastructures, in light of the structural reforms and power shifts discussed above, involves more than Cox's observation that the state has become, in effect, 'a transmission belt from the global to the national.'[10] Specifically in regard to information-based commodity activities, a more accurate description involves predominantly US-based interests constructing this transmission belt with tools (or structures) held by the American state. To extend this metaphor, repairs or major modifications to the belt will continue to require the direct participation of the United States. As Leo Panitch puts it, 'capitalism has not escaped the state but rather ... the state has, as always, been a fundamental constitutive element in the very process of extension of capitalism in our time.'[11]

The vested interests of the information economy have become the core constituents of an emerging transnational hegemonic bloc. But these interests and the relations now predominant in the international political economy remain dependent on the nation state to reproduce the new structures of global power involving ongoing reforms to world order through means ranging from coercion to consent. An emphasis on the former was apparent in US foreign policy in the 1980s. An emphasis on the latter is becoming apparent in part as a result of the institutionalization of a free-trade/free-flow information regime in the 1990s.


## 8.3  HEGEMONY, CULTURE AND MEDIATORS OF THE INTERNATIONAL POLITICAL ECONOMY

Assumptions regarding the strategic necessity of formulating counter-hegemonic challenges at a global level, while correctly focusing on the role of cultural and intellectual capacities in redressing dominant neo-liberal 'common-sense' assumptions,[12] not only remains a more difficult task than the mounting of a Gramscian war of position at the national level, but for the foreseeable future it is of secondary importance given the findings of the present study. Because the state is the essential mediator of 'globalization,' challenges to the contemporary world order first depend on capabilities forged at the national level. This is not to deny that transnational production and related activities, for example, are in themselves substantive and influential. Nor is it to challenge the fact that such structures have been and are extraordinarily important in relation to national and local policies and imaginations. It is important to recognize, as does Leo Panitch, that 'movement-building struggles arise in conjunctures that are...more than ever determined on a world basis. Movements in one country have always been informed and inspired by movements abroad.' However, Panitch also (accurately, I think) views such global forces in the context of a strategic historical perspective:

> There is no need to conjure up out of this an 'international civil society' to install a 'transnational democracy.' Rather, a series of movements will likely arise that will be exemplary for one another, even though national specificities will continue to prevail. Of course, one hopes that these movements will be, as far as possible, solidaristic with one another, even though international solidarity movements cannot be taken for alternatives, rather than as critical supplements, to the struggles that must take place on the terrain of each state.[13]

To focus on the assumed development of a global civil society, mediated by transnational communication technologies like DBS, international organizations, institutions and, still more abstractly, international regimes, as the means through which a counter-hegemonic consciousness and movement may arise is strategic folly. It is folly for at least two inter-related reasons. First, the nation state remains (through its legal, military and domestic welfare powers) the essential institution through which the international structures of globalization are forged, legitimized and potentially challenged. Second, the national and local remain the most cogent levels of cultural identity for the world's masses. As discussed in Chapter 2, culture is a complex expression of the way people live their lives. It also constitutes the context in which individual conceptual systems evolve and are applied to 'make sense' of both the information one receives as well as one's life conditions. The cultural process, over-simplified by Schiller and underdeveloped in Cox, involves significant disparities in how different classes, genders, ethnic groups and nations process the great variations in the information available to them (in addition to the experiences of day-to-day life). Before the final section of this final chapter addresses these conditions and capacities in light of DBS and global information infrastructure developments writ large, the role played by media (broadly defined) in the international political economy deserves some elaboration.

Throughout this book, the mediators of the international political economy have constituted an implicit analytical thread. The direct broadcast satellite has been the core technological mediator on which attention has been focused. The American state (and the nation state generally) has been the core institutional mediator. The International Telecommunications Union, UNESCO and the GATT/WTO have been core organizational media. More generally, the free flow/free-trade struggle has been the focus of a regime transition. Developments involving these media and many others have been addressed using a dynamic approach – changes in the GATT affected the ITU, DBS developments influenced the United Nations and so forth. This analysis also has been holistic in the sense that the micro processes at work – US State Department versus Commerce Department disputes; inter-corporate competitive and anti-competitive activities; the political economy of digital technology developments, to name just three – have been viewed in relation to the larger context of hegemonic crisis, the emergence of an information economy hegemonic bloc, and the still more general transition toward some form of post-Fordist world order. In all of this, an emphasis on the capacities of media – both as historical constructions and as limiting or facilitating structures – has enabled a relatively nuanced approach to understanding the assumptions held by policy agents as to what is do-able, feasible and imaginable. In other words, *the multiple and ever-changing mediators of the international political economy directly shape what is perhaps the essential concern of both Cox and Schiller – how consent is constructed, maintained and destroyed.*

Historic periods of disturbance or crisis usually compel the development of new or reformed media. The implicit and/or explicit purpose of some constructions or reforms is to create greater flexibility and/or stability for a ruling class or hegemonic bloc. These attempts often involve the use of various media to control territory and the people in it (control over space) and the maintenance of this control (control over time). The capacity to control space and time *and* the capacity to challenge hegemonic dominance involves the use of such media to undermine or accommodate critical thought. This is the essence of the cultural concerns implicit in this book: it is the essence of cultural imperialism and the construction of consent or its absence. Hegemonic rule involves more than the willingness of people to be ruled. It also involves the building and maintenance of 'the conditions for that willingness to be present.'[14] Both the construction or reform of key mediators in the international political economy thus constitute the necessary precondition for hegemonic rule – rule involving the capacity to compromise with counter-hegemonic forces in ways that will reinforce the naturalness of a favored world order. Without such media, a consensual hegemonic order would be impossible.

The hegemonic crisis facing America and the Fordist regime of accumulation, dating from the early 1970s, has involved conflicts among inter-and intra-class forces in the United States and challenges involving such media. Institutions such as international law, the structure and *raison d'être* of organizations like the ITU and challenges over the implementation of technologies like DBS, reflected and shaped the history of this struggle.

A central goal in such efforts to reform or restructure international media involves more than an attempt to influence what is on 'the agenda' or what kind of information will be produced and made available. More fundamentally, control over such media involves the shaping of conceptual systems through which elites and masses construct conciousness, and central to this process are the individual and cultural biases that such structures facilitate. For example, in the 1970s and 1980s, in the context of economic crisis and American hegemonic decline, the structural characteristics of the ITU facilitated the overtly 'political' concerns of less developed countries involving redistribution issues. From the perspective of particular US interests,

Union structures thus accommodated ways of imagining and potentially constructing a new world order that could undermine wealth and power opportunities stemming from new communication and information technology applications. But unlike the free flow of information, Western corporations could not conceive a realistic alternative to the Union. By the mid–1980s, the ITU was understood to be *the* necessary mediator of transnational telecommunications developments. Without the option of conservative entrenchment or an outright assault (as was leveled against UNESCO), the United States was compelled to focus on restructuring the ITU in ways that would produce favorable results in future Union-mediated conflicts.

Until the 1970s, the ITU had been a forum for engineers appointed by nation states. To put it crudely, Union personnel were the garage mechanics of international telecommunications, fixing frequency allocations and technical standards in accordance with the aspirations of public sector PTTs and private sector monopolies. Through threats tabled by the American state on behalf of mostly US-based corporations, the aggressive development of GATT negotiations on services, and the more general post-Fordist adoption of neo-liberal policy reforms, direct private sector participation in Union decision making has become the norm and the need to accommodate business and trade developments have become formally entrenched in ITU department mandates and activities. Other international organizations, such as the World Bank, have complemented this transformation through the granting of financial and technical assistance to countries that recognize the 'common sense' of an open market path to development. In the late 1990s, the ITU again has become the universally recognized 'neutral' mediator of international telecommunications.[15]

## 8.4  DBS AND THE TWENTY-FIRST CENTURY

At least until the end of 1990s, DBS will be the most cost-effective means of delivering electronic transmissions directly into homes. A US$1-billion investment in cable enables a company to reach several million households, whereas the same investment in DBS provides access to an entire continent.[16] In the United States, the introduction of a mass consumer high-power DBS system is under way due-to a number of competitive, technological and regulatory developments. In conjunction with the success of Star TV in Asia and the Astra system in Europe, the early success of DBS in North America – the most cabled continent in the world – will further raise the profile and significance of direct broadcast technologies among US government and corporate officials. Again, the essential importance of DBS lies in its status as a truly transnational communication system whose economics – involving enormous overheads and relatively minute per household delivery costs – impel the internationalization of information-based commodities.

Rather than technological advancements compelling the domestic re-regulation of US communication activities, 'inevitably' followed by the liberalization of international communications, the role of technology more accurately can be characterized as tools and/or catalysts accommodating corporate-based forces. Technological convergence and signal compression, both significantly advanced through digitalization, continue to facilitate the transnationalization of capitalist activities. To some extent, unlike the assumptions implied in the paradigm of cultural imperialism, ignorance has played an important role in the history of US foreign communication policy. Through the technological, legal and economic complexity of telesatellites and related developments, established corporate interests generally have benefited from the fragmentation and leadership vacuum that has characterized US policy. According to Edward Ploman, 'government, administrative, industrial and academic structures' have tended to 'work against frontier crossing between disciplines, technologies, bureaucracies – and mental categories.'[17] This, in turn, has facilitated the general movement away from behavioral regulation toward structural regulation, and this movement has been an expression of long-term TNC efforts to control rather than compete in the emerging information economy marketplace.

In relation to the intellectual capacities of mass publics to organize some form of sustained counter-hegemonic movement, the development of DBS provides little grounding for optimism. Despite the realisation of a *de facto* free flow of information regime and the practice of receiving information from around the world directly into one's living room or onto one's computer screen, it is unlikely that DBS or its use in conjunction with an inter-active information highway infrastructure will promote much more than a deepening of existing disparities. In less developed areas of the world, for example, beyond the availability of a supply of electricity, access to direct broadcast services will depend on the ability to purchase or gain access to a television set or computer monitor; the ability to pay for either a satellite dish or cable connection (assuming one is available);

and the leisure time and the cultural conceptualization of 'leisure' required to justify these investments. Even in relatively developed countries, a disparity in the availability of basic services, like the telephone, has grown as costs have increased.[18] Because relatively expensive information services often are themselves prerequisites to the development of the intellectual capacities needed to access and comprehend more specialized (and expensive) services, the ability to take full advantage of many information-based commodities is directly related to pre-existing intellectual, economic and/or organizational capacities.[19] In sum, what can be termed *the commoditization of information is reinforcing domestic and international social-economic disparities despite the presence of apparently more accessible communication technologies, information services, and their assumed liberalizing or liberating implications.*[20]

Beyond such outcomes and the insidious implications of world communications being dominated by relatively fewer and larger corporate entities (and the inherent difficulties of redressing monopoly behavior on a global scale), *we should not lose sight of the fact that nation states, as core institutional mediators, also can be centers (if not organizers) of resistance.* In the United States, for example, the Telecommunications Act generally has been applauded for apparently stimulating competition and its promotion of potentially seamless information highway developments. Its long-term international implications, however, ironically involve a world characterized by less competition and increasing disparities between large-scale and wealthy customers and the relatively poor and powerless. In this type of economic order, political and economic volatility becomes more probable as a result of potential disparities emerging between international corporations and national business and customer interests. This contradiction may well generate a resurgence of the popular authority of the nation state. In the telecommunications sector, the recently reformed ITU, for example, may well face difficulties maintaining its mask of objectivity. As the information economy becomes a truly transnational marketplace, and assuming a continuation of technical change and at least some competition involving a US 'champion' seeking access into overseas markets, and so forth, the Union could well become a forum of explicit private sector conflict. In other words, the structural reformulation of the ITU – itself designed to accommodate a range of information economy corporate interests– eventually may lead to the Union's political de-legitimation. Already, TNCs such as Motorola are sending personnel to act as officials in the national delegations of Canada, France, Australia and the United States.[21] Such instrumental relationships no doubt will problematize hegemonic aspirations for a consensual rather than a coercive world order. More generally, the World Trade Organization almost certainly will become *the* forum in which nation states will be hailed to challenge what they have only recently constructed: the 'inevitability' or 'naturalness' of neo-liberal developments and the apparent neutrality of free-trade and free flow international media. Paradoxically, in a world characterized by institutionalized state-mediated power disparities, the nation state remains the only institution through which the now seemingly unslayable conceptual giants called globalization and liberalization can be challenged.

The form in which such challenges and the mobilization of the nation will take place will involve the structural capacities of states and the related ability of public and private sector officials to recognize and redress structural problems. This, of course, will probably take place in periods of political and economic uncertainty as various domestic and international agents reassess their interests and engage in the struggle to reform, create or destroy domestic and international media. The economic, political and military position of the United States and the successful institutionalization of a free-trade/free flow regime involving new and reformed mediators is the basis of a potential period of consensual hegemony. But tensions and contradictions will continue to surface. The successful reassertion of some kind of *Pax Americana* thus will depend on the ability of the American state to respond to future crises in light of its cultural and other power capacities. As this study has shown, this struggle will unfold through domestic and international mediators and it will directly involve the cultural-power capabilities developed by domestic and international opponents during these formative years of the international information economy.

# NOTES

1  Personal interview with Janice Obuchowski, Freedom Technologies, 3 March 1994, Washington, DC.

2  Frederick Williams, *The New Telecommunications, Infrastructure for the Information Age* (New York: Free Press, 1991) pp. 11–12.

3  Interview with Eric Scheck.

4  Herbert I. Schiller in Preston et al., *Hope & Folly* (Minneapolis: University of Minnesota Press, 1989) p. 301.

5  Robert Cox quoted in Stephen Gill, 'Epistemology, Ontology and the "Italian School",' in Stephen Gill (ed.), *Gramsci, Historical Materialism and International Relations* (Cambridge: Cambridge University Press, 1993) p. 42 (emphases added).

6  See Robert W. Cox, 'The Global Political Economy and Social Choice,' in Daniel Drache and Meric S. Gertler (eds), *The New Era of Global Competition, State Policy and Market Power* (Montreal and Kingston: McGill-Queen's University Press, 1991) esp. pp. 337 and 343.

7  Robert W. Cox, *Production, Power, and World Order* (New York: Columbia University Press, 1987) p. 2.

8  *Ibid.*

9  The role of the USTR in representing International Intellectual Property Alliance interests in US–China software disputes during the mid-1990s serves as a reminder that the American state will remain the core agent through which the conditions required for international capital to operate will be policed and enforced. Suggestions that a diminution of state power has taken place as a result of internationalization processes also are challenged in light of the negligible independence of the foreign communication policy agencies examined in this book. Conceptualizing a reduction of state autonomy has little meaning in relation to a state that has rarely, if ever, enjoyed such autonomy.

10  Robert W. Cox, 'Global Perestroika,' in Ralph Miliband and Leo Panitch (eds), *Socialist Register 1992* (London: Merlin Press, 1992) p. 31.

11  Leo Panitch, 'Globalisation and the State' in Ralph Miliband and Leo Panitch (eds.), *Socialist Register 1994* (London: Merlin Press, 1994), p. 87.

12  Stephen Gill, 'Gramsci and Global Politics: Towards a Post-Hegemonic Research Agenda' in Stephen Gill (ed.), *Gramsci, Historical Materialism and International Relations* (Cambridge: Cambridge University Press, 1993) pp. 15–17.

13  Leo Panitch, 'Globalization, States, and Left Strategies,' *Social Justice*, 23 (1–2) (1996) 89.

14  Esteve Morera, 'Gramsci and Democracy,' *Canadian Journal of Political Science*, XXIII (1) (March 1990) 24.

15  Kelly Lee, *Global Telecommunications Regulation, A Political Economy Perspective* (London: Pinter, 1996) pp. 166–7 and 174.

16  David Bross, *DBS: Global Marketplace Analysis* (Potomac, Md.: Phillips Publishing, 1991) p. 8.

17  Edward W. Ploman, 'National Needs in an International Communication Setting,' *Transnational Data Report*, VI (5) (July – August 1983) 277.

18    Graham Murdock and Peter Golding, 'Information Poverty and Poli-
      tical Inequality: Citizenship in the Age of Privatized Communications,'
      *Journal of Communication*, 39 (3) (Summer 1989) 191.

19    As Murdock and Golding found in their study of public information
      and communication activity in England, 'economic barriers to develop-
      ing computer competence were often reinforced by social dynamics.
      Because there were fewer users in their neighbourhoods and they gen-
      erally worked in jobs that did not involve using computers, the less-well-
      off computer owners had only limited access to the kinds of advice and
      support networks enjoyed by more affluent users and therefore experi-
      enced more difficulty in sustaining commitment and developing skills.' –
      *ibid.*, p. 192.

20    Ian Parker, 'Economic Dimensions of Twenty-first-century Canadian
      Cultural Strategy,' in Ian Parker, John Hutcheson and Patrick Crawley
      (eds), *The Strategy of Canadian Culture in the twenty-first Century*
      (Toronto: TopCat Communications, 1988) p. 224.

21    Robin Mansell, 'Network Governance: Designing New Regimes' in
      Robin Mansell and Roger Silverstone (eds), *Communication by Design,
      The Politics of Information and Communication Technologies* (New
      York: Oxford, 1996) p. 199.

# Bibliography

## GENERAL

ALEXANDROWICZ, CHARLES Henry, *The Law of Global Communications*. New York: Columbia University Press, 1971.

ALPERT, MICHAEL S., 'Direct Broadcast Satellite (DBS) in the United States,' *Space Communications* 8 (1991) 365–74.

AMDUR, MEREDITH, 'Murdoch Star Deal Transforms Asia,' in *Broadcasting & Cable*, 123 (31) (2 August 1993) 34–5.

AMDUR, MEREDITH, 'US Broadcasters Berate GATT,' *Broadcasting & Cable*. 123 (51) (20 December 1993) 14.

ANDERSON, BENEDICT, *Imagined Communities, Reflections on the Origin and Spread of Nationalism*. London: Verso, 1990.

ANDREWS, EDMUND L., 'Senate Sends Bush Bill to Regulate Price of Cable TV,' *New York Times*, 23 September 1992, pp. A1 and C2.

ANG, IEN, *Desperately Seeking the Audience*. London: Routledge, 1991.

ANGUS, IAN and JHALLY, SUT (eds) *Cultural Politics in Contemporary America*. New York: Routledge, 1989.

ASANTE, MOLEFI KETE and GUDYKUNST, WILLIAM B. (eds) *Handbook of International and Intercultural Communication*. Newbury Park, Ca.: Sage, 1989.

ASSAEL, HENRY, and POLTRACK, DAVID F. 'Using Single Source Data to Select TV Programs Based on Purchasing Behavior,' *Journal of Advertising Research*, 31 (4) (August/September 1991) 9–17.

ATKINSON, JOE, 'Mass Communications, Economic Liberalism and the New Mediators,' *Political Science*, 41 (2) (December 1989) 85–108.

AUERBACH, STUART, 'Senators Introduce Trade Bill to Open Communications Markets,' *Washington Post*, 2 May 1984, pp. C1 and C12.

AUGELLI, ENRICO and MURPHY, CRAIG *America's Quest for Supremacy and the Third World, A Gramscian Analysis*. London: Pinter, 1988.

AULETTA, KEN, 'Raiding the Global Village,' *The New Yorker*, LXIX (24) (2 August 1993) 30.

BABE, ROBERT E., 'Information Industries and Economic Analysts: Policymakers Beware,' in Oscar H. Gandy, Jr, Paul Espinosa and Janusz A. Ordover (eds), *Proceedings from the Tenth Annual Telecommunications Policy Research Conference*. Norwood, NJ: Ablex, 1983, pp. 123–35.

BABE, ROBERT, *Telecommunications in Canada: Technology, Industry, and Government*. Toronto: University of Toronto Press, 1990.

BABE, ROBERT (ed.) *Information and Communication in Economics*. Boston: Kluwer, 1994.

BACKER Spielvogel Bates Media Department, *BSB Projections 2000, Media and Measurement Technology Predictions for the Coming Decade*. New York: Backer Spielvogel Bates, 1991.

BAGNALL, JAMES, 'AT&T's Crucial Charge into Canada, and Why it has been so Rough Going,' *Financial Times of Canada*, 14 August 1993, pp. 4–5.

BAILEY, JAMES Edwin, III, 'Current and Future Legal Uses of Direct Broadcast Satellites in International Law,' *Louisiana Law Review*, 45 (3) (1985) 701–20.

BAKER, BRENT, 'Decisions at the Speed of TV Satellites,' *Vital Speeches of the Day*, LVIII (19) (15 July 1992) 581–3.

BAKER, SIMON, 'An Audible Sigh of Relief,' *Cable and Satellite Europe*, 98 (February 1992) 42.

BARKER, PAUL, 'From Pariah to Paragon,' *Cable and Satellite Europe*, 16 (June 1992) 16–7.

BARKER, PAUL, 'Double Illumination,' *Cable and Satellite Europe*, 151 (July 1996) pp. 25–6.

BARKER, PAUL, 'A Meeting of Minds,' *Cable and Satellite Europe*, 150 (June 1996) 4.

BECKER, JORG, HEDEBRO, GORAN and PALDAN, LEENA (eds) *Communication and Domination: Essays in Honor of Herbert I. Schiller.* Norwood, NJ: Ablex, 1986.

BELL, DANIEL, *The Coming of Post-industrial Society: A Venture in Social Forecasting.* New York: Basic Books, 1973.

BELL, DESMOND and MEEHAN, NIALL, 'International Telecommunications Deregulation and Ireland's Domestic Communications Policy,' *Journal of Communication*, 38 (1) (Winter 1988) 70–84.

BENZ, STEPHEN F., 'Trade Liberalization and the Global Service Economy,' *Journal of World Trade Law*, 19 (1985) 95–120.

BERGER, PETER L. and LUCKMANN, THOMAS *The Social Construction of Reality, A Treatise in the Sociology of Knowledge.* Garden City, NY: Anchor Books, 1967.

BERGSTEN, C. FRED, HORST, THOMAS and MORAN, THEODORE H. *American Multinationals and American Interests.* Washington, DC: Brookings Institute, 1978.

BERLEUR, JACQUES and DRUMM JOHN (eds) *Information Technology Assessment, Proceedings of the 4th IFIP TC9 International Conference on Human Choice and Computers.* North Holland: Elsevier Science Publishers, 1991.

BERNARD, KEITH E., 'New Global Network Arrangements, Regulatory and Trade Considerations,' *Telecommunications Policy*, 18 (5) (July 1994) 378–96.

BERTRAMSEN, RENE BUGGE, 'From the Capitalist State to the Political Economy' in Bertramsen, Jens Peter Frolund Thomsen and Jacob Torfing, eds., *State, Economy and Society.* London: Unwin Hyman, 1991, pp. 94–145.

BHAGWATI, JAGDISH N., 'United States Trade Policy at the Crossroads' in *The World Economy.* Vol.12 No.4 (December 1989), pp. 439–79.

BINKOWSKI, EDWARD, *Satellite Information Systems.* Boston: G.K. Hall, 1988.

BLATHERWICK, DAVID E.S., *The International Politics of Telecommunications.* Berkeley, Cal.: Institute of International Studies, 1987.

'BLOCKING Scientific-technical Data Exports,' *Chronicle of International Communication*, VI (5) (June 1985) 1–2.

BLUMLER, JAY G., *Television in the United States: Funding Sources and Programming Consequences.* Unpublished study prepared by the British Centre for Television Research, University of Leeds, January 1986.

BLUMLER, JAY G., BRYNIN, MALCOLM and NOSSITER, T.J. 'Broadcasting Finance and Programme Quality, An International Review,' in Michael Gurevitch and Mark R. Levy (eds), *Mass Communication Review Yearbook?, vol. 6. Beverly Hills: Sage, 1987.*

BLUMLER, JAY G. and SPICER, CAROLYN MARTIN, 'Prospects for Creativity in the New Television Marketplace: Evidence from Program-Makers,' *Journal of Communication,* 40 (4) (Autumn 1990) 78–101.

BLUMLER, JAY G. and NOSSITER, T.J. (eds) *Broadcasting Finance in Transition, A Comparative Handbook.* New York: Oxford University Press, 1991.

BOGART, LEO, 'The American Media System and its Commercial Culture.' *Media Studies Journal,* 5 (4) (Fall 1991) 13–33.

BOWES, ELENA, 'Europe's Satellite TV Viewers Soar,' *Advertising Age,* 61 (39) (24 September 1990) 39.

BRAMAN, SANDRA, 'Information and Socioeconomic Class in US Constitutional Law,' *Journal of Communication,* 39 (3) (Summer 1989) 163–79.

BRAMAN, SANDRA, 'Trade and Information Policy,' *Media, Culture and Society,* 12 (3) (July 1990) 361–85.

BRANSCOMB, ANNE W., 'Communications Policy in the United States: Diversity and Pluralism in a Competitive Marketplace' in Patricia Edgar and Syed A. Rakim (eds), *Communication Policy in Developed Countries.* London: Kegan Paul International, 1983, pp. 25–51.

BRANSCOMB, ANNE W., 'Videotext: Global Progress and Comparative Policies,' *Journal of Communication,* 38 (1) (Winter 1988) 50–9.

BROSS, DAVID, *DBS: Global Marketplace Analysis.* Potomac, Md.: Phillips Publishing, 1991.

BROWN, DUNCAN H., 'Citizens or Consumers: US Reactions to the European Community's Directive on Television,' *Critical Studies in Mass Communications,* 8 (1) (March 1991) 1–12.

BROWN, RICH, 'Cable Sees Positives in Telco Ruling,' *Broadcasting & Cable,* 123 (35) (30 August 1993) 11.

BROWN, RICH, 'CellularVision, Bell Atlantic to Unwire NY,' in *Broadcasting & Cable,* 123 (32) (9 August 1993) 14.

BROWN, RICH, 'Telco-cable Giants Converge,' *Broadcasting & Cable* 123 (21) (24 May 1993) 6 and 16.

BROWNE, DONALD R., *International Radio Broadcasting.* New York: Praeger, 1982.

BRUCE, ROBERT R., 'Intelsat in Transition,' *Chronicle of International Communication,* VI (3) (April 1985) 5–7.

BURCH, DEAN, 'Public Utility Regulation: In Pursuit of the Public Interest,' *Public Utilities Fortnightly* (September 1973) 70.

BURNS, R.T., Confidential memorandum to N.C. Baker, Bell South Services. Unpublished mimeo, 14 June 1988.

'Cable Act Is Big Help to Direct Broadcast Satellites, Conference Told,' *Satellite Week,* 15 (8) (22 February 1993) 7.

'CANAL Plus, Putting Europe on the Box,' *The Economist*, 324 (7767) (11 July 1992) 70.

CANTON, BELINDA and DORDICK, HERBERT S., 'Information Strategies and International Trade Policy,' *Transnational Data Report*, V (6) (September 1982) 311–12.

CARNOY, MARTIN, CASTELS, MANUEL, COHEN, STEPHEN S. and CARDOSO, FERNANDO HENRIQUE, *The New Global Economy in the Information Age, Reflections on Our Changing World*. University Park, Pa.: Pennsylvania State University Press, 1993.

CARSE, PHILIP, and SHURMER, MARK, 'Why the US Standard will have the Clearest "Market Focus'," *InterMedia*, 21 (2) (March–April 1993) 31.

CARVETH, ROD, 'The Reconstruction of the Global Media Marketplace,' *Communication Research*, 19 (6) (December 1992) 705–23.

CHAN, JOSEPH MAN, 'Media Internationalization in China: Processes and Tensions,' *Journal of Communication*, 44 (3) (Summer 1994) 70–88.

CHAN, JOSEPH MAN, 'National Responses and Accessibility to Star TV in Asia,' *Journal of Communication*, 44 (3) (Summer 1994) 112–31.

'CHANGE and Chance at the Organizational Wheel,' *Chronicle of International Communication*, VI (1) (January–February 1985) 5–6.

CHASE, SCOTT, 'Horses for Courses,' *Cable and Satellite Europe*, 109 (January 1993) 30.

CHATTERJI, P.C., *Broadcasting in India*, New Delhi: Sage, 1991.

CHEVREAU, JONATHAN, 'Death of Local Subsidy Heralds New Phone Era,' *Financial Post*, 17 April 1993, p. 8.

CLARK, JOHN MAURICE, *Studies in the Economics of Overhead Costs*. Chicago: University of Chicago Press, 1937.

COHEN, G.A., *Karl Marx's Theory of History, A Defence*. Oxford: Oxford University Press, 1984.

COHEN, ROBERT B., *The US Policy Response to Europe's Changing Television and Film Market*. Unpublished report submitted to National Telecommunications and Information Administration Study on Globalization of Mass Media: Economic Policy Institute, 18 July 1990.

COHEN, ROBERT B. and DONOW, KENNETH, *Telecommunications Policy, High Definition Television, and US Competitiveness*. Washington, DC: Economic Policy Institute, 1989.

COLE, BARRY and OETTINGER, MAL, *Reluctant Regulators, The FCC and the Broadcast Audience*. Reading, Mass.: Addison-Wesley, 1978.

COLEMAN, WILLIAM, *Financial Services, Globalization and Domestic Policy Change: A Comparison of North America and the European Union*. London and New York: Macmillan and St Martin's Press, 1996.

COLLINS, RICHARD, *Satellite Television in Western Europe*. London: John Libbey & Company, 1990.

COLLINS, RICHARD, GARNHAM, NICHOLAS AND LOCKSLEY, GARETH, *The Economics of Television, The UK Case*. London: Sage, 1988.

'COMMUNICATIONS Satellites: An Introduction,' *Bulletin of the Atomic Scientists*, 23 (April 1967) 3.

COMOR, EDWARD, 'The Department of Communications under the Free Trade Regime,' *Canadian Journal of Communication*, 16 (2) (1991) 239–61.

COMOR, EDWARD A. (ed.) *The Global Political Economy of Communication: Hegemony, Telecommunication and the Information Economy.* London and New York: Macmillan and St Martin's Press, 1994 and 1996.

COMOR, EDWARD, 'Harold Innis's Dialectical Triad,' *Journal of Canadian Studies,* 29 (2) (Summer 1994) 111–27.

CORREA, LUIZ FELIPE de SEIXAS, 'Direct Satellite Broadcasting and the Third World,' *Columbia Journal of Transnational Law,* 13 (1974) 70–4.

COTTIER, THOMAS, 'The Prospects for Intellectual Property in GATT,' *Common Market Law Review,* 28 (2) (Summer 1991) 383–414.

COVAULT, CRAIG, 'NASA Urged to Study Satcom Program,' *Aviation Week & Space Technology,* 106 (14 March 1977) 41–2.

COWHEY, PETER F., 'Trade Talks and the Informatics Sector,' *International Journal,* XLII (Winter 1986–87) 107–37.

COX, ROBERT W., 'Ideologies and the New International Economic Order: Reflections on Some Recent Literature,' *International Organization,* 33 (2) (Spring 1979) 257–302.

COX, ROBERT W., 'Social Forces, States and World Orders: Beyond International Relations Theory,' *Millennium: Journal of International Studies,* 10 (2) (Summer 1981) 126–55.

COX, ROBERT W., 'Gramsci: Hegemony and International Relations: An Essay in Method,' *Millennium: Journal of International Studies,* 12 (2) (Summer 1983) 162–75.

COX, ROBERT W., *Production, Power, and World Order, Social Forces in the Making of History.* New York: Columbia University Press, 1987.

COX, ROBERT W., 'Global Perestroika,' in Ralph Miliband and Leo Panitch (eds), *Socialist Register 1992.* London: Merlin Press, 1992, pp. 26–43.

COX, ROBERT W., 'The Global Political Economy and Social Choice,' in Daniel Drache and Meric S. Gertler (eds), *The New Era of Global Competition, State Policy and Market Power.* Montreal and Kingston: McGill-Queen's University Press, 1991, pp. 335–50.

COX, ROBERT W., 'Real Socialism in Historical Perspective' in Ralph Miliband and Leo Panitch (eds), *Socialist Register 1991.* London: Merlin Press, 1991, pp. 169–93.

COX, ROBERT W. with TIMOTHY J. SINCLAIR, *Approaches to World Order.* Cambridge: Cambridge University Press, 1996.

CRAWFORD, MORRIS H., 'The US Mobilizes for WARC – but Bickers over Political Aims,' *Transnational Data Report,* V (6) (September 1982) 313.

'CRIMPING the Commitment,' *Chronicle of International Communication,* VI (5) (June 1985) 6–7.

CURRAN, JAMES, GUREVITCH, MICHAEL and WOOLLACOTT, JANET (eds), *Mass Communication and Society.* London: Arnold, 1977.

CUTLER, BLAYNE, 'Where does the Free Time Go?' *American Demographics,* 12 (11) (November 1990) 36–8.

DAVIES, SIMON TWISTON, 'Mandarin will be Plum,' *Cable and Satellite Europe,* 117 (September 1993) 20–1.

DAVIES, SIMON Twiston, 'The One that Got Away,' *Cable and Satellite Europe,* 120 (December 1993) 34–5.

DAVIS, HOWARD and WALTON, PAUL (eds) *Language, Image, Media.* London: Basil Blackwell, 1983.

DAVIS, MIKE, 'The Political Economy of Late-imperial America,' *New Left Review* 143 (January–February 1984) 6–38.

DAVIS, MIKE, 'Reaganomics' Magical Mystery Tour,' *New Left Review*, 149 (January–February 1985) 45–65.

DAVIS, MIKE, 'Why the US Working Class is Different' in Mike Davis, *Prisoners of the American Dream, Politics and Economy in the History of the US Working Class.* London: Verso, 1986, pp. 3–51.

'DBS, Fibre and Cable may be the Future Big Three, Say Panelists,' *Broadcasting*, 114 (16) (April 18 1988) 76–8.

'DBS Providers Hope to Eclipse Cable in Multichannel Future,' *Video Technology News*, 9 (9) (22 April 1996) n.p.

'DBS: The Next Generation,' *Broadcasting*, 118 (9) (26 February 1990) 27–31 and 55.

'DEAN Burch Heads INTELSAT,' *Transnational Data Report*, X (5) (May 1987) 8.

DE MOOIJ, MARIEKE K., *Advertising Worldwide.* New York: Prentice-Hall, 1991.

DE SONNE, MARCIA L., *Satellites & Broadcasting 1990, US Domestic and International Market Directions and Issues.* Washington, DC: National Association of Broadcasters, 1989.

DIEDERIKS-VERSCHOOR, I.H.Ph., *An Introduction to Space Law.* Deventer and Boston: Kluwer Law and Taxation Publishers, 1993.

DOUGAN, DIANA, 'Communications Satellites: Challenges of the Future'. Address to Society of Satellite Professionals, Washington, DC. Unpublished, 16 October 1987.

DOUGAN, DIANA, ' "Fortress Europe" of the Airways,' *Los Angeles Times*, 11 October 1989, p. B7.

DOUGAN, DIANA , 'The US and the Caribbean: Partners in Communication'. Address to the Caribbean Seminar on Space WARC and the Transborder Use of US Domestic Satellites. Montego Bay, 2 October 1984. Washington DC: US State Department, 1984.

DRAKE, WILLIAM J. and NICOLAIDIS, KALYPSO, 'Ideas, Interests, and Institutionalization: "Trade in Services" and the Uruguay Round,' *International Organization*, 46 1 (Winter 1992) 37–100.

DYSON, KENNETH and HUMPHREYS, PETER (eds) *The Politics of the Communications Revolution in Western Europe.* Totowa, NJ: Frank Cass & Co., 1986.

DYSON, KENNETH and HUMPHREYS, PETER with RALPH NEGRINE and JEAN-PAUL SIMON, *Broadcasting and New Media Policies in Western Europe.* New York: Routledge, 1988.

DYSON, KENNETH and HUMPHREYS, PETER (eds) *The Political Economy of Communications, International and European Dimensions.* London: Routledge, 1990.

DZIADUL, CHRIS, 'Another Dish on the Wall,' *Cable and Satellite Europe*, 109 (January 1993) 42–52.

EBANKS, KENNETH D., 'Pirates of the Caribbean Revisited: An Examination of the Continuing Problem of Satellite Signal Piracy in the Caribbean and Latin America,' *Law & Policy in International Business*, 21 (1) (1989) 33–52.

ELDER, ROBERT E., *The Information Machine, the United States Information Agency and American Foreign Policy*. Syracuse, NY: Syracuse University Press, 1968.

ELSON, DIANE, 'Market Socialism or Socialization of the Market?' *New Left Review*, 172 (November–December 1988) 3–44.

*EUROPEAN Satellite Broadcasting, Proceedings of the Conference Held in London, June 1989*. Middlesex: Blenheim Online Ltd, 1989.

EVANS, B.G. (ed.) *Satellite Communication Systems*. London: Peter Peregrinus, 1991.

EVANS, PETER B., RUESCHEMEYER, DIETRICH and SKOCPOL, THEDA,' On the Road toward a More Adequate Understanding of the State,' in P. Evans, D. Rueschemeyer and T. Skocpol, (eds), *Bringing the State Back In*. Cambridge: Cambridge University Press, 1985, pp. 347–66.

FALKENBERG, K.F., 'The Audio Visual Sector in the Uruguay Round'. Unpublished mimeo: 18–19 November 1994, pp. 242–6.

FEJES, FRED, 'Media Imperialism, An Assessment,' in D.Charles Whitney and Ellen Wartella (eds), *Mass Communication Review Yearbook*, vol. 3. Beverly Hills: Sage, 1982, pp. 345–54.

FINGER, SEYMOUR MAXWELL, 'Reform or Withdrawal,' *Foreign Service Journal*, 61 (6) (June 1984) 18–23.

FISHER, DAVID I., *Prior Consent to International Direct Broadcast Satellite Broadcasting*. Dordrecht: Martinus Nijhoff Publishers, 1990.

FISKE, JOHN, *Television Culture*. New York: Methuen, 1987.

FISKE, JOHN and HARTLEY, JOHN. *Reading Television*. London: Methuen, 1982.

FJORDBAK, SHARON L., 'The Internationsl Direct Broadcast Satellite Controversy,' *The Journal of Air Law and Commerce*, 55 (4) (Summer 1990) 903–38.

FLYNN, BARRY, 'The Scramble for Europe,' *Cable and Satellite Europe*, 118 (October 1993) 46–8.

FOISIE, GEOFFREY, 'Banking on Syndication,' *Broadcasting* (21 January 1992) 51.

FOISIE, GEOFFREY and MOSHAVI, SHARON D., 'TV Advertising's Brave New World,' *Broadcasting*, 122 (16) (13 April 1992) 44–6.

'FOR the Record and Subject to Change,' *Chronicle of International Communication*, V (10) (December 1984) 7.

FORESTER, TOM, *'High-Tech Society,' The Story of the Information Technology Revolution. Cambridge, Mass.: MIT Press, 1987.*

'FORMIDABLE Barriers Seen to Media Trade,' *Transnational Data Report*, VIII (1) (January–February 1985) 11.

FOWLER, MARC, 'Free Markets for Telecommunications: US View,' *Transnational Data Report*, VIII (3) (April/May 1985) 137.

FOX, BARRY, 'Satellite Broadcasters Battle in the Sky,' *New Scientist*, 120 (1635) (22 October, 1988) 48–52.

FREDERICK, HOWARD H., *Global Communication & International Relations*. Belmont, Cae.: Wadsworth, 1993.

'FREEDOM of Business Communication Vital,' *Transnational Data Report*, VI (6) (September 1983) 302–5.

FREEMAN, HARRY L., 'Impeding the Flow of Information Damages National Interests,' *Transnational Data Report*, VI (1) (January–February 1983) 19.

FREIMAN, MARK J., 'Consumer Sovereignty and National Sovereignty in Domestic and International Broadcasting,' in *Canadian–U.S. Conference on Communications Policy, Cultures in Collision*. New York: Praeger, 1984, pp. 104–21.

FRIEDEN, ROB, 'Much Ado about Bandwidth,' *Satellite Communications*, 17 (2) (February 1993) 24–8.

FROW, JOHN, 'Knowledge and Class,' *Cultural Studies*, 7 (2) (May 1993) 240–81.

GADBAW, R. MICHAEL and GWYNN, ROSEMARY E., 'Intellectual Property Rights in the New GATT Round,' in R.M. Gadbaw and Timothy J. Richards (eds), *Intellectual Property Rights, Global Consensus, Global Conflict?* Boulder, Col.: Westview Press, 1988, pp. 38–88.

GADDIS, JOHN LEWIS, *Strategies of Containment*. New York: Oxford University Press, 1982.

GALBRAITH, JOHN KENNETH, *The Affluent Society*. 2nd ed. New York: Signet, 1969.

GALLOWAY, JONATHAN F., *The Politics and Technology of Satellite Communications*. Toronto: Lexington Books, 1972.

GALTUNG, JOHAN, 'A Structural Theory of Imperialism,' in Michael Smith, Richard Little and Michael Shackleton (eds), *Perspectives on World Politics*. London: Croom Helm, pp. 301–12.

GANDY, OSCAR H., Jr, 'Toward a Political Economy of Personal Information,' *Critical Studies in Mass Communication*, 10 (1) (March 1993) 70–97.

GANDY, OSCAR H., Jr, Espinosa, Paul and Ordover, Janus A. (eds), *Proceedings from the Tenth Annual Telecommunications Policy Research Conference*. Norwood, NJ: Ablex, 1983.

'THE GANG that Wouldn't Shoot Straight,' *Chronicle of International Communication*, V (10) (December 1984) 1–3.

GARNHAM, NICHOLAS, *Capitalism and Communication, Global Culture and the Economics of Information*, Fred Inglis (ed.). London: Sage, 1990.

GARNHAM, NICHOLAS, 'Communication Technology and Policy,' in Michael Gurevitch and Mark R. Levy (eds), *Mass Communication Review Yearbook*, vol. 5. Beverly Hills, Cal.: Sage, 1985, pp. 65–74.

GAVENTA, JOHN, *Power and Powerlessness, Quiescence and Rebellion in an Appalachian Valley*. Urbana: University of Illinois Press, 1980.

GERBNER, GEORGE, MOWLANA, HAMID and NORDENSTRENG, KAARLE (eds), *The Global Media Debate: Its Rise, Fall, and Renewal*. Norwood, NJ: Ablex, 1993.

GERSHON, RICHARD A., 'Telephone–Cable Cross-Ownership,' *Telecommunications Policy*, 16 (2) (March 1992) 110–21.

GILL, STEPHEN, *American Hegemony and the Trilateral Commission*. Cambridge: Cambridge University Press, 1990.

GILL, STEPHEN, 'Intellectuals and Transnational Capital,' in Ralph Miliband, Leo Panitch and John Saville (eds), *Socialist Register 1990*. London: Merlin Press, 1990, pp. 290–310.

GILL, STEPHEN, 'Economic Globalization and the Internationalization of Authority: Limits and Contradictions,' *Geoforum*. (23 3) (1992), 269–83.

GILL, STEPHEN (ed.) *Gramsci, Historical Materialism and International Relations*. Cambridge: Cambridge University Press, 1993.

GILL, STEPHEN, 'Neo-Liberalism and the Shift towards a US-Centered Transnational Hegemony,' in Henk Overbeek (ed.), *Restructuring Hegemony in the Global Political Economy*. London: Routledge, 1993, pp. 246–82.

GILL, STEPHEN and LAW, DAVID, 'Global Hegemony and the Structural Power of Capital,' *International Studies Quarterly*, 33 (1989) 475–99.

GILLESPIE, ANDREW and ROBINS, KEVEN, 'Geographical Inequalities: The Spatial Bias of the New Communications Technologies,' *Journal of Communication* 39 (3) (Summer 1989) 7–18.

GITLIN, TODD, 'Prime Time Ideology: The Hegemonic Process in Television Entertainment' *Social Problems*, 26 3 (February 1979) 251–66.

GITLIN, TODD, *The Whole World Is Watching, Mass Media in the Making and Unmaking of the New Left*. Berkeley: University of California Press, 1980.

GOLD, MARC and LEYTON-BROWN, DAVID (eds) *Trade-Offs on Free Trade, The Canada–US Free Trade Agreement*. Toronto: Carswell, 1988.

GORDON, GEORGE N. and FALK, IRVING A., *The War of Ideas: America's International Identity Crisis*. New York: Hastings House, 1973.

GORE, AL and BROWN, RONALD H., *Global Information Infrastructure: Agenda for Cooperation*. Washington, DC: US Government Printing Office, 1995.

GRAMSCI, ANTONIO, *Selections from the Prison Notebooks*. Quintin Hoare and Geoffrey Nowell Smith (eds). New York: International Publishers, 1985.

GREGG, DONNA C., 'Capitalizing on National Self-Interest: The Management of International Telecommunication Conflict by the International Telecommunication Union,' *Law and Contemporary Problems*, 45 (1) (Winter 1982) 37–52.

GUREVITCH, MICHAEL, BENNETT, TONY, CURRAN, JAMES AND WOOLLACOTT, JANET (eds), *Culture, Society and the Media*. London: Routledge, 1990.

GUREVITCH, MICHAEL, and LEVY, MARK R. (eds.), *Mass Communication Review Yourbook*, Vol. 5. Beverly Hills: Sage, 1985.

HAGLAND, DAVID G. and HAWES MICHAEL K., *World Politics, Power, Interdependence & Dependence*. Toronto: Harcourt Brace Jovanovich, 1990.

HALL, PETER A., *Governing the Economy, The Politics of State Intervention in Britain and France*. New York: Oxford University Press, 1986.

HALL, STUART, 'Encoding/Decoding' in Stuart Hall et al. (eds), *Culture, Media, Language: Working Papers in Cultural Studies, 1972–79*. London: Hutchinson, 1980, pp. 128–38.

HALL, STUART, CRITCHER, CHAS, JEFFERSON, TONY, CLARKE, JOHN AND ROBERTS, BRIAN *Policing the Crisis: Mugging, the State and Law and Order*. London: Macmillan, 1978.

HALLIDAY, FRED, *The Making of the Second Cold War*. London: Verso, 1983.

HAMELINK, CEES J., *Cultural Autonomy in Global Communications: Planning National Information Policy*. London: Centre for the Study of Communication and Culture, 1988.

HAMPLE, DALE, 'Communication and the Unconscious,' in Brenda Dervin and Melvin J. Voigt (eds), *Progress in Communication Sciences*, vol. viii. Norwood, NJ: Ablex, 1987, pp. 83–121.

'HANGING on a Brighter Star,' *Cable and Satellite Europe*, 150 (June 1996) 80.

HANSEN, ALLEN C., *USIA, Public Diplomacy in the Computer Age*. New York: Praeger Publishers, 1984.

HANSON, JARICE, CONROY, THOMAS J. AND DONNELLY, DAVID 'Initiatives and Ownership, HDTV and the Influence of Corporatism in the United States,' *Communication Research*, 19 (6) (December 1992) 806–18.

HARTZ, LOUIS, *The Liberal Tradition in America, An Interpretation of American Political Thought since the Revolution*. New York: Harvest/Harcourt Brace Jovanovich, 1955.

HARVEY, DAVID, *The Condition of Postmodernity, An Enquiry into the Origins of Cultural Change*. Oxford: Basil Blackwell, 1990.

HAULE, JOHN JAMES, 'United States Foreign Telecommunications Policy Goals–Issues, Explanations and Prospects,' *Gazette, International Journal for Mass Communication Studies*. 44 (1) (July 1989) 27–43.

HAVICK, JOHN J. (ed.) *Communications Policy and the Political Process*. Westport, Conn.: Greenwood Press, 1983.

'HDTV Uses Go Beyond Broadcasting,' *Broadcasting*, 118 (26) (25 June 1990) 69–70.

HILLS, JILL, *Deregulating Telecoms, Competition and Control in the United States, Japan and Britain*. London: Frances Pinter, 1986.

HILLS, JILL, 'Dynamics of US International Telecom Policy,' *Transnational Data Report*, XII (2) (February 1989) 14–21.

HILLS, JILL, *The Democracy Gap, The Politics of Information and Communication Technologies in the United States and Europe*. New York: Greenwood Press, 1991.

HOGGART, RICHARD, *The Uses of Literacy, Aspects of Working-class Life with Special Reference to Publications and Entertainments*. London: Penguin, 1990.

HOLMES, BRADLEY P., 'US Reactions to EC Telecom Policy,' *Transnational Data and Communications Report*, XIII (4) (April 1990) 15–16.

HOWARD, DONALD G. and RYANS, JOHN K., 'The Probable Effect of Satellite TV on Agency/Client Relationships,' *Journal of Advertising Research*, 28 (6) (December 1988/January 1989) 41–6.

HORWITZ, ROBERT B., 'The First Amendment Meets Some New Technologies, Broadcasting, Common Carriers, and Free Speech in the 1990s,' *Theory and Society*, 20 (1) (February 1991) 21–72.

HORWITZ, ROBERT B., *The Irony of Regulatory Reform, The Deregulation of American Telecommunications*. New York: Oxford University Press, 1989.

HSIUNG, JAMES CHIEH, 'Status and Implications of Federal Regulation of Direct Broadcast Satellite.' Unpublished PhD dissertation: Bowling Green State University, 1984.

HUDSON, HEATHER, *Communication Satellites: Their Development and Impact.* New York: Free Press, 1990.

HYMER, STEPHEN, 'Economics of Imperialism – Discussion,' *The American Economic Review,* LX (2) (May 1970) 243–6.

HYMER, STEPHEN, 'The Efficiency (Contradictions) of Multinational Corporations,' *The American Economic Review,* LX (2) (May 1970) 441–8.

HYMER, STEPHEN, 'The Internationalization of Capital,' *Journal of Economic Issues* VI (1) (March 1972) 91–111.

'IF One Conference Fails, the US Has Alternatives,' *New York Times,* 4 December 1990, p. C5.

IMBER, MARK F., *The USA, ILO, UNESCO and IAEA, Politicization and Withdrawal in the Specialized Agencies.* Houndmills: Macmillan, 1989,

'INFORMATION Flow Vital to Global Economy,' *Transnational Data Report,* VI (5) (July–August 1983) 239–42.

INNIS, HAROLD A., 'The Role of Intelligence,' *Canadian Journal of Economics and Political Science,* I (2) (May 1935) 280–7.

INNIS, HAROLD A., *Political Economy in the Modern State.* Toronto: Ryerson Press, 1946.

INNIS, HAROLD A., *Empire and Communications.* Toronto: University of Toronto Press, 1972.

INNIS, HAROLD A., *Essays in Canadian Economic History.* Mary Q. Innis (ed.). Toronto: University of Toronto Press, 1973.

INNIS, HAROLD A., *The Cod Fisheries, The History of an International Economy.* Toronto: University of Toronto Press, 1978.

INNIS, HAROLD A., *The Bias of Communication.* Toronto: University of Toronto Press, 1982.

INNIS, HAROLD A., *The Fur Trade in Canada.* Toronto: University of Toronto Press, 1984.

INTERNATIONAL Communications Studies Program, *Communications Policy: Issues for the New Administration.* Washington, DC: Center for Strategic and International Studies, 1993.

INTERNATIONAL Intellectual Property Alliance, 'People's Republic of China Tops IIPA's Special 301 Target List with almost $830 Million in Estimated Losses due to Piracy'. Washington: IIPA Press Release, 18 February 1994.

'ITU Restructuring Is Intended to Make it More "Market-Oriented",' *Satellite Week,* 15 (7) (15 February 1993) 5–6.

JAMES, WILLIAM L. and HILL, JOHN S., 'International Advertising Messages: To Adapt or not to Adapt (That is the Question),' *Journal of Advertising Research.* 31 (3) (June–July 1991) 65–71.

JANISCH, HUDSON N., 'The Canada–US Free Trade Agreement, Impact on Telecommunications,' *Telecommunications Policy,* 13 (2) (1989) 99–103.

JASENTULIYANA, NANDARIRI, 'Direct Satellite Broadcasting and the Third World,' *Columbia Journal of Transnational Law,* 13 (1974) 68–70.

JEFFERSON, DAVID J., 'Average Price of Hollywood Movie Hits All-time High of $28.8 Million,' *Globe and Mail*. 13 March 1993, p. C3.

JESSELL, HARRY A., 'White House Calls for Video Dialtone,' *Broadcasting*, 122 (23) (1 June 1992) 26.

JESSELL, HARRY A., 'FCC Calls for Telco TV,' *Broadcasting*, 122 (30) (20 July 1992) 3 and 8.

JESSELL, HARRY A., 'Telcos Want Bigger Stake in Programming,' *Broadcasting*, 122 (31) (27 July 1992) 24.

JESSELL, HARRY A., 'Going for it in DBS,' *Broadcasting & Cable*, 126 (19) (29 April 1996) 6.

JESSELL, HARRY and LAMBERT, PETER 'The Uncertain Future of DBS,' *Broadcasting*, 116 (11) (13 March 1989) 42–4.

JESSELL, HARRY et al., 'Special Report: Domestic Satellites, Dawning of a New Generation,' *Broadcasting*, 115 (3) (18 July 1988) 39–59.

JHALLY, SUT, 'The Spectacle of Accumulation,' *The Insurgent Sociologist*, 12 (3) (Summer 1984) 41–57.

'JOHN Malone's TV-Dinner,' *The Economist*, 328 (7819) (10 July 1993) 59.

JOHNSON, LELAND L. and Castleman, Deborah R., *Direct Broadcast Satellites, A Competitive Alternative to Cable Television?* Santa Monica, Cal.: Rand Corporation, 1991.

JOHNSON, LELAND L. and REED, DAVID P. 'Telephone Company Entry into Cable Television, An Evaluation,' *Telecommunications Policy*, 16 (2) (March 1988) 122–34.

JUSSAWALLA, MEHEROO, 'Economics and Global Impact of Telecom Deregulation,' *Transnational Data and Communications Report*, XI (3) (March 1988) 10–16.

JUSSAWALLA, MEHEROO, OKUMA, TADAYUKI and ARAKI, TOSHIHIRO (eds), *Information Technology and Global Interdependence*. New York: Greenwood Press, 1989.

KATZENBACH, NICHOLAS, 'Framing Telecommunication Policy – An IBM View,' *Transnational Data Report*, VIII (3) (April–May 1985) 167–8.

KEGLEY, CHARLES W., Jr and WITTKOPF, EUGENE R., *American Foreign Policy, Patterns and Process*. 3rd ed. New York: St Martin's Press, 1987.

KEGLEY, CHARLES W., Jr and WITTKOPF, EUGENE R., *World Politics, Trend and Transformation*. 3rd ed. New York: St Martin's Press, 1989.

KELM, ELLEN ELIZABETH JAKES, *The Commercial Viability of Direct Broadcast Satellites in the United States*. Unpublished PhD dissertation: Northwestern University, 1985.

KEREVER, ANDRÉ, 'Satellite Broadcasting and Copyright,' *Copyright Bulletin*, XXIV (3) (1990) 6–22.

KINSLEY, MICHAEL E., *Outer Space and Inner Sanctums: Government, Business, and Satellite Communication*. New York: John Wiley & Sons, 1976.

KOSTYRA, RICHARD, 'Communications in the Future, The Changing Media Environment,' *Vital Speeches of the Day*, LVII (1) (15 October 1990) 21–4.

KOTHARI, RAJNI, 'The Yawning Vacuum: A World without Alternatives,' *Alternatives*, 18 (2) (1993) 119–39.

KRAATZ, KLAUS-JURGEN, 'GATT and Telecommunications,' *International Business Lawyer*, 18 (11) (December 1990) 516–18.

KRASNER,STEPHEND.,*DefendingtheNationalInterest,RawMaterialsInvestmentsandUSForeignPolicy.*Princeton:Princeton UniversityPress,1978.

KRASNER, STEPHEN D., 'Global Communications and National Power, Life on the Pareto Frontier,' *World Politics*, 43 (3) (April 1991) 336–66.

KUPCHAN, CHARLES A., 'Empire, Military Power, and Economic Decline,' *International Security*, 13 (4) (Spring 1989) 36–53.

KURTH, JAMES R., 'The United States and Western Europe in the Reagan Era,' in Morris H. Morley (ed.), *Crisis and Confrontation, Ronald Reagan's Foreign Policy.* Totowa, NJ: Rowman & Littlefield, 1988, pp. 46–79.

LACHMANN, LUDWIG M., *Capital and its Structure.* London: G. Bell & Sons, 1956.

LAMBERT, PETER, 'HDTV Push Feels like Shove to Broadcasters,' *Broadcasting*, 122 (27) (29 June 1992) 3 and 13.

LAMBERT, PETER, 'Digital Compression Now Arriving on the Fast Track,' *Broadcasting*, 122 (31) (27 July 1992) 40–6.

LAMBERT, PETER, 'Video Dialtone: First the Copper Age,' *Broadcasting*, 122 (45) (2 November 1992) 62.

LARSEN, PETER (ed.) *Import/Export: International Flow of Television Fiction.* Paris: UNESCO, 1990.

LEAFFER, MARSHALL A., 'Protecting United States Intellectual Property Abroad: Toward a New Multilateralism,' *Iowa Law Review*, 76 (2) (January 1991) 273–308.

LEE, CHIN-CHUAN, *Media Imperialism Reconsidered, The Homogenizing of Television Culture.* Beverly Hills, Cal.: Sage, 1979.

'LEE Cites Need Now to Start Shaping Ground Rules for Direct Satellites,' *Broadcasting*, 85 (9) (27 August 1973) 38.

LEE, KELLY, *Global Telecommunications Regulation, A Political Economy Perspective.* London: Pinter, 1996.

LEE, PAUL SIU-NAM, 'Communication Imperialism and Dependency: A Conceptual Clarification,' *Gazette, International Journal for Mass Communication Studies*, 41 (2) (1988) 69–83.

LEESON, KENNETH W., *International Communications, Blueprint for Policy.* Amsterdam: Elsevier Science Publishers, 1984.

LEISS, WILLIAM, KLINE, STEPHEN and JHALLY, SUT, *Social Communication in Advertising, Persons, Products & Images of Well-being.* Scarborough: Nelson Canada, 1990.

LERNER, N.C., 'Telecommunications Privatization and Liberalization in Developing Countries,' *Telecommunication Journal*, 58 (6) (May 1991) 279–86.

LESSING, LAWRENCE, 'Cinderella in the Sky,' *Fortune*, LXXVI (5) (October 1967) 131–3 and 196–208.

LEVINE, JONATHAN B. and GROSS, NEIL, 'HDTV: Europe May Already be an Also-Ran,' *Business Week* (Industrial/Technology edn), 3255 (13 January 1992) 46.

LEVINE, JONATHAN B., 'This Satellite Company Runs Rings Around Rivals,' *Business Week* (Industrial/Technology edn), 3199 (11 February 1991) 74–5.

LEVINSON, PAUL, *Mind at Large: Knowing in the Technological Age.* Greenwich: Jai Press, 1988.

LIVANT, BILL, 'The Audience Commodity,' *Canadian Journal of Political and Social Theory*, 3 (1) (Winter 1979) 91–106.

'LOWERING the Voice,' *Newsweek* (9 July 1973) 60–1.

LUKES, STEPHEN, *Power, A Radical View.* London: Macmillan, 1979.

LUTHER, SARA FLETCHER, *The United States and the Direct Broadcast Satellite.* New York: Oxford University Press, 1988.

LUXENBERG, BARBARA and MOSSINGHOFF, GERALD J., 'Intellectual Property and Space Activities,' *Journal of Space Law*, 13 (1) (1985) 8–21.

LYON, DAVID, *The Information Society: Issues and Illusions.* Cambridge: Polity Press, 1988.

MCANANY, EMILE G. and WILKINSON, KENTON T., 'From Cultural Imperialists to Takeover Victims? Questions on Hollywood's Buyouts from the Critical Tradition,' *Communication Research*, 19 (6) (December 1992) 724–48.

MACBRIDE, SEAN, ABEL, ELIE, BEUVE-MERY, HUBERT, *et al. Many Voices, One World, Towards a New More Just and More Efficient World Information and Communication Order. Report by the International Commission for the Study of Communication Problems.* Paris: Kogan Page/ UNESCO, 1984.

MCCHESNEY, ROBERT W., 'The Global Struggle for Democratic Communication,' *Monthly Review*, 48 (3) (July–August 1996) 1–20.

MCCONVILLE, JIM, 'DBS at Top of Murdoch Wish List,' *Broadcasting & Cable*, 126 (15) (8 April 1996) 16.

MCDOWELL, STEPHEN D., *Globalization, Liberalization and Policy Change: A Political Economy of India's Communications Sector.* London and New York: Macmillan and St Martin's Press, 1996.

MCMAHAN, JEFF, *Reagan and the World, Imperial Policy in the New Cold War.* New York: Monthly Review Press, 1985.

MCQUAIG, LINDA, *The Quick and the Dead, Brian Mulroney, Big Business and the Seduction of Canada.* Toronto: Viking, 1991.

MAGDOFF, HARRY, 'Militarism and Imperialism,' *The American Economic Review*, LX (2) (May 1970) 237–42.

MAGNANT, ROBERT S., *Domestic Satellite: An FCC Giant Step.* Boulder, Col.: Westview Press, 1977.

'MAKING Room at the Table of Organization,' *Chronicle of International Communication*, V (5) (June 1984) 1–2.

MALMGREN, HAROLD B., 'Negotiating International Rules for Trade in Services,' *World Economy*, 8 (1) (1985) 11–26.

MANET, ENRIQUE GONZALEZ, 'Technology, TDF and a New International Information Order,' *Transnational Data Report*, V (4) (June 1982) 205–8.

MANSELL, ROBIN, 'Telecommunications and Productivity,' *Canadian Journal of Communication*, 8 (1) (June, July, August 1981) 56–60.

MANSELL, ROBIN, 'Is Policy Research an Irrelevant Exercise? The Case of Canadian DBS Planning,' *Journal of Communication*, 35 (2) (Spring 1985) 154–66.

MANSELL, ROBIN and SILVERSTONE, ROGER (eds) *Communication by Design, The Politics of Information and Communication Technologies.* New York: Oxford University Press, 1996.

MAREMONT, MARK, 'Rupert Murdoch's Rendezvous in Space,' *Business Week* 3188 (19 November 1990) 63–4.

'MARKETPLACE News,' *Cable and Satellite Europe*, 146 (February 1996) 52.

MARTINEZ, LARRY, *Communication Satellites: Power Politics in Space.* Dedham, Mass.: Artech House, 1985.

MARX, KARL, *Capital, A Critique of Political Economy* vol. I. Moscow: Progress Publishers, 1977.

MARX, KARL, *Capital, A Critique of Political Economy*, vol. II. Moscow: Progress Publishers, 1978.

MARX, KARL, *Capital, A Critique of Political Economy*, vol. III. Moscow: Progress Publishers, 1966.

MARX, KARL, *The Communist Manifesto.* Harmondsworth: Penguin, 1979.

MARX, KARL and ENGELS, FREDERICK, *Karl Marx and Frederick Engels Collected Works*, vols 28 and 29. New York: International Publishers, 1986 and 1987.

MARX, KARL and ENGLES, FREDERICK *The German Ideology.* C.J. Arthur (ed.), New York: International Publishers, 1984.

MARX, KARL, and ENGLES, FREDERICK, *Pre-Capitalist Socio-economic Formations, A Collection.* Moscow: Progress Publishers, 1979.

MASSACHUSETTS Institute of Technology Communication Forum, *Direct Broadcast Satellites.* Unpublished Seminar Notes: 1 November, 1990.

MATTELART, ARMAND, *Advertising International, The Privatisation of Public Space.* Michael Chanan (trans.), London: Routledge, 1991.

MATTELART, ARMAND and SIEGELAUB, SETH (eds) *Communication and Class Struggle*, vol. 1. *Capitalism, Imperialism.* New York: International General, 1979.

MATTELART, ARMAND and SIEGELAUB, SETH (eds) *Communication and Class Struggle*, vol. 2. *Liberation, Socialism.* New York: International General, 1983.

MAYO, JOHN S., 'Communications after 2000 AD, The American Scene,' *Vital Speeches of the Day*, LVIII (19) (15 July 1992) 599–603.

MELODY, WILLIAM H., SALTER, LIORA and HEYER PAUL (eds) *Culture, Communication and Dependency.* Norwood: Ablex, 1981.

MEYER, NOEL, 'In Units We Trust,' *Cable and Satellite Europe*, 148 (April 1996) 72, 74–6.

MILL, JOHN STUART, *On Liberty.* New York: The Liberal Arts Press, 1956.

MILLER, EDYTHE S., 'Some Market Structure and Regulatory Implications of the Brave New World of Telecommunications,' *Journal of Economic Issues*, XXVII (1) (March 1993) 19–39.

MILLS, MIKE, 'The New Kings of Capitol Hill, Regional Bells Use Lobbying Clout to Push for New Markets,' *Washington Post*, 23 April 1995, pp. H1 and H5.

MIRABITO, MICHAEL M. and MORGENSTERN, BARBARA L. *The New Communications Technologies.* Boston: Focal Press, 1990.

MITTELMAN, JAMES H. and PASHA, MUSTAPHA KAMAL, *Out from Underdevelopment Revisited: Changing Global Structures and the Remaking of the Third World.* London and New York: Macmillan and St Martin's Press, 1996.

MOORES, SHUAN, 'Satellite TV as Cultural Sign: Consumption, Embedding and Articulation,' *Media, Culture and Society*, 15(4) (October 1993) 621–39.

MORAN, MICHAEL, *The Politics of the Financial Services Revolution, The USA, UK and Japan.* London: Macmillan, 1991.

MORERA, ESTEVE, 'Gramsci and Democracy,' *Canadian Journal of Political Science* XXIII (1) (March 1990) 23–37.

MORGAN, GEORGE, MORGAN, KAREN and PARKER, ALAN, 'Industrial Policy and the Case of High Definition Television,' *Challenge*, 33 (5) (September/October 1990) 55–7.

MORLEY, DAVID, *Family Television: Cultural Power and Domestic Leisure.* London: Comedia, 1986.

MORLEY, DAVID, 'Changing Paradigms in Audience Studies,' in Ellen Seiter, Hans Borchers, Gabriele Kreutzner and Eva-Maria Warth (eds), *Remote Control, Television, Audiences, and Cultural Power.* London: Routledge, 1989.

MORNER, ANNA, 'The GATT Uruguay Round and Copyright,' *Copyright Bulletin*, XXV (2) (1991) 7–17.

MOSCO, VINCENT, 'Toward a Theory of the State and Telecommunication Policy,' *Journal of Communication*, 38 (1) (Winter 1988) 107–24.

MOSCO, VINCENT, 'Who Makes US Government Policy in World Communications?' *Journal of Communication*, 29 (1) (Winter 1979) 158–64.

MOSCO, VINCENT, *The Pay-Per Society.* Toronto: Garamond Press, 1989.

MOSCO, VINCENT, *The Political Economy of Communication.* London: Sage, 1996.

MOSCO, VINCENT and WASKO, JANET (eds), *The Critical Communications Revue*, vol. II: *Changing Patterns of Communications Control.* Norwood: Ablex, 1984.

MOSCO, VINCENT and WASKO, JANET (eds) *The Political Economy of Information.* Madison: University of Wisconsin Press, 1988.

MOTION Picture Association of America, 'Comments'. Submission to National Telecommunications and Information Administration for Globalization of the Mass Media Study. Unpublished: 30 May 1990.

MOTION Picture Association of America, Inc., *Trade Barriers to Exports of US Filmed Entertainment.* Report to the United States Trade Representative. Unpublished: February 1992.

MOTION Picture Export Association of America, *Comments Regarding EC Proposal for a Council Directive on Copyright Aspects of Satellite Broadcasting and Cable Retransmission.* Report submitted to the Legal Affairs Committee of the European Parliament. Unpublished: 25 March 1992.

'MOVING up the Timetable on DBS, *Broadcasting*, 119 (8) (20 August 1990) 27–8.

MOWLANA, HAMID, *Global Communication in Transition, The End of Diversity?* Thousand Oaks: Sage, 1996.

MOWLANA, HAMID and WILSON, LAURIE J. *Communication Technology and Development*. Paris: UNESCO, 1988.

MUELLER, MILTON, 'Telecommunications as Infrastructure: A Skeptical View,' *Journal of Communication*, 43 (2) (Spring 1993) 147–59.

MULGAN, GEOFF J., *Communication and Control*. New York: The Guilford Press, 1991.

MURDOCK, GRAHAM and GOLDING, PETER, 'Information Poverty and Political Inequality: Citizenship in the Age of Privatized Communications,' *Journal of Communication*, 39 (3) (Summer 1989) 180–95.

MURPHY, CRAIG N., *International Organization and Industrial Change, Global Governance since 1850*. Cambridge: Polity Press, 1994.

MUSOLF, LLOYD D. (ed.) *Communications Satellites in Political Orbit*. San Francisco: Chandler, 1968.

NATIONAL Association of Broadcasters, 'Comments of the National Association of Broadcasters'. Unpublished submission to National Telecommunications and Information Administration for Globalization of Mass Media Study: 30 May 1990.

NATIONAL Cable Television Association, 'Reply Comments of the National Cable Television Association, Inc.' Unpublished submission to National Telecommunications and Information Administration for Globalization of Mass Media Study: 11 July 1990.

NATIONAL Cable Television Association, 'Facts at a Glance: International Cable'. Washington, DC: NCTA Research and Policy Department, March 1991.

NATIONAL Cable Television Association, 'Cable Television Developments'. Washington, DC: NCTA Research and Policy Department, May 1992.

NATIONAL Cable Television Association, *Cable Television and America's Telecommunications Infrastructure*. Washington, DC: NCTA, April 1993.

NEGRINE, RALPH, *Satellite Broadcasting, The Politics and Implications of the New Media*. London: Routledge, 1988.

NEGRINE, RALPH and PAPATHANASSOPOULOS, S. 'The Internationalization of Television,' *European Journal of Communication*, 6 (1) (March 1991) 9–32.

NEWBERG, PAULA R. (ed.) *New Directions in Telecommunications Policy*, vol.1: *Regulatory Policy: Telephony and Mass Media*. Durham, NC: Duke University Press, 1989.

NEWBERG, PAULA R. (ed.) *New Directions in Telecommunications Policy*, vol.2: *Information Policy and Economic Policy*. Durham, NC: Duke University Press, 1989.

NEWELL, GREGORY J., 'FY 1984 Assistance Requests for Organizations and Programs,' *Department of State Bulletin* (May 1983) 79–80.

NEWELL, GREGORY J., 'Perspectives on the US Withdrawal from UNESCO,' *Department of State Bulletin* (January 1985) 53–6.

NEWELL, GREGORY J., 'Freedom of the Press: The Need for Vigilance,' *Department of State Bulletin* (January 1985) 62–4.

NEWELL, GREGORY J., 'The New US Observer Role in UNESCO,' *Department of State Bulletin* (March 1985) 73–4.

NEWELL, GREGORY J., 'Keeping International Cooperation Alive,' *Society*, 22 (September/October 1985) 15–20.

NEWS Corporation International, 'Comments of the News Corporation Limited on the Globalization of the Mass Media Firms'. Unpublished submission to National Telecommunications and Information Administration for Globalization of Mass Media Study: 30 May 1990.

NORDENSTRENG, KAARLE and SCHILLER, HERBERT I. (eds) *National Sovereignty and International Communication*. Norwood, NJ: Ablex, 1979.

NORDENSTRENG, KAARLE, *The Mass Media Declaration of UNESCO*. Norwood, NJ: Ablex, 1984.

NORDLINGER, ERIC A., *On the Autonomy of the Democratic State*. Cambridge, Mass.: Harvard University Press, 1981.

O'BRIEN, RITA CRUISE, 'Information Emerging as Key North-South Issue,' *Transnational Data Report*, V (6) (September 1982) 317–19.

OSTERGAARD, BERNT STUBBE and KLEINSTEUBER, HANS J., 'The Technology Factor,' Karen Siune and Wolfgang Truetzschler (eds), *Dynamics of Media Politics, Broadcast and Electronic Media in Western Europe*. London: Sage, 1992, 57–74.

'PANAMSAT Likely Will Attract a Host of Aerospace, Telco Suitors,' in *Satellite News*, 19 (15) (8 September 1996) n.p.

'PANELISTS Discuss Future of DBS,' *Broadcasting*, 118 (15) (9 April, 1990) p. 59.

PANITCH, LEO, 'Globalisation and the State,' in Ralph Miliband and Leo Panitch (eds.), *Socialist Register 1994*. London: The Merlin Press, 1994, 60–93.

PANITCH, LEO, 'Globalization, States, and Left Strategies,' *Social Justice*, 23 (1–2) (1996) 79–90.

PANITCH, LEO, 'Rethinking the Role of the State in an Era of Globalization'. Toronto: unpublished mimeo, n.d.

PAPATHANASSOPOULOS, STYLIANOS, 'The EC: "Television Without Frontiers" But With Media Monopolies?' *InterMedia*, 18 (3) (June–July 1990) 27–30.

PARKER, IAŃ, 'Harold Innis, Karl Marx and Canadian Political Economy,' *Queen's Quarterly*, 84 (4) (Winter 1977) 545–63.

PARKER, IAN, 'The National Policy, Neoclassical Economics, and the Political Economy of Tariffs,' *Journal of Canadian Studies*, 14 (3) (Fall 1979) 95–110.

PARKER, IAN, 'Staples, Communications and the Economics of Capacity, Overhead Costs, Rigidity, and Bias,' in Duncan Cameron (ed.), *Explorations in Canadian Economic History*. Ottawa: University of Ottawa Press, 1985.

PARKER, IAN, 'Editor's Introduction,' in W. Thomas Easterbrook, *North American Patterns of Growth and Development: The Continental Context*. Ian Parker (ed.). Toronto: University of Toronto Press, 1990.

PARKER, IAN, HUTCHESON, JOHN and CRAWLEY, PATRICK (eds) *The Strategy of Canadian Culture in the 21st Century*. Toronto: TopCat Communications, 1988.

PARTRIDGE, JOHN, 'Pub-and-Club Viewing on Tap for the Future,' *Globe and Mail*, 29 June 1991, B1-B2.

PATEL, VIRAT, 'Broadband Convergence, A View of the Regulatory Barriers,' *Telecommunications Policy* 16 (2) (March 1992) 98–104.

PATEMAN, CAROLE, *Participation and Democratic Theory*. Cambridge: Cambridge University Press, 1983.

PAUL, JOEL R., 'Images from Abroad: Making Direct Broadcasting by Satellite Safe for Sovereignty,' *Hastings International Comparative Law Review*, 9 (2) (Winter 1986) 329–75.

PEARCE, ALAN , 'Telecom Policy and the White House,' *Telecommunications* (November 1980) 16.

PEARCE, ALAN, 'Bush's Policy-making Team One Year Later,' *Network World*, 7 (34) (20 August 1990) 1, 31–3 and 37.

PEARCE, KEVIN, 'The World is my Franchise,' *Channels*, 10 (18) (3 December 1990) 30–1.

PEERS, MARTIN, 'TCI: Regulatory Climate Improving for Cable Giant,' *Atlanta Constitution* (31 August 1995), F4.

PETERSMANN, ERNST-ULRICH, 'International Competition Rules for the GATT-MTO World Trade and Legal System,' *Journal of World Trade*, 27 (6) (December 1993) 43–81.

PEYRET, PATRICE J.Y., 'Defeating Pay-TV Pirates with Smart Cards' in IEEE 1990, *International Conference on Consumer Electronics, Digest of Technical Papers*, Rosemont, Ill.: IEEE, 1990, 316–17.

PICHLER, MARIE HELEN, *Copyright Problems of Satellite and Cable Television in Europe*. London: Graham & Trotman/Martinus Nijhoff, 1987.

PIJL, KEES Van Der, 'Ruling Classes, Hegemony, and the State System,' *International Journal of Political Economy*, 19 (3) (Fall 1989) 7–35.

PIPE, RUSSELL G., 'Telecommunications Services: Considerations for Developing Countries in Uruguay Round Negotiations,' in United Nations Conference on Trade and Development, *Trade in Services: Sectoral Issues*. New York: United Nations, 1989, 49–111.

PLOMAN, EDWARD W., 'National Needs in an International Communication Setting,' *Transnational Data Report*. VI (5) (July–August 1983).

PLOMAN, EDWARD W., *Space, Earth and Communication*. Westport, Conn.: Quorum Books, 1984.

PORTER, HENRY, 'Keeper of the Global Gate,' *Manchester Guardian Weekly*, 155 (26) (29 December 1996) 16–17.

PORTER, VINCENT, 'Film and Television in the Single European Market – Dreams and Delusions,' *Journal of Media Law & Practice*, 13 (1) (1992) 148–57.

PORTER, VINCENT, 'The Re-regulation of Television: Pluralism, Constitutionality and the Free Market in the USA, West Germany, France and the UK,' *Media, Culture and Society*, 11 (1) (January 1989) 5–27.

POWELL, JON T., 'Towards a Negotiable Definition of Propaganda for International Agreements Related to Direct Broadcast Satellites,' *Law and Comtemporary Problems* 45 (1) (Winter 1982) 3–35.

PRATT, LARRY, 'The Reagan Doctrine and the Third World,' in Ralph Miliband, Leo Panitch and John Saville, (eds), *Socialist Register, 1987*. London: Merlin Press, 1987, 61–96.

PRESTON, WILLIAM, Jr, HERMAN, EDWARD S. AND SCHILLER, HERBERT I. *Hope & Folly, The United States and UNESCO 1945–1985*. Minneapolis: University of Minnesota Press, 1989.

PRITCHARD, WILBUR L. and OGATA, MUTSUO, 'Satellite Direct Broadcast,' *Proceedings of the IEEE*, 78 (7) (July 1990) 1116–40.

PRITCHARD, WILBUR L. and RADIN, HARLEY W., 'Direct Broadcast Satellite Service by Direct Broadcast Satellite Corporation,' *IEEE Communications Magazine*, 22 (3) (March 1984) 19–25.

PROCEEDINGS of the European Conferences on Satellite Broadcasting and Satellite Communications 1987, *Satellite Communications & Broadcasting 87*. London: Online, 1988.

'QUARTERLY Connections,' *Cable and Satellite Europe*, 153 (September 1996) 50.

QUEENEY, KATHRYN M., *Direct Broadcast Satellites and the United Nations*. Leyden: Sijthoff & Noordhoff, 1978.

QUESTER, GEORGE H., *The International Politics of Television*. Lexington, Mass.: Lexington Books, 1990.

QUINONES, ROBERTO ALVAREZ, 'Decolonization of Information,' *Transnational Data Report*, VII (8) (December 1984) 443.

RAINA, ASOKA, 'Star-struck,' *Cable and Satellite Europe*, 112 (April 1993) 42 and 44–5.

RAINGER, PETER, GREGORY, DAVID N., HARVEY, ROBERT V. AND JENNINGS, ANTHONY, *Satellite Broadcasting*. Chichester: John Wiley & Sons, 1985.

REEVES, GEOFFREY, *Communications and the 'Third World'*. London: Routledge, 1993.

REINHART, EDWARD E., 'Satellite Broadcasting and Distribution in the United States,' *Telecommunication Journal*, 57 (6) (June 1990) 407–18.

'RE-REGULATION Frenzy,' *The Economist*, 322 (7746) (15, February 1992) 25–6.

RICHARDSON, BONNIE (MPAA), letter to Donna R. Koehneke (US International Trade Commission) 2 May 1994. Unpublished.

'THE RIGHT Stuff, Ambassador Diana Lady Dougan,' *Broadcasting* (18 March 1985) n.p.

RITCHIE, CYNTHIA, 'Prime Focus: DirecTV,' *Cable and Satellite Europe*, 116 (August 1993) 29–30.

RITCHIE, CYNTHIA, 'Turning Defence into Offense,' *Cable and Satellite Europe*, 116 (August 1993) 26–7.

RITCHIE, L. DAVID, 'Another Turn of the Information Revolution: Relevance, Technology, and the Information Society,' *Communication Research*, 18 (3) (June 1991) 412–27.

ROACH, COLLEEN, 'The US Position on the New World Information and Communication Order,' *Journal of Communication*, 37 (4) (Autumn 1987) 36–51.

ROBINSON, EUGENE, 'Rupert Murdoch: Global Gatekeeper,' *Washington Post*, 2 October 1993, p. C6.

ROBINSON, GLEN O. (ed.) *Communications for Tomorrow, Policy Perspectives for the 1980s*. New York: Praeger Publishers, 1978.

ROBINSON, KENNETH, 'The Significance of Telecom 2000' in Harvey M. Sapolsky, Rhonda J. Crane, W. Russell Neuman and Eli M. Noam (eds., *The Telecommunications Revolution, Past, Present, and Future*. London: Routledge, 1992, 28–38.

ROBINSON, PETER, 'The International Dimension of Telecommunications Policy Issues,' *Telecommunications Policy*, 15 (2) (April 1991) 95–100.

ROBINSON, PETER, SAUVANT, KARL P. AND GOVITRIKAR, VISH-
WAS P. (eds), *Electronic Highways for World Trade, Issues in Telecommunication and Data Services*. Boulder Col.: Westview Press, 1989.

ROOBEEK, ANNEMIEKE J., 'The Crisis in Fordism and the Rise of a New
Technological Paradigm,' *Futures*, 19 (2) (April 1987) 129–54.

ROSENBERG, NATHAN, 'Marx as a Student of Technology,' in Les Levi-
dow and Bob Young, *Science, Technology and the Labour Process*. Oxford:
Blackrose Press, 1981, 8–31.

ROSS, BRIAN L., ' "I Love Lucy," But the European Community Doesn't:
Apparent Protectionism in the European Community's Broadcast Market,'
*Brooklyn Journal of International Law*, XVI (3) (1990) 529–60.

ROTSTEIN, ABRAHAM, 'Economics and Culture: Separation without
Divorce,' in Harry Hillman Chartrand, William S. Hendon and Claire
McCaughey (eds), *Cultural Economics 88: A Canadian Perspective*. Akron,
Oh.: Association for Cultural Economics, 1989, 21–30.

RUSSETT, BRUCE, 'The Mysterious Case of Vanishing Hegemony; or, Is
Mark Twain Really Dead?' *International Organization*, 39 (2) (Spring 1985)
207–31.

RUSSETT, BRUCE and HANSON, ELIZABETH C., *Interest and Ideology,
The Foreign Policy Beliefs of American Businessmen*. San Francisco: W.H.
Freeman Company, 1975.

RUTH, STEVEN, 'The Regulation of Spillover Transmissions from Direct
Broadcast Satellites in Europe,' *Federal Communications Law Journal* 42 (1)
(December 1989) 107–29.

RUTKOWSKI, ANTHONY M., 'Role of Direct Broadcasting Satellites in
the Integrated Communications Environment,' *Transnational Data Report*,
VI (1) (January–February 1983) 41–2.

SAHIN, HALUK and ROBINSON, JOHN P., 'Beyond the Realm of Necessity, Television and the Colonization of Leisure,' in D. Charles Whitney
and Ellen Wartella (eds), *Mass Communication Review Yearbook, vol. 3.
Beverly Hills, Cal.: Sage, 1982*.

SALWEN, MICHAEL B., 'Cultural Imperialism: A Media Effects
Approach,' *Critical Studies in Mass Communications*. 8 (1) (March 1991)
29–38.

SANDBANK, C.P., 'The Emergence of Digital Television,' in C.P. Sandbank,
(ed.), *Digital Television*. Chichester: John Wiley & Sons, 1990, 1–20.

SARNOFF, ROBERT W., 'Freedom to Communicate'. Address to the
Executives' Club of Chicago, 9 February 1973. New York: RCA, 1973.

SARNOFF, ROBERT W., 'Satellite Communications Concepts for a New
Age'. Keynote address to the 2nd World Telecommunications Exhibition in
Geneva, 2 October 1975. New York: RCA, 1975.

SATELLITE Broadcasting and Communications Association of America,
'Comments in the Matter of Telephone Company–Cable Television Cross-
ownership Rules'. Submitted to the Federal Communications Commission.
Unpublished: 3 February 1991.

SATELLITE Broadcasting and Communications Association of America,
'Fact Sheet'. Alexandria: SBCA, n.d.

SATELLITE Systems Engineering, Inc., *International Direct Broadcast Satellites*. Potomac, Md.: Phillips Telecommunications Research, 1989.

SAUVANT, KARL P., 'The Potential of Multinational Enterprises as Vehicles for the Transmission of Business Culture,' in K. Sauvant and Farid G. Lavipour (eds), *Controlling Multinational Enterprises, Problems, Strategies, Counterstrategies.* Boulder, Col.: Westview Press, 1976, 39–78.

SAUVANT, KARL P., *International Transactions in Services: The Politics of Transborder Data Flows.* Boulder, Col.: Westview Press, 1986.

SAUVANT, KARL P., *Trade and Foreign Direct Investment in Data Services.* Boulder, Col.: Westview Press, 1986.

SCHAEFER, DAVID J., and ATKIN, DAVID, 'An Analysis of Policy Options for High-Definition Television,' *Telecommunications Policy*, 15 (5) (October 1991) 411–28.

SCHILLER, DAN, *Telematics and Government.* Norwood, NJ: Ablex, 1982.

SCHILLER, DAN, 'Privatization Trends in World Communications,' *Transnational Data Report*, VI (2) (March 1983) 105–8.

SCHILLER, HERBERT I., *Mass Communications and American Empire.* Boulder, Col.: Westview Press, 1969.

SCHILLER, HERBERT I., *Communication and Cultural Domination.* New York: M.E. Sharpe, 1976.

SCHILLER, HERBERT I., *Information and the Crisis Economy.* Norwood, NJ: Ablex, 1984.

SCHILLER, HERBERT I., *Culture, Inc., The Corporate Takeover of Public Expression.* New York: Oxford University Press, 1989.

SCHILLER, HERBERT I., 'Not Yet the Post-Imperialist Era,' *Critical Studies in Mass Communications*, 8 (1) (March 1991) 13–28.

SCHILLER, HERBERT I., *Mass Communications and American Empire*, 2nd ed. Boulder Col.: Westview Press, 1992.

SCHILLER, HERBERT I., 'Transnational Media: Creating Consumers Worldwide,' *Journal of International Affairs*, 47 (1) (Summer 1993) 47–58.

SCHINE, ERIC, 'Digital TV: Advantage, Hughes,' *Business Week*, 3415 (13 March 1995) n.p.

SCHLEGAL, JOCHEN K.H., 'Competition in International Communications,' *Transnational Data and Communications Report*, X (5) (May 1987) 19–20.

SCHOTT, CHARLES, 'Convergence of Telecoms and Broadcasting Regulation,' *InterMedia*, 19 (1) (January–February 1991) 27–8.

SCHULTZ, JAMES B., 'Reliable Survivable Satellites Seen as Key Link in United States Security,' *Satellite Communications* (June 1980).

SCOTT, MARGARET, 'Dishing the Rules,' *Far Eastern Economic Review*, 148 (24) (14 June 1990) 34–40.

SCOTT, WILLIAM B., 'Satellites Key to "Infostructure",' *Aviation Week & Space Technology* (14 March 1994) 57–8.

SCULLY, SEAN, 'The "Grand Alliance" Becomes Reality,' *Broadcasting & Cable*, 123 (22) (31 May 1993) 59–60.

SCULLY, SEAN, 'Local DBS is on the Beam,' *Broadcasting & Cable*, 123 (28) (12 July 1993) 60.

SIDER, GERALD M., 'The Ties that Bind: Culture and Agriculture, Property and Propriety in the Newfoundland Village Fishery,' *Social History*, 5 (1) (January 1980) 1–39.

SIGNITZER, BENNO, *Regulation of Direct Broadcasting from Satellites, The UN Involvement.* New York: Praeger Publishers, 1976.

SIKES, ALFRED C., 'Deregulation's Irreversible Momentum,' *Transnational Data and Communication Report*, XI (4) (April 1988) 20.

SILBERMAN, CHARLES E., 'The Little Bird that Casts a Big Shadow,' *Fortune*, LXXV (2) (February 1967) 108–11 and 223–6.

SILVERSTONE, ROGER, 'From Audiences to Consumers: The Household and the Consumption of Communication and Information Technologies,' *European Journal of Communication*, 6 (2) (June 1991) 135–54.

SINGLETON, LOY A., *Global Impact, The New Telecommunication Technology*, New York: Harper & Row, 1989.

SIWEK, STEPHEN E. and FURCHTGOTT-ROTH, HAROLD, *Copyright Industries in the US Economy, 1993 Perspective*. Washington, DC: International Intellectual Property Alliance, October 1993.

SIWEK, STEPHEN E. and FURCHTGOTT-ROTH, HAROLD, *Copyright Industries in the US Economy, 1977–1993*. Washington, DC: International Intellectual Property Alliance, January 1995.

SKOCPOL, THEDA, EVANS, PETER B. and RUESCHEMEYER, DIETRICH (eds), *Bringing the State Back In*. Cambridge: Cambridge University Press, 1985, 3–37.

'SKY Money Machine,' *Cable and Satellite Europe*, 154 (October 1996) 12 and 14.

SLACK, JENNIFER DARYL, 'Surveying the Impacts of Communication Technologies,' in Brenda Dervin and Melvin J. Voigt (eds), *Progress in Communication Sciences*, vol. V. Norwood, NJ: Ablex, 1984, 73–109.

SMART, TIM, 'Knights of the Business Roundatable, Tracking Big Business,' Agenda in Wahington,' *Business Week*, 3075 (21 October 1988) 39–42.

SMITH, DELBERT D., *Communication via Satellite: A Vision in Retrospect*. Leyden: A.W. Sijthoff, 1976.

SOLOMON, JONATHAN, 'The ITU in a Time of Change,' *Telecommunicatios Policy*, 15 (4) (August 1991) 372–5.

SPERO, JOAN EDELMAN, 'Information: The Policy Void,' *Foreign Policy*, 48 (Fall 1982) 139–56.

STALSON, HELENA, *Intellectual Property Rights and US Competitiveness in Trade*. Washington, DC: National Planning Association, 1989.

STANBURY, W.T. (ed.) *Telecommunications Policy and Regulation, The Impact of Competition and Technological Change*. Montreal: Institute for Research on Public Policy, 1986.

STEWART, M. LESUEUR, *To See the World, The Global Dimension in International Direct Television Broadcasting by Satellite*. Dordrecht: Martinus Nijhoff Publishers, 1991.

STOKES, MARK, 'Canada and the Direct Broadcast Satellite: Issues in the Global Communications Flow,' *Journal of Canadian Studies*, 27 (2) (Summer 1992) 82–96.

STRANGE, SUSAN, 'The Persistent Myth of Lost Hegemony,' *International Organization*, 41 (4) (Autumn 1987) 553–74.

STRANGE, SUSAN, *States and Markets*. London: Pinter Publishers, 1988.

STRAUBHAAR, JOSEPH D., 'Beyond Media Imperialism: Assymetrical Interdependence and Cultural Proximity,' *Critical Studies in Mass Communications*, 8 (1) (March 1991) 39–59.

SUKOW, RANDY, 'House Beats Up on Cable,' *Broadcasting*, 122 (31) (27 July, 1992) 3 and 14.

'SUMMARY Excerpts SIG Report to NSC,' *Chronicle of International Communication*, V (9) (November 1984).

'SUMMER Theatre on the Hill,' *Chronicle of International Communication*, V (4) (May 1984) 4–5.

SUNKEL, OSVALDO and FUENZALIDA, EDMUNDO F. 'Transnationalization and its Consequences,' in José J. Villamil (ed.), *Transnational Capitalism and National Development, New Perspectives on Dependence*. Atlantic Highlands, NJ: Humanities Press, 1979, 67–93.

SVENDSON, KNUT DIDRIK GALSCHIODT, *The Impact of Direct Broadcast Satellites on National Communication Policies in Western Europe*. Unpublished MA dissertation: Bowling Green State University, 1991.

TAISHOFF, MARIKA NATASHA, *State Responsibility and the Direct Broadcast Satellite*. London: Francis Pinter, 1987.

TARJANNE, PEKKA, 'The ITU Responds to New Concepts for Public Policy in the Global Information Society,' *InterMedia*, 20 (6) (November–December 1992) 12–14.

'TELCO'S Video Fortunes,' *Broadcasting*, 122 (44) (26 October 1992) 49.

'TELEVISION Goes Global, Footprints in the Sand,' *The Economist*, 307 (7555) (18 June, 1988) 95–6.

THOMAS, HELEN, 'Federal Exec Doubles as Ranch Hand,' UPI Release (19 December 1982) n.p.

THOMAS, HELEN, 'Commerce Administrator-Ranch Hand Resigns,' UPI Release (7 November 1983) n.p.

TIME Warner, Inc., 'Response to National Telecommunications and Information Administration Request for Comments'. Unpublished: 30 May 1990.

TOMLINSON, JOHN, *Cultural Imperialism, A Critical Introduction*. Baltimore: The Johns Hopkins University Press, 1991.

'TRACKING Red Television Beams,' *Chronicle of International Communication*, VI (4) (May 1985) 5–6.

TRITT, ROBERT, 'GATS, Son of GATT: A New Rule Book for Cross-Border Competition,' *InterMedia*, 20 (6) (November–December 1992) 15–16.

'TUNE Up for Term Two,' *Chronicle of International Communication*, V (6) (July–August, 1984) 1 and 7–8.

TUNSTALL, JEREMY, *The Media are American*. New York: Columbia University Press, 1977.

TUNSTALL, JEREMY, *Communications Deregulation, The Unleashing of America's Communications Industry*. Oxford: Basil Blackwell, 1986.

TUROW, JOSEPH, 'The Organizational Underpinnings of Contemporary Media Conglomerates,' *Communication Research*, 19 (6) (December 1992) 682–704.

UDWIN, GERALD E., 'The FCC's "Video Dialtone Decision...Has Opened a Door for Television Stations",' *Broadcasting* 122 (31) (27 July 1992) 18.

UNDERHILL, GEOFFREY (ed.) *Making Markets: The New World Order in International Finance*. London and New York: Macmillan and St Martin's Press, 1996.

'US Development Communications Assistance Programs,' *Chronicle of International Communication*, V (9) (November 1984) 1.

VANGRASSTEK Communications, 'Trade-related Intellectual Property Rights: United States Trade Policy, Developing Countries and the Uruguay Round,' in United Nations Conference on Trade and Development, *Uruguay Round: Further Papers on Selected Issues*. New York: United Nations, 1990, 79–128.

VEBLEN, THORSTEIN, *Imperial Germany and the Industrial Revolution*. New York: The Viking Press, 1954.

WALKER, MARTIN, 'Foreign Policy Goes to Market,' *Manchester Guardian Weekly*, (12 January 1997) p. 6.

WASCO, JANET, PHILLIPS, MARK AND PURDIE, CHRIS, 'Hollywood Meets Madison Avenue: The Commercialization of US Films,' *Media, Culture and Society*, 15 (2) (April 1993) 271–93.

WEBSTER, DAVID, 'New Communications Technology and the International Political Process,' in Simon Serfaty (ed.) *The Media and Foreign Policy*. Houndmills. Macmillan, 1990.

WEBSTER, DAVID, *Building Democracy: New Broadcasting Laws in East and Central Europe*. Washington, DC: The Annenberg Washington Program, 1992.

WESTLAKE, MICHAEL, 'Reach for the Stars,' *Far Eastern Economic Review*, 151 (22) (30 May 1991) 61.

WHEELER, JAMES O. and MITCHELSON, RONALD L. 'The Information Empire,' *American Demographics*, 13 (3) (March 1991) 41–3.

WIGAND, ROLF T., 'Satellite Communication: Policy and Regulatory Issues,' in Brenda Dervin and Melvin J. Voigt (eds), *Progress in Communication Sciences*, Vol. VIII. Norwood, NJ: Ablex, 1987, 231–62.

WILDMAN, STEVEN S. and SIWEK, STEPHEN E., *International Trade in Films and Television Programs*. Cambridge, Mass.: American Enterprise Institute/Ballinger, 1988.

WILLIAMS, FREDERICK, *The New Telecommunications, Infrastructure for the Information Age*. New York: The Free Press, 1991.

WILLIAMS, RAYMOND, 'Culture and Civilization,' in Paul Edwards (ed.), *The Encyclopedia of Philosophy*, vol. 2. New York: Macmillan and The Free Press, 1967, 273–6.

WILLIAMS, RAYMOND, *Communications*. London: Chatto & Windus, 1969.

WILLIAMS, RAYMOND, *Problems in Materialism and Culture*. London: Verso, 1982.

WILLIAMS, RAYMOND, *Television, Technology and Cultural Form*. Ederyn Williams (ed.). London: Routledge, 1990.

WILLIAMS, SYLVIA MAUREEN, 'Direct Broadcast Satellites and International Law,' *International Relations*, 8 (3) (May 1985) 245–69.

WILLIAMS, WILLIAM APPLEMAN, *The Tragedy of American Diplomacy*. New York: Dell Publishing, 1982.

WILSON, F.A., *An Introduction to Satellite Television*, rev. edn, London: Bernard Babani, 1989.

WINTER, HARVEY J., 'The Role of the United States Government in Improving International Intellectual Property Protection,' *The Journal of Law & Technology*, 2 (2) (Fall 1987) 325–32.

WOLFE, DAVID, 'Socio-political Contexts of Technological Change: Some Conceptual Models,' in Brian Elliott (ed.), *Technology and Social Process*. Edinburgh: Edinburgh University Press, 1988, 131–51.

WOLFF, RICHARD D., 'Economics of Imperialism, Modern Imperialism: The View from the Metropolis,' *The American Economic Review*, LX (2) (May 1970) 225–30.

WOLFHARD, ERIC, 'International Trade in International Property: The Emerging GATT Regime,' *University of Toronto Faculty of Law Review*, 49 (1) (Winter 1991) 106–51.

WOOD, ELLEN MEIKSINS, 'Marxism Without Class Struggle?' in Ralph Miliband and John Saville (eds), *Socialist Register 1983*. London: Merlin Press, 1983, 239–71.

WOOD, JAMES, *Satellite Communications and DBS Systems*. Oxford: Focal Press, 1992.

WOOD, STEPHEN (ed.) *The Transformation of Work? Skill, Flexibility and the Labour Process*. London: Unwin Hyman, 1989.

WOOD, WILLIAM and O'HARE, SHARON L., 'Paying for the Video Revolution: Consumer Spending on the Mass Media,' *Journal of Communication*, 41 (1) (Winter 1991) 24–30.

WOODROW, R. BRIAN, 'Tilting Towards a Trade Regime, The ITU and the Uruguay Round Services Negotiations,' *Telecommunications Policy*, 15 (4) (August 1991) 323–42.

WORLD Administrative Radio Conference for Space Telecommunications, *Final Acts*, Geneva: International Telecommunications Union, 1971.

'YES It Was a Fudge,' *Cable and Satellite Europe*, 92 (August 1991) 42.

ZAMPARUTTI, ELEONORA and MUSCARA, PIERO, 'Code Red,' *Cable and Satellite Europe*, 149 (May 1996) 42, 44 and 45.

## US PUBLIC SECTOR DOCUMENTS AND HEARINGS

BORTNICK, JANE, 'International Telecommunications and Information Policy: Selected Issues for the 1980s'. Report prepared for the US Senate, Committee on Foreign Affairs. Unpublished: 1983.

DEGNAN, KIM E., DUNMORE, KENNETH R. and SARDELLA, VINCENT, 'Direct Broadcast Satellites: Policies, Prospects, and Potential Competition'. Unpublished: US Department of Commerce, 1981.

FASCELL, DANTE R., 'Modern Communications and Foreign Policy'. Report by the US House of Representatives Committee on Foreign Affairs. Unpublished: 13 June 1967.

FEDERAL Communications Commission, 'Policies for Regulation of Direct Broadcast Satellites'. Staff Report. Unpublished: 2 October 1980.

FEKETEKUTY, GEZA, 'The Telecommunications and Services Market Worldwide: A US View'. Unpublished mimeo: Office of the United States Trade Representative, 1985.

INFORMATION Infrastructure Task Force, 'The National Information Infrastructure: Agenda for Action'. Washington, DC: National Telecommunications and Information Administration, 15 September 1993.

MCGOVERN, GEORGE, 'The Role and Control of International Communications and Information'. Report to the United States Senate Committee on Foreign Relations, Subcommittee on International Operations. Washington, DC: US Government Printing Office, 1977.

NATIONAL Telecommunications and Information Administration, *Policy Implications of Information Technology*. Washington, DC: US Government Printing Office, 1984.

NATIONAL Telecommunications and Information Administration, *NTIA Competition Benefits Report*. Washington, DC: US Government Printing Office, 1985.

NATIONAL Telecommunications and Information Administration, *NTIA Telecom 2000, Charting the Course for a New Century*. Washington, DC: US Government Printing Office, 1992.

OFFICE of the Federal Register, National Archives and Records Administration, *The United States Government Manval 1991/92*. Lanham, MD: Bernan Press, 1991

PRESIDENTIAl, Commission on International Radio Broadcasting, *The Right to Know*. Washington, DC: US Government Printing Office, 1973.

*President's Task Force on Communications Policy, Final Report*. Washington, DC: US Government Printing Office, 7 December 1968.

SETZER, FLORENCE and LEVY, JONATHAN, *Broadcast Television in a Multichannel Marketplace*. Office of Plans and Policy Working Paper 26. Washington, DC: Federal Communications Commission, 1991.

UNITED States Congress. House. Committee on Science and Astronautics. Hearings on 'Commercial Communications Satellites'. 87th Congr., 2nd sess., 18 September 1962.

UNITED States Congress. House. Committee on Foreign Affairs. Subcommittee on International Organizations and Movements. Hearings on 'Winning the Cold War: the US Ideological Offensive'. 88th Congr., 1st sess., 28, 29 March 1963; 2, 3 April 1963; 11, 13, 14 September 1963.

UNITED States Congress. House. Committee on Foreign Affairs. Subcommittee on International Organizations and Movements. Hearings on 'Modern Communications and Foreign Policy'. 90th Congr., 1st sess., 8, 9 February 1967.

UNITED States Congress. House. Committee on Foreign Affairs. Subcommittee on National Security Policy and Scientific Developments. Hearings on 'Satellite Broadcasting: Implications for Foreign Policy'. 91st Congr., 1st sess., 13, 14, 15, 22 May 1969.

UNITED States Congress. House. Committee on Foreign Affairs. Subcommittee on National Security Policy and Scientific Developments. Hearings on 'Foreign Policy Implications of Satellite Communications'. 91st Congr., 2nd sess., 23, 28, 30 April 1970.

UNITED States Congress. House. Committee on International Relations. Subcommittee on International Organizations. Hearings on 'UNESCO: Challenges and Opportunities for the United States'. 94th Congr., 2nd sess., 14 June 1976.

UNITED States Congress. House. Committee on Energy and Commerce. Subcommittee on Telecommunications, Consumer Protection, and Finance.

Hearings on 'Satellite Communications/Direct Broadcast Satellites,' 97th Congr., 1st sess., 15 December 1981.

UNITED States Congress. House. Committee on Energy and Commerce. Subcommittee on Commerce, Transportation, and Tourism. Hearings on 'General Trade Policy'. 98th Congr., 1st sess., 15 March; 5 April; 25 May; 22 June, 1983.

UNITED States Congress. House. Committee on Ways and Means. Subcommittee on Trade. Hearings on 'US Trade Deficit'. 98th Congr., 2nd sess., 28, 29 March; 5, 10, 12, 25 April 1984.

UNITED States Congress. House. Committee on Banking, Finance and Urban Affairs. Subcommittee on Economic Stabilization. Hearings on 'Service Industries: the Future Shape of the American Economy'. 98th Congr., 2nd sess., 8, 12, 14, 28 June 1984.

UNITED States Congress. House. Committee on Energy and Commerce. Subcommittee on Telecommunications, Consumer Protection, and Finance. Hearings on 'International Satellite Issues'. 98th Congr., 2nd sess., 13 June; 25, 26 July 1984.

UNITED States Congress. House. Committee on Foreign Affairs. Subcommittees on International Operations and on International Economic Policy and Trade. Hearings on 'Foreign Policy Implications of Competition in International Telecommunications'. 99th Congr., 1st sess., 19 February; 6, 28 March 1985.

UNITED States Congress. House. Committee on Energy and Commerce. Subcommittee on Oversight and Investigations. Hearings on 'Unfair Trade Practices'. 101st Congr., 1st sess., 1 and 14 March 1989.

UNITED States Congress. House. Committee on the Judiciary. Subcommittee on Courts, Intellectual Property, and the Administration of Justice. Hearings 'Intellectual Property, Domestic Productivity and Trade'. 101st Congr., 1st sess., 25 July 1989.

UNITED States Congress. House. Committee on Energy and Commerce. Subcommittee on Telecommunications and Finance. Hearings on 'Television Broadcasting and the European Community'. 100th Congr., 1st sess., 26 July 1989.

UNITED States Congress. 'Modern Communications and Foreign Policy'. Report prepared for House of Representatives Committee on Foreign Affairs. 90th Congr., 1st sess., 13 June 1967.

UNITED States Congress. Office of Technology Assessment, *Intellectual Property Rights in an Age of Electronics and Information*. Washington, DC: US Government Printing Office, 1986.

UNITED States Congress. Office of Technology Assessment, *Multinationals and the National Interest, Playing by Different Rules*. Washington, DC: US Government Printing Office, September 1993.

UNITED States Congress. Senate. Select Committee on Small Business. Subcommittee on Monopoly. Hearings on 'Space Satellite Communications,' 87th Congr., 1st sess., 2, 3, 4, 9, 10 and 11 August, 1961.

UNITED States Congress. Senate. Committee on the Judiciary. Subcommittee on Antitrust and Monopoly. Hearings on 'Antitrust Problems of the Space Satellite Communications System'. 87th Congr., 2nd sess., 12 April 1962.

UNITED States Congress. Senate. Committee on Foreign Relations 'Hearings on the Communications Satellite Act of 1962,' 87th Congr., 2nd sess., August 3, 6, 7, 8 and 9, 1962.

UNITED States Congress. Senate. Committee on Foreign Relations. Subcommittee on International Operations. Hearings on 'The Role and Control of International Communications and Information'. 95th Congr., 1st sess., June 1977.

UNITED States Congress. Senate. Committee on Foreign Relations, *The Role and Control of International Communications and Information.* Report prepared for Subcommittee on International Operations. Washington, DC: US Government Printing Office, 1977.

UNITED States Congress. Senate. Committee on Commerce, Science, and Transportation. Subcommittee on Communications. Hearing on 'The International Telecommunications Act of 1983'. 98th Congr., 1st sess., 10, 11 May 1983.

UNITED States Congress. Senate. Committee on Foreign Relations. Subcommittee on Arms Control, Oceans, International Operations and Environment. Hearings on 'International Communication and Information Policy'. 98th Congr., 1st sess., 19, 31 October 1983.

UNITED States Congress. Senate. Committee on Commerce, Science, and Transportation. Subcommittee on Communications. Hearing on 'International Telecommunications'. 100th Congr., 1st sess., 28 February 1987.

UNITED States Department of Commerce, 'Comprehensive Study of the Globalization of Mass Media Firms'. Notice of Inquiry issued by National Telecommunications and Information Administration, February 1990 (Docket No.900241–0041).

UNITED States Department of Commerce. *Globalization of the Mass Media.* Washington, DC: National Telecommunications and Information Administration, January 1993.

UNITED States Department of Commerce. 'Long-range Goals in International Telecommunications and Information, An Outline of United States Policy'. Unpublished: National Telecommunications and Information Administration, 1983.

UNITED States Department of Commerce, *NTIA.* Information pamphlet: n.d.

UNITED States Department of State, *Bureau of International Communications and Information Policy.* Department of State Publication 9860: March 1991.

UNITED States General Accounting Office, *US Communications Policy: Issues for the 1990s.* Washington, DC: G.A.O. Information Management and Technology Division, October 1991.

UNITED States Government, *US National Study on Trade in Services: A Submission by the United States Government to the General Agreement on Tariffs and Trade.* Washington, DC: Government Printing Office, 1984.

UNITED States Government, Interagency Working Group on Transborder Data Flow, 'Communications and Transborder Data Flows in the United States: A Background Paper'. Unpublished mimeo. Washington, DC: Interagency Working Group on TDF, 1985.

UNITED States Information Agency, *Telling America's Story to the World.* Washington, DC: USIA, January 1993.
UNITED States National Security Council, 'National Security Decision Directive Number 130'. 6 March 1984.


## OTHER PUBLIC SECTOR DOCUMENTS

COMMUNICATIONS Canada, *Communications for the Twenty-first Century.* Ottawa: Minister of Supply and Services, 1987.
COMMUNICATIONS Canada, *Vital Links: Canadian Cultural Industries.* Ottawa: Minister of Supply and Services, 1987.
EUROPEAN Community, *Television Without Frontiers, Green Paper on the Establishment of the Common Market for Broadcasting, Especially by Satellite and Cable.* Brussels: Office for Official Publications of the European Communities, 1984.
LOCKSLEY, GARETH, *TV Broadcasting in Europe and the New Technologies.* Luxembourg: Office for Official Publications of the European Communities, 1988.
ORGANIZATION for Economic Cooperation and Development, *Report by the High Level Group on Trade and Related Problems.* Paris: OECD, 1973.
ORGANIZATION for Economic Co-operation and Development, *Interdependence and Co-operation in Tomorrow's World.* Paris: OECD, 1987.
ORGANIZATION for Economic Co-operation and Development, *Information Technology and New Growth Opportunities.* Paris: OECD, 1989.
*STATE of New York* v. *Primestar Partners LP*, 'Complaint Draft No. 6'. Unpublished: 22 December 1991.


## PERSONAL INTERVIEWS

ALLEN, CATHY A., Vice President, Technology Office, Citicorp International. In New York City, 23 April 1993.
ALPERT, MICHAEL S., President, Alpert & Associates. In Washington, DC, 2 September 1992.
ATTAWAY, FRITZ, Vice President, Motion Picture Association of America. In Washington, DC, 1 September 1992.
BOWER, VINTON, Vice President, HBO Satellite Services. In New York City, 23 April 1993.
BRUMFIELD, CYNTHIA, Director of Research and Policy, National Cable Television Association. In Washington, DC, 8 September 1992.
BYKOWSKY, MARK, Senior Economist, National Telecommunications and Information Administration, United States Department of Commerce. In Washington DC, 1 September 1992.
BYWATER, SHARON, Special Policy Assistant, Office of International Affairs, National Telecommunications and Information Administration,

United States Department of Commerce. In Washington, DC, 1 September 1992.

DE SONNE, MARSHA, Director of Technology Research, National Association of Broadcasters. In Washington, DC, 1 September 1992.

DONOW, KENNETH, Communications Policy Consultant. In Washington, DC, 4 September 1992.

DOUGAN, DIANA, Senior Advisor and Chair of the International Communications Studies Program, Center for Strategic and International Studies. In Washington, DC, 3 September 1992.

FITCH, MICHAEL, Assistant Coordinator, International Communications and Information Policy, United States Department of State. In Washington, DC, 9 September 1992.

GILSERNAN, JOHN, Deputy Director for Radio Spectrum Policy, United States Department of State. In Washington, DC, 3 March 1994.

GLICKFIELD, CHERYL R., Senior Telecommunications Policy Attorney, National Telecommunications and Information Administration, United States Department of Commerce. Telephone interview, 18 August 1992.

HILL, EILEEN, Senior International Economist, Office of International Organizations, National Telecommunications and Information Administration, United States Department of Commerce. In Washington, DC, 10 September 1992.

LEVY, JONATHAN, Senior Economist, Office of Plans and Policy, Federal Communications Commission. In Washington, DC, 2 September 1992.

MARGULIS, LES, International Media Director, BBDO Worldwide. In New York City, 21 April 1993.

MCKEE, JOHN, President, DirecTV Canada. In Toronto, 21 June 1993.

OBUCHOWSKI, JANICE, President, Freedom Technologies. In Washington, DC, 3 March 1994.

PRUITT, JEAN, Associate Administrator for International Affairs, National Telecommunications and Information Administration, United States Department of Commerce. In Washington, DC, 4 March 1994.

ROSATI, DINO, Computer Engineering Consultant. In Toronto, 18 September 1992 and 16 November 1994.

SCHECK, ERIC, International Media Supervisor, BBDO Worldwide. In New York City, 21 April 1993.

SIGMUND, JOHN, Senior Economist, International Trade Administration, United States Department of Commerce. In Washington, DC, 10 September 1992.

SIMON, EMORY, Deputy Assistant United States Trade Representative, Office of the United States Trade Representative. In Washington, DC, 9 September 1992.

SOLBERG, MARK, Attorney, Video Services Division, Federal Communications Commission. In Washington, DC, 9 September 1992.

STEELE, GEORGE, President, Viacom MGS Services. In New York City, 23 April 1993.

THIBEDAU, HARRY W., Manager of Industry and Technical Affairs, Satellite Broadcasting and Communications Association. In Alexandria, Virginia, 31 August 1992.

TURNER, LESLIE, Director of International Programming, The Discovery Channel. In Bethesda, Maryland, 10 September 1992.

WEBSTER, DAVID, International Communications Consultant/President, Trans Atlantic Dialogue on European Broadcasting. In Washington, DC, 11 September 1992.

WHITEHEAD, CLAY 'TOM,' Communications Consultant. In Washington, DC, 2 September 1992.

# Index

Abel, John, 191 n
advertising and marketing, 140, 149,
    157 n, 179–82, 184–5, 189 n,
    191 n, 195
Aetna, 60
    *see also* Satellite Business Systems
Algeria, 135
Alpert, Michael, 191 n
American Broadcasting Company
    (ABC), 49, 55, 68 n, 71 n
American Express, 118, 121, 127 n,
    128 n, 136
American Screen Actors Guild, 71 n
American Telephone and Telegraph
    Company (AT&T), 5, 9–10, 20,
    43, 44–5, 46–51, 53–61, 64, 65,
    71 n, 72 n, 98, 109, 110, 116, 119,
    126 n, 131, 134–6, 144, 152–3 n,
    162, 163, 166, 176, 178, 182, 185,
    186, 187 n, 198
    divestiture of, 131, 132, 152–3 n,
        161–3, 185
Astra, 166, 172, 174, 175, 182, 207
Attaway, Fritz, 169, 189 n

Baldridge, Malcolm, 122
BBDO Worldwide, 179, 184, 192 n
Bell Atlantic, 153 n, 187 n
Bell South, 153 n
Bertelsmann, 5, 182
Blatherwick, David, 82
Boeing, vii
Bortnik, Jane, 120, 161–2, 173
Bower, Vinton, 182
Braman, Sandra, 157 n
Brazil, 80–1, 89–90, 104 n, 139,
    142
Bretton Woods, 93
British Broadcasting Corporation
    (BBC), 183
British Telecom, 5, 182, 185
Brownlee, Dennis, 172
Brzezinski, Zbigniew, 115
BSkyB, 4, 166, 172

*see also* News Corporation
    International, Rupert
    Murdoch
Bundy, McGeorge, 68 n
Burch, Dean, 57, 72 n
Bush, George/Bush
    administration, 190 n, 194
Business Roundtable, 127 n
Butler, Richard, 135–6, 147

Cable News Network (CNN), 125 n
Cable & Wireless, 159 n
Canada, 52, 85, 89, 110, 119, 146,
    157 n
Canada-United States Free Trade
    Agreement, 127 n, 141, 156 n
    *see also* North American Free
        Trade Agreement (NAFTA)
Canal Plus, 5, 182, 184
Carter, Jimmy/Carter
    administration, 56, 93, 114–5,
    122, 196
Columbia Broadcasting System
    (CBS), 57, 62, 63, 71 n, 73 n,
    190 n
Chase Manhattan Bank, 72 n
Chile, 81
Citicorp, 164, 177
class, concept of/relations, 27, 31,
    34, 36, 200, 201, 205, 206,
    208–09, 212 n
Clinton, Bill/Clinton
    administration, 4, 146, 164, 203
Cohen, Robert B., 190–1 n
Cold War, vii, 78, 91, 106 n, 150,
    190 n
    the New Cold War, 96, 97
    policies of 'containment' and
        'enlargement', vii
    *see also* Soviet Union
Colombia, 142
Communications Satellite
    Corporation (Comsat/
    COMSAT), 20, 46–51, 53, 55,

56–8, 60, 61, 64, 65, 68 n, 69 n, 77, 78, 81, 82, 98, 108–10, 115, 116, 119, 134, 191 n, 193, 198
*see also* Satellite Business Systems, Satellite Television Corporation
Continental Cablevision, 165
Control Data Corporation, 128 n
Coopers and Lybrand, 175
corporate mergers and acquisitions, 163, 179–80, 182, 187 n
Corporation for Public Broadcasting, 121
Correa, Luiz Felipe de Seixas, 17
Cox, Robert W., 12, 23–7, 31–2, 33, 35, 38, 199–206
on culture, 23–4
on hegemony, 23–4, 199
on historic bloc, 31, 32
on 'ideas', 26
on the internationalizing state, 32, 35, 200–1
Crawford, Morris H., 116
Cuba, 142, 160 n
cultural imperialism, viii, 7, 8, 12, 18–22, 29, 33, 36, 38, 97–8, 123, 129 n, 170, 185–6, 196–9, 206, 208
*and* capitalism, 21–2, 33
definition of, 18
media imperialism, 39 n
*and* United States foreign policy, 22, 33, 123, 146, 186, 196–200
culture, 21–8, 37, 38, 185, 204, 205, 209
*and* conceptual systems, 25, 27–8, 205, 206, 209
culture-power, 21, 25–6, 50, 51, 54, 59, 63, 64, 75, 77, 78, 84, 88, 91, 96, 108, 111, 150, 171–2, 173, 180–1, 184–5, 193, 198–9, 206, 210
definition of, 27, 28, 39 n, 205
*and* information, 25–8
*and* knowledge, 25–7, 31, 36, 38, 205, 206, 208
Czechoslovakia, 82

DDB Needham Worldwide, 180
deButts, John D., 72 n
digital technologies/digitalization, 6, 58, 70 n, 146–7, 164–6, 171, 172, 173–7, 182, 183, 185, 186, 190 n, 205, 208
*and* convergence, 109, 112, 117, 180–1, 182, 185, 194, 208
*see also* high definition television (HDTV)
Dingman, James T., 47
direct broadcast satellite (DBS)
ATS system, 41, 53, 54, 75, 78, 82
*and* culture-power, 25, 51, 54, 59, 63–4, 66 n, 77, 149, 150
educational uses of, 51–4, 64, 75, 77, 82, 88, 126 n
*and* globalization, 29, 59, 108, 146–7, 149, 179–87
technological capabilities of, 4–6, 50–1, 52–3, 59, 63, 69–70 n, 81–2, 88, 96, 146–7, 165–6, 172, 175, 183–5, 188 n, 194
*see also* propaganda, telecommunication satellites
Direct Broadcast Satellite Corporation, 73 n, 189 n
DirecTV, 4, 5, 110, 166, 167–8, 171, 172, 177
*see also* Hughes Communications
Disney, 168, 191 n
Dizard, Wilson, 51
Domino's Pizza, 181, 191 n
Donow, Kenneth, 190–1 n
Dougan, Diana Lady, 120–2, 126 n, 129 n
Doyle, Stephen, 85
Drake, William, 117

Eisenhower, Dwight/Eisenhower administration, 19, 42
Elder, Robert, 77
Electronic Data Systems, 170
European Community/Union, 141, 142, 145, 146, 157 n, 174–5, 176, 184, 186–7

Fairchild Industries, 41
Fascell, Dante R., 107, 129 n

Feketekuty, Geza, 128 n
Fly, James Lawrence, 69 n
Focus Broadcast Corporation,
    73 n
Fordism/Post-Fordism, 10, 34, 90,
    164, 203, 205–7
  *and* advertising and marketing,
    180–1
  *and* General Motors, 170–1
  *and* information and
    communication
    commodities, 182, 186
  *and* labor costs, 183
  *and* United States
    Telecommunications Act, 185
foreign direct investment, 155–6 n
Fowler, Marc, 120
France, 81, 83, 89, 102 n, 103 n, 146,
    174
free flow of information policy, 3,
    7–11, 18, 27–9, 75, 77, 79–80,
    83–5, 87–91, 92, 94–9, 105 n,
    109, 111, 113, 116–23, 127 n,
    128 n, 133–4, 135, 139–40, 148,
    149–52, 155 n, 162, 186, 195,
    196, 200–10
  *and* international law, 75, 79–90,
    103 n, 107, 123, 134–5, 141,
    193, 200, 201, 206
'free trade', 11, 26, 27, 29, 133, 137,
    151–2, 164, 177, 185, 187, 195,
    197, 201, 210
  *and* free flow of information
    policy, 133, 136–7, 140–1,
    150–2, 186, 193, 204, 205,
    210
  *see also*, General Agreement on
    Tariffs and Trade (GATT),
    United States Trade
    Representative (USTR)

Gardner, Michael R., 135, 136
Gardner, Richard N., 108
Garin, Michael, 182
General Agreement on Tariffs and
    Trade (GATT), 2, 11, 27, 33,
    35, 119, 122, 136, 137, 138–9,
    141–52, 154 n, 156–9 n, 201, 203,
    205

  *and* intellectual property, 11, 26,
    35, 120, 128 n, 142–52, 154 n,
    157–9 n, 164, 195
  most favored nation, 145, 146
  national treatment, 146, 158 n
  *and* services, 11, 26, 35, 127 n,
    128 n, 138–9, 141–5, 149, 152,
    154–9 n, 164, 178, 186, 195,
    202, 207
  World Trade Organization
    (WTO), 28, 35, 149, 151, 164,
    178, 195, 205, 210
General Dynamics, 53
General Electric, 52, 53, 167, 168
  GE Americom, 167
General Instruments, 73 n
General Motors (GM), vii, 5, 59,
    170–1, 180
  *see also* Hughes Communications
Gill, Stephen, 23, 24, 28, 31
Gillette, 179
Global Information Infrastructure
    (GII), 4–6, 12, 134, 164, 185,
    196, 205
globalization, vii, 8, 12, 21, 28–9,
    117, 137, 151–2, 179–87, 195,
    202–3, 204–10
Golding, Peter, 212 n
Goldwater, Barry, 120
Gore, Al, 164, 185, 196
Graphic Scanning, 73 n
Green, Harold H., 131, 153 n

Halliday, Fred, 96
Hargrove, John L., 103 n
Hechler, Ken, 45
hegemony, 23–38, 187, 194–210
  *and* cultural imperialism, 21–2,
    196–200, 206
  definition of, 8, 23, 199
  *and* global civil society, 204
  hegemonic bloc, 12, 29, 31, 37,
    203, 205, 206
  *and* knowledge, 26–7, 31, 38, 152,
    194–5
  *and* liberalism, 194–5, 199,
    210
  *and* the United States, viii, 8, 10,
    12–3, 27, 33–4, 50, 84, 90–1,

95–7, 99, 107–08, 143, 152, 187, 193–5, 198–210
*see also* nation state
Hennelly, Edward P., 95
Heritage Foundation, 94, 95
high definition television (HDTV), 62, 70n, 164, 173–7, 186, 190–1n
description of, 14n
*see also* digital technologies
Hills, Jill, 59, 152n, 153n
Hollywood, vii, 146, 169, 184, 191n
*see also* Motion Picture Association of America (MPAA)
Home Box Office (HBO), 60, 167–9, 182, 189n
Homet, Roland S., 1, 134
Hong Kong, 169, 171, 183
Hughes Aircraft, 9, 41, 43, 46, 53, 57, 65, 68n, 82, 115, 170
Hughes Communications, 4, 5, 167–8, 170–1, 185
*see also* DirecTV, General Motors (GM)
Hutchison Whampoa, 181

India, 42, 54, 139, 142, 171, 189n
information and communication commodities, 1–3, 12, 30, 34–5, 38, 59, 90–1, 93, 98, 99, 114, 116, 117–9, 121, 127n, 132, 133, 137, 138, 144, 146, 151, 153n, 161–4, 170–1, 173, 176–87, 193–203, 208–10
*and* 'free trade', 11, 34, 107, 117, 119, 121, 122, 136–7, 145–6, 151, 156n, 193
propagation of, 6, 27, 149, 150, 173, 197
services, 2, 117–19, 127n, 128n, 133, 136–9, 153n, 155–6n, 158n, 161, 162, 164, 173, 177, 185, 186, 209
*and* United States foreign policy, 12, 19, 93, 94, 107–10, 114, 117, 119, 120, 123, 124, 128n, 132–3, 135–52, 186–7, 193–200, 203, 210

Institute for Contemporary Studies, 94
International Broadcast Systems, 149
International Business Machines (IBM), 59, 60–1, 65, 72n, 104n, 136, 162, 186
*see also* Satellite Business Systems (SBS)
International Chamber of Commerce, 122, 127n
International Intellectual Property Alliance (IIPA), 144, 151, 159n, 211n
International Monetary Fund (IMF), 145
International Program for the Development of Communications (IPDC), 94, 106n, 196–7
International Telecommunications Satellite Organization (Intelsat), 49–50, 51, 69n, 82, 92, 98, 110, 132, 134
International Telecommunications Union (ITU), 35, 61, 79–81, 84–6, 90, 94, 97, 98, 100–1n, 108, 113, 116, 117, 121, 123, 133, 135–7, 147–8, 151, 154n, 159n, 201, 203, 205, 206–7, 209
World Administrative Radio Conference (WARC), 61–2, 69n, 89, 94, 113–7, 123, 126n
World Administrative Radio Conference on Space Telecommunications (WARC-ST), 84–5, 89
World Administrative Telegraph and Telephone Conference (WATTC), 136–7, 154n
International Television Service (ITV), 77
Irmer, Thomas, 148
Israel, 95, 103n, 135, 141, 154

Jamaica, 142
Japan, 88, 119, 132, 141, 150, 153n, 162, 173–7, 186, 187

Japanese Broadcasting Corporation (NHK), 175
Johnson, G. Griffith, 45
Johnson, Lyndon/Johnson administration, 56, 59
Jones, Earl L., 149

K-Prime Partners, 166–7, 168
*see also* Primestar
Kennedy, John F./Kennedy administration, 48, 68 n
Keogh, James, 77, 100 n
Keynesian economics, 34, 93

League of Nations Treaty, 79
Lebanon, 135
LeBlanc, Dennis, 1, 3, 13, 121
Lee, Robert E., 66 n
Less Developed Countries (LDCs), 7, 22, 51, 53, 54, 64, 75–6, 77, 82–4, 92–8, 107, 113, 114, 116, 120, 126 n, 129 n, 135–42, 144, 145, 148–9, 154 n, 156 n, 158 n, 171, 181, 196–7, 200, 208
Conference of Ministers of Non-Aligned Countries, 7
'Group of Ten', 142, 149
'Group of Twenty', 142
*see also* New World Information and Communication Order (NWICO)
Loevinger, Lee, 47
Lugar, Richard, 129 n

*MacNeil-Lehrer Report*, 183
Margulis, Les, 179, 181
Markey, David, 132
Marks, Leonard H., 78
Marshall Plan, 99 n
Mass Communications Inc. (MCI), 5, 163, 182
Mayor, Fredico, 148
M'Bow, Amadou Mahtar, 95
McGovern, George, 92, 93–4
McNamara, Robert, 106 n
Meese, Edwin, 94
Mexico, 81, 203
Microsoft, vii

Mitchell, John, 71 n
Mobil Oil, 95
Morse, Wayne, 48
Mosbacher, Robert A., 156 n
Motion Picture Association of America (MPAA), 144, 146, 157 n, 158 n, 169
*see also* Hollywood
Motorola, 126 n, 209
Murdoch, Rupert, 4, 182
*see also* BSkyB, News Corporation International, StarTV
Murdock, Graham, 212 n
Murphy, C. Gordon, 44, 45, 67 n
Murray, Simon, 172
Music Television (MTV), 167, 183, 184

nation state, vii–viii, 3, 8, 9, 12, 28, 32, 33, 37, 79, 80, 86, 151–2, 186–7, 199–200, 202–7, 209–10
*and* globalization, 8, 28, 32, 186–7, 195–6, 199–200, 202, 209
national sovereignty, 3, 79–86, 90, 96–7, 103 n, 127 n, 134, 136–7
prior consent, 3, 81, 84–92, 95–9, 140, 141, 200
state theory, 8, 22–4, 27, 28–38, 40 n, 90–1, 107–10, 120, 123, 124, 152, 196–207, 210, 211 n
*see also* free flow of information policy, United Nations
National Academy of Sciences (NAS), 42, 88
National Association of Broadcasters (NAB), 53, 54, 58, 60, 62, 65, 73 n, 98, 169, 175, 191 n
National Broadcasting Company (NBC), 20, 71 n
National Committee for a Free Europe, 77
*see also* Radio Free Europe (RFE), Radio Liberty (RL)
National Foreign Trade Council, 139
National League of Cities, 168
National Science Foundation, 190 n
New International Economic Order (NIEO), 93, 149

New World Information and
  Communication Order
  (NWICO), 7, 10, 39 n, 76, 92–7,
  106 n, 114, 133, 148–9, 197
  mandate of, 92
  *see also* free flow of information
    policy, Less Developed
    Countries (LDCs), New
    International Economic Order
    (NIEO)
Newell, Gregory, 135, 154 n
News Corporation International,
  4–5, 170, 171–3, 181, 182, 185
  *see also* BSkyB, Rupert Murdoch,
    News Datacom, StarTV
News Datacom, 5, 172
  *see also* News Corporation
    International
Nichols, Richard B., 135–6
Nicolaidis, Kalypso, 117
Nixon, Richard/Nixon
  administration, 54, 56, 57, 65,
  71 n, 77, 114
North American Free Trade
  Agreement (NAFTA), 145,
  156 n
  *see also* Canada-United States
    Free Trade Agreement
Nynex, 153 n, 187 n

Obuchowski, Janice, 194
Onstead, Phillip C., 128 n
open skies policy, 57–9, 65, 71 n,
  72 n, 110
Organization for Economic
  Cooperation and Development
  (OECD), 138–9, 147
Organization of Petroleum Exporting
  Countries (OPEC), 34, 93
Outer Space Treaty, 86–7, 103 n

PanAmSat, 5
Panitch, Leo, vii, 203, 204
Parker, Ian, 25
Pastore, John, 48
People's Republic of China
  (PRC), 151, 171–2, 211 n
Philips, 174, 175
Playboy Entertainment, 168

Ploman, Edward, 208
Porter, Vincent, 173
Presidential Commission on
  International Radio
  Broadcasting, 78
Preston, William, 92
Primestar, 166–8, 189 n
  *see also* K-Prime Partners
Propaganda, 76–8, 86, 91, 98, 111,
  150
  *and* DBS, 51–5, 75, 77–8, 84, 150
  *see also* Radio Free Europe (RFE),
    Radio Liberty (RL), United
    States Information Agency
    (USIA)
Prudential Insurance, 73 n
Pruitt, Jean, 172
Pucket, Allen E., 43–4

Radio Corporation of America
  (RCA), 19, 20, 43, 44, 52, 60,
  62, 63, 65, 73 n
Radio Free Europe (RFE), 77, 78,
  150
  *see also* Central Intelligence
    Agency (CIA)
Radio Liberty (RL), 77, 78, 150
  *see also* Central Intelligence
    Agency (CIA)
Rancho del Cielo, 1
Rand Corporation, 66 n
Reagan, Ronald, 1, 10, 11, 13,
  94–5, 97, 105 n, 110, 113,
  120–1, 132–6, 141, 162,
  194
  Reagan doctrine, 96
  'Reaganomics', 34
Regional Bell Operating Companies
  (RBOCs), 131, 153 n, 161–3,
  178, 187 n
Reinhard, Keith L., 180
Republic of Korea, 157 n
Richardson, John, 77
Robinson, Glenn, 114–15
Rostow, Eugene, 56
  Rostow Commission/Report,
    56–7, 59, 65, 117
Ruddy, F.S., 83
Rusk, Dean, 48

Sarnoff, David, 52, 65
  *see also* Radio Corporation of
    America (RCA)
Satellite Business Systems, 60–1,
    104 n, 126 n
Satellite Television Corporation
    (STC), 62–3
Sauvant, Karl, 119, 143, 155–6 n
Scheck, Eric, 184–5, 192 n, 195
Schiller, Herbert I., 7, 18–23, 25, 38,
    97, 98, 123, 150, 196–8, 199, 201,
    205, 206
  *see also* cultural imperialism
Services Policy Advisory
    Committee, 139
Shultz, George, 120, 122
Simon, Emory, 150
Skocpol, Theda, 30, 31
Smith, Delbert D., 41
Snow, Tony, 160 n
Solomon, Jonathan, 159 n
Sony, 177
Soviet Union (USSR), 6, 12, 35, 42,
    46–51, 63–4, 65, 77–8, 80, 81, 85,
    86, 89, 91, 93, 94, 96, 98, 106 n,
    116, 150, 195
Spero, Joan Edelman, 118–19,
    128 n
Sprint, 163
StarTV, 4, 169, 171–2, 181–4, 189 n,
    207
  *see also* Rupert Murdoch, News
    Corporation International
Stockman, David, 105 n
Stoil, Michael, 114
Strange, Susan, 26, 27
Sweden, 85, 89, 104 n

Tarjanne, Pekka, 147–8
*Teenage Mutant Ninja Turtles*, 181,
    191 n
Tele-Communication Incorporated
    (TCI), 165, 166, 185, 187 n,
    189 n
Tempo Satellite, 167
telecommunication satellites
    (telesatellites)
  Advent, 43
  Anik, 62–3

costs, 6, 46, 47, 49, 53, 55, 56–7,
    59, 61, 63, 67 n, 71 n, 72 n, 75,
    134, 165–6, 188 n, 208
  Echo, 42
  geostationary orbit, 14 n, 43–5
  Intersputnik, 116
  K-1, 167, 168
  Relay, 43
  Satcom, 60
  Sputnik, 42, 50, 66 n
  Syncom, 43–5, 67 n
  technology, 14–15 n, 43–4, 48–9,
    52, 58, 60, 78, 84–5, 88, 132
  Telecom, 132
  Telstar, 43, 45, 48, 55
  Vista, 52
  *see also*, direct broadcast satellite,
    propaganda
Thomson, 174
Thomson, Robert, 185
Time-Warner, 165, 180, 189 n
  Time Inc., 121
  Warner Cable, 166
TRW Systems, 53
Tunstall, Jeremy, 63
Turner, Ted, 125 n
  Turner Broadcasting, 168
  *see also* Cable Network News
    (CNN)

United Arab Republic (UAR), 81
United Kingdom, 136, 154 n, 166,
    175, 212 n
United Nations, 75, 76, 79–82, 84,
    86, 90–4, 97, 98, 101 n, 108, 117,
    141, 143, 148, 197, 205
  Conference on the Peaceful Uses
    of Outer Space
    (COPUOS), 81–5, 89–90,
    104 n
  General Assembly, 6, 80, 86,
    89–90, 92, 104 n
  United Nations Conference on
    Trade and Development
    (UNCTAD), 141
  United Nations Educational,
    Scientific and Cultural
    Organization
    (UNESCO), 13 n, 17, 41, 90,

91–5, 97, 98, 105–6 n, 113,
133, 135, 136, 148, 151, 197,
201, 205, 207
United Satellite Communications
Incorporated (USCI), 62–3,
73 n
United States Academy of
Engineering, 173
United States Chamber of
Commerce, 122, 144
United States Council for
International Business, 127 n,
144
United States Democratic Party, 46,
63
United States government
Central Intelligence Agency
(CIA), 75, 77, 78, 91, 95, 98,
113, 150
Department of Commerce, 1, 56,
103 n, 109–16, 119, 122, 132,
135, 139, 150, 152, 172, 173,
194, 205
Department of Defense
(DoD), 20, 21, 41–5, 50, 55,
58, 64, 65, 66 n, 75, 82, 106 n,
113, 115, 117–18, 127 n, 134,
190 n
Department of Justice (DoJ),
47–9, 57, 71 n, 131, 161, 163,
167
Department of State, 46, 56, 64,
76, 78, 87, 93, 95–9, 106 n,
108–16, 120–2, 123, 126 n,
129 n, 132–5, 151, 152, 205;
Bureau of International
Communications and
Information Policy
(ICIP), 114, 122, 126 n; Office
of the Coordinator for
International Communication
and Foreign Policy, 120–2;
Office of International
Communications Policy,
114
Federal Communications
Commission (FCC), 10–11,
44–9, 51, 55–65, 71 n, 72 n, 97,
99, 109, 110–11, 112–16, 120,

125 n, 133, 135, 151, 162, 167,
168–9, 170, 175–7
foreign policy, structural
conditions, 108–24, 131–3,
136, 149, 151, 152, 170, 186,
193–4, 198, 200, 201–3, 206,
208, 210, 211 n
General Accounting Office
(GAO), 1
Intellectual Property
Committee, 144
Interagency Working Group on
Transborder Data
Flow, 139–40
legislation: Cable Regulation
Act, 168, 189 n;
Communications Act, 110,
153 n; Communications
Satellite Act, 9, 41, 46, 47, 49,
55, 63–5, 68 n, 98; Omnibus
Trade and Competitiveness
Act, 142–3, 146, 158 n, 159 n;
Satellite Home Viewer
Act, 168;
Telecommunications Act, 12,
153 n, 163–4, 177–8, 185,
187 n, 209; Trade and Tariff
Act, 139, 141
National Aeronautics and Space
Administration (NASA),
41, 42, 48, 50, 52–4, 65,
66 n, 75, 78, 82, 88, 106 n,
113, 173
National Security Agency
(NSA), 113
National Security Council
(NSC), 113, 123, 150
National Telecommunications and
Information Administration
(NTIA), 56, 111–12, 114, 115,
121, 122, 133, 151
Office of Telecommunications
Policy (OTP), 56, 57, 71 n,
111, 114, 117
Office of the United States Trade
Representative (USTR),
11, 112–13, 126 n, 128 n,
138–45, 150–2, 186, 193, 194,
211 n

Senior Interagency Group for
International
Communications and
Information Policy
(SIG), 113, 120, 123
trade policy, 2, 98, 107, 113, 117,
118–24, 128 n, 132–3, 136–52,
157 n
United States Information Agency
(USIA), 45, 50, 51, 55,
68 n, 75, 77, 78, 83,
95, 98, 99 n, 100 n, 109, 111,
115, 150; *see also*
International Television
Service (ITV), Voice of
America (VoA)
Voice of America (VoA), 76–8,
114, 115, 150; *see also* United
States Information Agency
(USIA)
Working Group on
Telecommunications
Services, 144–5

United States Republican Party, 121
United States Satellite Broadcasting
(USSB), 73 n, 172
Universal Declaration of Human
Rights, 80, 83, 87
US West, 153 n

Video Satellite Systems, 73 n
Vietnam war, 34
Von Laue, Theodore H., 97

Wasilewski, Vincent T., 73 n
Webb, James, 106 n
Webster, David, 183, 184
Weinberger, Caspar, 94
Western Union, 60, 62, 63, 71 n,
73 n, 126 n
Whitehead, Clay, 71 n
Woldman, Joel, 107
Woodrow, R. Brian, 147
World Bank, 197, 207
World Press Freedom
Committee, 105 n